Sidney Nolan
SUCH IS LIFE

Sidney Nolan
SUCH IS LIFE

A BIOGRAPHY BY BRIAN ADAMS

Hutchinson of Australia

Century Hutchinson Australia Pty Ltd
16—22 Church Street, Hawthorn, Victoria 3122

Melbourne Sydney London
Auckland Johannesburg
and agencies throughout the world

First published 1987
© Brian Adams 1987
Designed by Derrick I. Stone Design
Typeset by Setrite Typesetters Ltd., Hong Kong
Printed and bound Impact Printing Pty Ltd, Victoria

National Library of Australia
Cataloguing in Publication Data:
Adams, Brian, 1934—
  Sidney Nolan: such is life, a biography.

  Bibliography.
  Includes index.
  ISBN 0 09 157360 2.

  1. Nolan, Sir Sidney, 1917—   . 2. Painters —
Australia — Biography. 3. Artists — Australia —
Biography. I. Title.

759.994

Contents

For Elizabeth Betson

Acknowledgements

An illustrated biography such as this is possible only through the diverse contributions of many people, everything from chance remarks heard at dinner parties to the hours of recorded reminiscences with the subject himself. Then there are the masses of books, exhibition catalogues, and newspaper and magazine clippings to be studied for background information. A select bibliography lists the most important books in this regard, and for access to much of the other published reference material I am indebted to the State Library of New South Wales; the Mitchell Library, Sydney; the State Library of Victoria; the La Trobe Library, Melbourne; the libraries of the Art Gallery of New South Wales and the Art Gallery of South Australia; the *West Australian*, Perth; and Australian Consolidated Press.

Albert Tucker and Barrett Reid, both of Melbourne, gave me valuable comments about the Heide circle and assisted in locating contemporary photographs. Additional pictures of the artist and his works came from Mary Andrews of Sydney; the Australian Opera; the Australian National Gallery, Canberra; the National Gallery of Victoria, Melbourne; the Nolan Gallery at Lanyon; Heide Park and Art Gallery, Melbourne; the Art Gallery of New South Wales, Sydney; the Australian War Memorial, Canberra; the Australian Archives of the Dance, Melbourne; News Limited, and the artist's sister, Mrs Lorna Goslin of Melbourne. Unless otherwise indicated, works reproduced in this book are from the private collection of Sir Sidney Nolan.

My particular thanks go to Neil Mundy of NVC Arts International for suggesting the title of this book, to my sister Elizabeth Betson for allowing me to use her London home as an office, and to Loraine Brown for research assistance. The manuscript was ably unravelled from chaotic drafts and typed by Kaye Osborne, and Elizabeth Douglas gave invaluable assistance at all stages of the book's production.

Finally, *Such is Life* would not have eventuated without the generous hospitality and stoical patience of the artist and his wife during my incessant questioning while staying as their guest at The Rodd on several occasions during the twelve months from June 1985.

Brian Adams
Sydney 1986

Introduction

When Ned Kelly, the notorious bushranger, was about to be hanged in Melbourne Gaol on 11 November 1880, his last words before the trapdoor was sprung were reported to be 'Such is life'. The demise of the former petty criminal, whose horse-stealing activities had led to his gang murdering three policemen, produced Australia's most famous folk hero. His name soon achieved mythical proportions, becoming lauded or despised — but rarely ignored — because such spirit reflected a facet of the national character, summed-up in the expression 'game as Ned Kelly', in admiration of the underdog.

The same ironic comment as Kelly's was used by Joseph Furphy for the title of his unconventional and entertaining novel written under the pseudonym of the central character, Tom Collins, and first published in 1903. It mirrored many of the new nation's rural philosophies and aspirations, told by a cast of colourful characters — an Australian brotherhood of man — in a loose federation of bush yarns described by the author as 'temper, democratic; bias, offensively Australian'.

Those three words, 'Such is life', continue to epitomise many of the characteristics inherent in the national personality; an intriguing fusion of stoicism, individuality and pride. As the Sydney-born art critic Robert Hughes points out, Ned Kelly's expression is 'a shrug that echoes through the nation's history'.

Sidney Nolan has interpreted many of his country's myths, including Kelly and Furphy, and on the way to becoming Australia's best-known painter fabricated a few more of his own. This biography does not attempt a critical study of his work — although there is urgent need for a new one. Instead, it reveals for the first time, as told to Brian Adams, the eventful life of an extraordinarily creative person, who can shrug his own shoulders with the pride of achievement and comment, like Kelly and Furphy, 'Such is life'.

Sir Sidney Robert Nolan, OM, Kt, CBE, and his wife Mary have now settled in rural England at one end of a well-travelled axis that has remained the principal source of his inspiration. With countless side trips to China and Kenya,

Greece and the Middle East, Cambodia and New Guinea, Nolan has emerged as an inveterate traveller, although these peripatetic inclinations have led to sustained criticism of his extensive output, making him a controversial figure. During a career embracing half a century Nolan has become the most honoured artist in his country's history and has gained a niche in the pantheon of world art. Whether he is the *best* painter Australia has produced is a topic of frequent discussion there, where his pictures of arid landscapes peopled by quirky characters and littered with the detritus of a developing nation, contrast vividly with his view from The Rodd, as his English house is named.

The Nolans live close to Presteigne in the peaceful countryside bordering Wales, the owners of a fine Elizabethan manor whose origins are lost in the mists of medieval time. At the age of seventy, the painter plays the part of a benevolent country squire rather than lord of the manor, his slight body still trim with a feline quality of movement, white hair thinning on top, and electric-blue eyes missing nothing. He scans his adopted countryside with the look of a man who still has truths to discover about nature and life. His gentle exterior masks an intellectually tough, self-contained person, with acute vision and acerbic wit, whose avuncular appearance leaves many unprepared for the Australian larrikin who still loves to gatecrash parties, but hesitates to use his considerable influence for gaining personal favours.

It was the experience of growing up in Melbourne during the 1920s and 1930s that moulded Nolan into a successful painter whose reputation would range far beyond the shores of Port Phillip Bay. But at the time of his birth into a working-class family towards the end of the Great War, the chances of outstanding achievement in any form of endeavour must have seemed remote in a world rent by conflict and confusion, where art had been one of the casualties.

CHAPTER ONE

A Celtic Larrikin

§

During 1916 a bright new comet in the constellation of Cetus was first noticed in the heavens and was interpreted by many as a harbinger of dramatic change, perhaps foretelling the end of hostilities after nearly two bitter years of war in Europe. It became known as the Peace Comet. By the first quarter of the following year accord still eluded the warring industrial nations of the world as the fiery body showed itself off brighter than ever, trailing a brilliant tail across the skies, just as Halley's Comet had done seven years before. Astronomers said the Peace Comet had been travelling towards earth for 400 days and predicted its imminent departure from the galaxy to disappear far out into the universe and not return for another 60,000 years.

This phenomenon was apparent in Australia low on the northern horizon for an hour each night during a spell of fine autumn weather as Melbourne prepared to celebrate a long weekend to mark the 61st anniversary of Eight Hours Day. The city's work stopped on this weekend in late April and would not resume until the day after Monday's traditional union march through the streets. It was a muted holiday mood, however, because nearly every family had loved ones away at the war, or had already lost relatives who had volunteered to join the Australian Infantry Force and fight in defence of the British Empire. Despatches from the Front published in the daily newspapers described the Anglo-French campaign against the Germans as proceeding satisfactorily, with the Allies capturing hundreds of enemy guns and taking 33,000 prisoners after an eleven-day attack. A service to honour the entry of the United States into the conflict had just been held at St Paul's Cathedral in London, adding to optimism that the war might soon draw to a close, comet or no comet. But there was also the bad news that while Germany was admitting huge troop losses on the Western Front, she was retaliating at sea with the indiscriminate sinking of hospital ships carrying wounded soldiers to British ports.

At home, the nation's dynamic leader, Billy Hughes, arrived in Melbourne from Tasmania where he had been campaigning for the forthcoming federal election with frequent speechmaking to anyone who would listen, except 'certain British naturalised subjects born in an "enemy country"' who, according to the official government gazette, were disqualified from voting. It would be an interrupted week because, following a return to work on Tuesday, there would be another holiday on the Wednesday to commemorate the second anniversary of the famous landing at Anzac Cove in the Dardanelles, where the Australian and New Zealand soldiers were defeated by the Turkish forces. A huge military parade would be held in the centre of Melbourne with 7,000 men taking part, including survivors of the bloody Gallipoli campaign, where 10,000 Australian and New Zealand troops perished.

It was against this background of uncertain times that in the Melbourne suburb of Carlton on 22 April 1917 Dora Irene Nolan gave birth to her first child, a son who would be given the name Sidney Robert. Mrs Nolan could never have imagined that her baby with his shock of dark hair and lusty cries would one day weave his mercurial way through the constellation of the arts with the brilliance of the Peace Comet, bearing strange star patterns as a result of being born on the cusp of Aries and Taurus.

Some two decades before, around the turn of the century, the infant's grandfather, a former policeman, was working as a stock manager for an estate near Rushworth in northern Victoria. Its grand mansion, named Dhurringile, had been built by a businessman as a suitable residence to impress the young bride he was bringing out from England. She died during the long sea journey, however, and never saw her new home with its stained glass windows depicting kangaroos and its broad pastures. Grandfather Nolan's family included three sons and by the time they grew into young men, it was decided to take up a large block of uncleared land at Nagambie and attempt to wrest a family farm from virgin scrub. A selection such as this cost little in cash, but inflicted backbreaking toil on the owners for its clearing and the planting of crops. The challenge of the frontier was strong, however, and the Nolans went to their block with the will to succeed and the determination to have a place of their own. They erected a bark hut, started to fell trees and cut out the stringy scrub so that a few sheep could be run at first. This arduous progress would take three years and in the middle of the period of cutting and burning, one of the sons, Sidney, married his sweetheart, Dora Sutherland, also a fifth generation Australian. Conditions at Nagambie remained rough and when they were expecting their first child it was decided to send her to stay with relations in Melbourne for the confinement.

During her few weeks in the city, Dora Nolan experienced the tensions felt by a nation fighting a distant war and she was anxious to return to the quiet of the bush as soon as possible. She quickly regained strength and took her healthy young boy back to an admiring father and family circle. As the land was cleared

4

further it produced indifferent soil, gravelly and thin, difficult for growing a reasonable grass cover for feeding sheep and virtually impossible for crops. The family was forced to face the harsh fact that it could hardly survive as a farm of any sort in the violently alternating weather patterns of drenching rain and searing drought. Somebody suggested there might be gold and, although there were a few successful strikes in other parts of the district, the Nolans' search was unsuccessful. Perhaps only those with a resilient Celtic heritage would have embarked on the unpromising scheme in the first place and persevered with such stamina and blinkered determination. After several generations in Australia, the Nolans remained essentially Irish. They were lapsed Roman Catholics whose belief in God had been substituted by the will to succeed in carving out a living from this inhospitable land. Their combined efforts were doomed in the unyielding environment, however, and a year after Sidney was born they were forced to accept defeat, just as the Allies were claiming victory in Europe and Australia was about to face an uncomfortable adjustment to peacetime. The Nolans retreated to the city as a family unit, where all three sons of the pioneering grandfather were fortunate to find jobs with the Melbourne and Metropolitan Tramways Board.

The infant's family moved into a small house in Pakington Street, in the bayside suburb of St Kilda. Two daughters and a son were added to the family at two-year intervals, but Sidney's development was somewhat detached from them, separated by the age difference that became magnified to the young. His first impressions were of the beach and they, like many other early memories, would stay vividly with him throughout his life. It was a long walk for a young lad from Pakington Street down to the broad promenade which had the appearance, if not the atmosphere, of a typical English seaside resort of the Victorian era. On summer weekends the pier, the ornamental gardens and the sandy beach would be thronged with visitors. The seagulls wheeled overhead, there was noise and bustle and laughter making a cosmopolitan outlet for a rather formal, unbending city whose pleasures were not always apparent. St Kilda provided a sort of Blackpool for this Manchester in the sun, although Sidney's hedonistic days of splashing in the calm waters of the bay and then baking his lithe body on the hot sand were typically Australian diversions. St Kilda was enjoying something of a renaissance, which had begun during the royal tour of 1920 when the Prince of Wales had landed at the pier, a day which people still talked about. There were some curious sights at St Kilda, and one that stuck in young Sidney's mind was a man who balanced upside-down on one hand with a row of ties for sale draped over the other arm. Sidney and his friends crowded around watching the performance, which in spite of repeated efforts they were unable to copy. This impressive act always attracted considerable attention but seemed to sell few ties.

Sidney's first few visits to the beach each season resulted in bad blisters which had to be treated by his mother with a poultice of flour and water until the sensitive skin built up its resistance to the glare and could be coaxed into a resilient tan. His father revelled in an active life as a member of the Tramways lifesaving club, which was trained to a keen pitch by an inspector named Robey, who also looked after the football team and a gymnasium group. There were sixteen of these fit and enthusiastic men from the local Tramways area, all with growing families, who visited the turreted and domed baths on the St Kilda foreshore every Sunday during the warmer months. This famous establishment, opened in 1860, was divided into a large swimming and sunbathing area lined with dressing cubicles for the men and a smaller pool for women. Most of the men bathed naked and young Nolan became accustomed to being among these bronzed figures, a couple of hundred of them looking like Greek heroes, each Sunday afternoon.

The boy was known affectionately by his parents as 'Siddy' or 'the young feller'. He got to know his father's regular mates and was soon calling them by their nicknames, although his inherent shyness led to an occasional stammer. The men competed as a lifesaving team around the bayside beaches and also in the more serious competition in New South Wales. During the winter their leisure-time energies were concentrated on the well-equipped Tramways' gymnasium, where young Nolan was introduced to the parallel bars and, because of his strong light body, became the team mascot when they formed their human pyramids. Being hauled to the top was a horrifying experience at first, swaying twenty feet above the wooden floor, perched precariously on sweaty shoulders, but it proved a good mental discipline and quickly eliminated his fear of heights. Soon he was making daredevil leaps from the diving tower at the baths, and it was the sheer enjoyment of this athletic life that began to monopolise most of Sidney's thoughts and energies. His attendance at the local primary school, the Brighton Road State School, seemed like an interlude between holidays when he could be outside with his own young friends or the Tramways men, enjoying the sun and exercise. He proved to be a bright pupil, however, quietly rebellious and full of pranks.

Although Sidney's father often made jokes about his family having been lapsed Catholics for 300 years, the lad's upbringing was surrounded by religious influences. His mother, rather against her husband's wishes, had begun to take Sidney to meetings at the fundamentalist Christian Church, situated just a short distance along Pakington Street and run principally by a lay teacher who was a local furniture removalist. He read the lessons and instructed the children in scripture studies with the intention of entering them in contests of Bible knowledge with other young Christians across the State. There were also social activities connected with the church, including picnics down the bay at Rickett's

Sidney, aged 4 (Lorna Goslin)

Sidney, 6; Marjorie, 4; Lorna, 2; at Pakington Street, St Kilda (Lorna Goslin)

Point or Half Moon Bay, where the children were taken in the removal van. Sidney was too young to realise that the older children were being closely watched on these Sunday school outings for signs of early puberty and an interest between the sexes, which was considered unhealthy. Instead, his curiosity was channelled into religious experiences reminiscent of revivalist meetings. During services, members of the congregation were encouraged to shout out when the spirit moved them and it was common for believers to jump to their feet and cry 'I have seen the Lord!' Young Nolan was taught to follow this example. The day came when he was considered ready to be accepted fully into the church and at a special baptism service, a bath was set up on the stage of the church hall. At the appropriate moment he stood up and shouted 'I have seen the Lord', the congregation repeated the line and the boy was led to the bath and immersed in the lukewarm water by the preacher. Sidney spluttered back onto the bare boards, was wrapped in a towel and led away shivering to a stove at the back of the hall to dry off. Young Nolan had seen the light before the age of ten, if only briefly, and then ceased to attend the church because he had more interesting things to do.

Most children in Melbourne were introduced to the almost legendary folk hero Ned Kelly by being taken to see the armour he wore at his final shoot-out at Glenrowan. It was one of the prize exhibits at the Aquarium where the bushranger's famous helmet and breastplate fashioned from the mould boards of ploughs were hung on a wooden stand rather like a coat rack. On the way to see the fish, the children would pass the armour, knocking on the iron mask and asking if Ned was inside. Nolan took special pride in boasting to friends that his grandfather had chased the Kelly gang and, when he really wanted to impress, embroidered the story by claiming that grandfather Nolan was responsible, almost single-handed, for the gang's capture.

The family outgrew their cottage and moved to a larger home in the heart of the St Kilda shopping district near Acland Street, just around the corner from the Village Belle Hotel and a few minutes walk from the huge funfair of Luna Park and the beach. Young Sidney's two uncles — the elder Billy, the younger Louis — and his father, Sid, all considered themselves lucky to be working as gripmen on the cable trams. It was a job that required skill and dedication and in return offered a reasonable wage and the satisfaction of providing a reliable service. Billy Nolan — tall, strong and angular — was regarded as a first-class gripman with an excellent record, as was Nolan's father. But Louis had not bothered to acquire the skills of his older brothers; two smashed grips were recorded against his name and on both occasions he suffered the ignominy of his tram having to be towed back to the depot to have its shattered claw extracted in the workshop then hung up on a rack, like a carcass, waiting for repairs. Eventually, Louis was dismissed when his tally of disasters reached three, but the other two Nolans continued their jobs with unblemished reputations. Sidney was proud of the assured manner in which his father drove a tram, often taking long rides across town with him, feeling superior to the other passengers because he did not have to pay, as the conductor with a bell on his ticket-punch passed him with a wink instead of collecting the fare. The boy was fascinated to watch the passengers sitting on the slatted wooden benches of the dummy car when the tram approached a corner, hoping to see them fall off as the underground cable was thrown and the vehicle allowed to coast under its own momentum until the grip was re-engaged on the straight. On approaching a bend the tram developed a rocking motion and his father called out, 'Mind the curve!' to warn unwary passengers to guard against being shaken off. Young Nolan expertly waited until the last moment to clutch a restraining strap as the brown and cream coloured cars lurched around the corner.

He was happy in the easy environment of tramdriving, swimming, lifesaving, football, gymnastics and cycling and enjoyed the camaraderie of his father's friends. School was something to be endured, like medicine, between the physical activities of life at St Kilda, although he was also becoming increasingly

Standing: Sidney, Lorna, Mr Nolan
In front: Raymond, Marjorie (Lorna Goslin)

Mr Nolan with two conductors and electric tram (Lorna Goslin)

interested in words and language. The uncles and their families lived in Abbotsford and Collingwood, a long tram ride away on the opposite side of the city, but there were regular family gatherings and longer journeys two or three times a year to relatives in the Goulburn Valley, who also visited the city occasionally. There were a dozen families who circulated socially with plenty of company for the children — cousins to play with, barn dances to attend and the older boys looking for kissing cousins. The prevailing mood within the various families that made up the Nolans' social circle — those in Melbourne and those in the Goulburn Valley — was Irish, even if the connection with Ireland was tenuous. It was a relaxed, but structured, working-class atmosphere with card games once a week and the races on most Saturdays when the dressing was as stylish as their incomes would allow.

As the effects of the worldwide depression began to settle on Australia, a tram driver's wages were barely enough to maintain and feed a family with certain expectations from life. Nolan's father saw an opportunity of easing the economic strictures by becoming an SP bookmaker in his spare time and this illegal activity began to engage the boy during his early teens, giving him an insight into a completely new world. While the rest of the community seemed to be facing severe problems making ends meet, the Nolans acquired a new style and affluence, demonstrated by a car parked outside the house and regular visits from a tailor, because a bookmaker needed to look responsible to his clients and respectable to the rest of the community. Sidney was introduced under the tutelage of his father to the shady world of betting on the horses as well as to the competitive delights of cycle racing. Young Nolan was too slight and his legs were not long or strong enough to maintain the stamina needed for distance races, but he compensated for that by becoming an excellent tactician and winning a number of cups and medals for sprint races.

The bookmaking business flourished in spite of sporadic attempts to snuff it out. Nolan was instructed in the accounting operations which took place as the members of the syndicate sat around the dining room table of the St Kilda house late into Saturday night with bottles of beer and plates of crayfish in front of them while the books were carefully balanced. On busy race days it could mean staying up until 4 a.m. to discover what profits had been made. Nolan's father did most of his touting in and around the Tramways depot at Dorcas Street in South Melbourne and the work was brought home, to the discomfort of Dora who loathed the thought of a police raid and the social stigma that would result from a conviction. It was always a tense time in the household on Saturday nights, reckoning the syndicate's profits and losses, working out doubles and places — all quite complicated calculations, many of which were entrusted to a youth who showed little interest in mathematics at school. Occasionally there would be a cursory visit from the police, but an aunt in the family was married to a member of the Victoria Police Force and there always seemed to be ample notice of these calls. It was best to play safe, however, and one of Nolan's tasks was to act swiftly when there was a knock on the door. He knew how to secrete the money in the cistern above the lavatory bowl, quickly and efficiently, where it would remain safe, if soggy, until the visit was over. The police were invited to the dining room with a friendly formality as if attending a card party. There was idle banter about their right to enter private property without a search warrant and that was always laughed off in an unvarying dialogue that nobody should worry too much about rights. The police officers sat at the table drinking beer and finishing off the crayfish until it was time to continue their rounds, leaving the syndicate to get on with the bookkeeping. Nolan then went through his routine of climbing on the toilet seat and fishing out the sodden banknotes, which had to be placed between sheets of newspaper to dry off a little before being pegged on a line strung across the fireplace.

Dora Nolan detested her husband's bookmaking activities, fearing they would frustrate her aspirations for the children, but she welcomed the extra income at a time when many families in the street had to worry about where their next meal was coming from. And there was the compensation of having a car, which most working-class families regarded as an unattainable dream. The big black Hupmobile stood proudly outside their house, often the only motor car in sight. This second-hand vehicle in good condition was Mr Nolan's pride and joy, and it received his loving care for an hour or two every Sunday when the week's accumulation of salt spray would be washed away and the black duco buffed and polished. For most of the time life was good for the Nolan family, although a different side revealed itself every now and then. Being a bookmaker meant there was usually money around, but on other occasions a series of losses plunged Mr Nolan to depths of despair and the children would hear him weeping in his bedroom.

Most of the Nolan family entertainment was dictated by Dora, who had an insatiable love of the cinema as well as the live theatre. On Saturday nights they usually attended a local vaudeville show known as 'pops' and went to a midweek film at St Kilda's Empress Theatre. Mrs Nolan was a good mother to her well-spaced brood, practical and loving, and her personal escape from the mundane world of the 1930s was centred on the exploits of the leading Hollywood stars. For years she took young Sidney shopping with her every Friday along Acland Street, followed by waffles at Coles' cafeteria and then a matinee at the Empress. For a long time the school ignored the boy's regular absences at the end of the week but finally an inspector was sent to discover the reason for Sidney's truancy. However, Mrs Nolan remained adamant that he should accompany her and the matinee visits continued.

Later, at Brighton Technical School, language and its patterns intrigued him and he became friendly with the English teachers, discovering what books to read, becoming interested in the styles of the various authors. Nolan was rarely without a book in his hand or beside his bed. He could also manage mathematics reasonably well because the training as a bookmaker's accountant provided a good grounding in figures, although as an abstract subject without the direct application of calculating odds and sorting cash it did not hold his interest. He showed little aptitude for painting or modelling, receiving miserable marks for the subject, which was not surprising because most of the lessons seemed to be spent splashing paint over his trousers and throwing missiles of modelling clay around the classroom when the teacher's back was turned. The school was attended by mainly working-class children from the area. It had a tough reputation, although its training in the practical skills of carpentry, metalwork and plumbing made it one of the best schools of its type in Australia and young Nolan's time there was not wasted.

From an early age Nolan found himself to be something of a loner. He was just as interested in youthful pranks as the other St Kilda lads, but he entered into these activities in a more calculated way. Participation was part of the code and it was essential to be seen to belong to one street gang or another, taking part in continuous exercises to prove oneself. If the task was set, the pressures to conform, even in this junior society, demanded that an attempt must be made to carry it out, whatever the risk. One of the dares involved digging up a tree fern from somebody's front garden and planting it in front of the police sergeant's house without being detected. Another involved ringing all the door bells in a nominated street without being caught, or even seen. There were also street brawls between rival gangs with punch-ups, bloodied noses and ritual throwings off St Kilda pier.

In this atmosphere, Nolan developed as a cagey, discriminating kind of semi-delinquent, managing to remain part of a group by participating in the minimum amount of pranks and rumpus necessary to retain his standing and avoid ostracism. This was in the face of homilies from his father. 'No matter how smart you are', he would lecture his eldest son, 'and no matter how dumb a policeman is, remember there are always a hundred policemen to one of you and sooner or later the law will get you if you play up'. They were the beliefs of a man whose family, going back over many generations to County Clare, had always maintained a strong sense of law and order and had produced many policemen. Young Nolan maintained a healthy respect for established order while continuing to be a larrikin because he knew the rules for survival and could take care of himself. His attitude to other forms of society was equally calculating and he used the activities of the clubs to which Dora insisted he belong as a means of escape into a wider world of experience. He developed an energetic life as an amateur athlete, particularly as a cyclist, which allowed him to explore the eastern Victorian countryside, often riding alone, developing his own thoughts.

During the winter months Melbourne would be preoccupied by Australian Rules football, with intense rivalry between suburban clubs playing for the annual premiership. The games attracted large attendances and Nolan was a regular supporter of the local team, known as the Saints, who played their home matches on a ground located at St Kilda junction. To a lad growing up in Melbourne, the Saturday afternoon ritual of the footy was a highlight of the week. He admired the players' ability to jump impossibly high when taking a mark. It was a spine-tingling moment as the big men in their striped guernseys appeared to fly, reaching for the spinning oval ball with a grace that seemed to occur in slow motion.

The only threat for Nolan to the accepted code of living concerned girls. There was a harmless flirtation with one of the family cousins, amounting to nothing more than a friendship, but Nolan's father took him aside to warn about an unhealthy and unacceptable interest in the opposite sex. He told an apocryphal tale of what happened in such circumstances in Ireland when the young men of County Clare were roped down the cliffs to collect gannet eggs and if any of them was seen to be getting too fond of his cousin, he was let drop to his death. This far-fetched story made its impression on young Nolan. The greatest opportunity to satisfy his curiosity in the opposite sex occurred at Luna Park, which had the reputation of being a place to pick up girls. The

Luna Park, 1986   *St Kilda Baths, 1986*

atmosphere of repressed sexuality there reminded him of the American films he saw and the books he read, which he found closer to his experience than many English films and books.

Nolan left school at fourteen in 1931, having exhibited little of the potential his mother had expected. The easy-going nature of his father and the stricter demands imposed by his mother had left him in no better situation than thousands of other young people looking for jobs at a time during the early days of the depression when employment prospects were at their bleakest. After failing to get a job, he decided to attend the Prahran Technical College, continuing a correspondence course he had begun in the design and crafts departments, which had the reputation of being among the best in Australia. One of his teachers was a promising young painter named William Dargie who questioned a monogram design Nolan was toying with, incorporating a lagoon and a yacht that was unashamedly copied from a printed advertisement. Dargie suspected its source and said he was not at all impressed with such work. Nolan also dabbled in jewellery and became interested in carpentry and metalwork classes, but decided the art course was the most interesting, although at first it involved little more than copying furniture designs. He persisted, however, and his progress was promising enough for him to get special dispensation to work in the life class, a full two years before it was usually allowed.

Nolan's first encounter with the nude female form was a chubby woman who sat on a simple upright chair, her buttocks overflowing the narrow slatted seat, while the students, arrayed around her in a semi-circle, drew and painted in twenty-minute sessions, after which she retired behind a screen for a short break to smoke a cigarette and drink a cup of tea. After one of these rest periods she returned sooner than usual, wearing a red kimono-style gown hanging loose and dangling a cigarette from the corner of her mouth. Nolan looked up from his drawing at the Arabian Nights fantasy before him and was astonished to see hanging on her outstretched arm a row of ties for sale at 6d and 9d each. He was suddenly transported to the time years before when he had watched with admiration as the man stood on his hands outside the St Kilda baths with ties for sale. This almost surreal image was repeating itself and he would store it away in his mind for future use.

While attending classes at Prahran, Nolan continued to look for a job. He was a member of the YMCA where he became an excellent table tennis player and took part in the club's swimming competitions. The YMCA ran a service each morning where members could assemble and hear of any work being offered. On previous occasions when Nolan had attended there was nothing available, until one morning he finally landed a job with three other young men distributing leaflets to houses in various suburbs for the Aspro company. Employed at last, he set off with considerable enthusiasm for the task, although the quartet began to wilt as the hot day progressed and energies flagged. There were many stops for cooling drinks and then finally, in a fit of rebelliousness, most of the leaflets found their way into the Yarra river at Richmond. Fortunately, no one found out and the engagement led to an introduction to the company's advertising manager whose brother, Leyshon-White, ran a flourishing commercial art studio in the city.

Nolan was able to convince the man that he had, in fact, received extensive training in commercial art at Prahran and had his heart set on such a career. Leyshon-White was impressed with such enthusiasm and set him to work on some drawings for an advertising feature for the P & O shipping company. Nolan found it rather boring to be depicting liners at sea and paid more attention to the processes of making silk screen posters, some of the first printing of this kind in Australia. They were not a great success, however, because paint was sticking to the screens and had to be thoroughly cleaned off in baths after each print was struck. Nolan's lack of interest in his job resulted in some scrappy maritime illustrations which Leyshon-White rejected, asking him to try again. In a large room at the back of the studio there were six artists sitting at tilted easels engaged in drawing up newspaper advertisements and from the speed and quality of their work Nolan realised he could never match their techniques. It was simply the case that they were good at drawing, and he was not.

The owner's business was commercial art, but his real love was painting and he kept a small studio for his indulgence next door to the commercial premises. Nolan wandered in there one day to find a vastly different atmosphere, with Leyshon-White dressed in a paint-spattered smock, wielding an extensive palette as he worked away at a canvas on a large easel. Reclining in front of him on a platform decorated with red velvet was a nude model surrounded by the smell of whisky which was strong enough to dominate the pungency of the paints. The model saw Nolan and gestured to the painter that they had a visitor. Leyshon-White wheeled round and asked him what he wanted, surprised that one of the workers had dared to enter his inner sanctum. It was a situation which required some quick thinking from Nolan. 'Well, you are quite right', he said, 'I am simply no good at drawing ships and neckties and cut glass decanters because I am also a real painter and want to be doing exactly what you are at this moment.' He had to admit to himself he could think of nothing more exciting than painting a good-looking nude, languidly desporting herself on red velvet, with both artist and model pausing to take an occasional sip of whisky from a paint-streaked glass, although he had never tasted the drink. The artist smiled, disarmed at the young man's frankness and his obvious delight at seeing this scene. 'You can't expect to become a painter overnight', he told him. 'It takes years of study and hundreds of canvases before you can begin to work like this.' He pointed theatrically to a poorly composed representation of the model, who was now sitting up, still naked, smoking a cigarette. The painter stumbled and dropped several of his brushes to the ground. As he bent down to pick them up, flicking off the dust, he tried to cover up his embarrassment by suggesting that Nolan might find some other work with him, 'as a prelude to you becoming a fully-fledged painter'. He regained his composure and said, 'I know, I'll put you in charge of my school since you're not very good at ships or ties'.

Nolan found himself in the remarkable situation of running Leyshon-White's correspondence school of art, with a lucrative clientele who lived mostly in the rural areas of Victoria and paid the considerable sum of £30 a course as the means to fulfil their dreams of becoming artists. Most of the addresses were in the Gippsland region and the envelopes containing their exercises would come in from Bairnsdale and Morwell, Omeo and Moe, many of them pathetic little drawings from coal workers and farm labourers who yearned for their talents to be discovered so they could release themselves from the workaday world. Nolan found himself unable to take any of this seriously and he gained a perverse enjoyment from issuing dismissive advice to the students, referring them to the work of the great European masters for guidance and inspiration, knowing they were never likely to see a real Leonardo or a Cézanne. He soon found himself a more interesting job, however, and left before letters of complaint came flooding in from the unfortunate clients.

Headwear was big business in Melbourne during the 1930s, an essential item of clothing for the man in the street; without a hat he would feel as undressed as going trouserless. It was the age of Akubra, the great national brand, but there were also dozens of other manufacturers in competition to supply the local demand and Nolan's new job was in the display department of a company named Fayrfield Hats on the far side of the city at Abbotsford. Here he found work to suit his temperament, where he could use his hands and brain in dealing with colour and form. It entailed assisting in the design and construction of advertising signs and display stands, which were sent to stores throughout the State.

On fine mornings Nolan would get up at 6 o'clock and walk down to the beach when there was nobody around except a few bathers and draw huge abstracts in the sand. On his way to work he stood up in the tram as it passed along the upper esplanade and looked down on his efforts. By the time he came home the tide had washed them away ready for further attempts the next day. At work, he eagerly applied himself to mastering techniques of spray painting, learning how to build up layers of colour to give striking effects, and there were other influences at hand to add to his appreciation of art and design. The advertising manager of the company, Vernon Jones, subscribed to a number of American magazines which were left in the department for reference. One of them in particular attracted Nolan, a luxurious publication called *Apparel Arts* crammed with samples of suiting materials, twills and silks for shirts and with advertisements for the latest designs for fabrics and fashions in the United States. Jones, who was something of a visionary, also received *The Studio* from England, as well as various art books which combined to form a sizeable library. By these means Nolan had access to monographs on the leading contemporary painters of Europe and by the age of sixteen was becoming more familiar with international trends than most of the people who belonged to the small art world outside the factory. He began to be influenced by what he saw in the magazines and books, composing small abstracts in the style of Moholy-Nagy and Paul Klee. He also experimented with photography, although the spray gun was his main instrument of expression, and he became proficient in making bold shapes and shadowy forms that could be incorporated in the advertising for Fayrfield Hats.

When he was unsupervised, Nolan began using the techniques he was developing to make a series of illustrations for James Joyce's *Ulysses*, which he was reading at the Victorian State Library. He spent weeks reading the book which, as an art student now enrolled for part-time study at the National Gallery School, he was able to obtain on special request, for it was unavailable to the general public under Australia's stifling censorship regulations. Between his design activities Nolan spent as much time as he could reading in a small shed at the factory which contained a compressor for the spray guns. The building was just outside the studio and doubled as a watchman's hut at night, being furnished with a desk and comfortable chair. It had a small window looking out into the courtyard so that anyone approaching could be observed. Nolan would sit reading with one finger on the compressor button so that if anybody came he could start the machine, wander out of the hut and return to the studio, leaving his book hidden in a corner. It was an unconventional location to read all the novels of Theodore Dreiser but the strong imagery of *An American Tragedy*, *Sister Carrie*, *The Financier* and *The Genius* seemed to be enhanced by the atmosphere of this industrial background.

Vernon Jones continued to supply Nolan with art books from America and England, and Nolan experimented with the photograms and photomontage he read about. He devised a system of stencils for spray painting which, with a quick mental twist, could be turned from straight commerical illustration to his own abstract images which were unlike anything else he saw in Melbourne. This was far more exciting to his receptive mind than the dull classes at the National Gallery School where he and hundreds of other hopeful artists were enrolled, either in full-time courses or part-time during the evening. Nolan preferred to miss many of the art classes and instead wandered upstairs to the State Library where he read as many of the thousands of volumes ranged around the walls as he could manage. He began the philosophy section from the end shelves, starting with the Zs, grasping some of the concepts of the world's greatest thinkers, stopping and digesting more thoroughly when a particular writer interested him such as Alfred North Whitehead with his *Symbolism, its Meaning and Effect* and *Adventures of Ideas*. He then attempted to relate these philosophical concepts to the work of novelists such as Joyce, striving to create a visual link between them.

Nolan realised that he was far too young to be taken seriously as an artist and that his experiments were destined to be ridiculed in a society whose art displayed only the mildest of modern influences. For a painter in Melbourne opportunities to exhibit were limited, confined to the premises of the stuffily conservative Victorian Artists Society, the Athenaeum Gallery and a couple of small display galleries that were little more than craft shops. Opportunities were even more restricted if the artist did not produce traditional pastoral pictures. Arthur Streeton was undisputed king of the local painters, even though his long reign was approaching its end. In fact, he was a monarch and Lord High Executioner rolled into one, because his position as art critic on the *Argus* made his an influential voice. Most of the younger painters regarded his work, once so fresh and vigorous, as staid and unexciting. His writings were reactionary, but in the wrong direction, comprising a constant diatribe against the influences of modernism that Streeton saw as threatening to destroy the wholesomeness of art as practised so demonstrably well by himself. Nolan had seen a recent Streeton exhibition at the Athenaeum Gallery and he could not forget a little painting that stood out from the predictable landscapes. It was a street scene done in his late manner, loosely painted; in the foreground was a large pile of used matchsticks with red paint all over them ringed by some scumbly, badly abstracted figures. It was a limp attempt to deride modern art and all it did for Nolan was make him glad that on occasions he and some of the other students furtively spat on the artist's post-1900 work when they passed it in the National Gallery.

Nolan was regarded by his fellow students as something of a dilettante because he studied part-time at the National Gallery School and seemed to lack the burning ambition of the others to win the coveted travelling scholarship that enabled a generous period of study overseas. He displayed few touches of the Bohemian, always appearing well-dressed for his visits to the school and library. His friends such as Arthur Reed and Francis Brabazon saw his sporadic attendance and sparse results as amusingly pointless, failing to appreciate the enthusiastic talk and torrent of ideas behind Nolan's lack of work. Superficially, he gave the impression of a loner whose interests remained rooted in physical pursuits, resulting in endless games of table tennis with anyone who would challenge him. The intense reading activity and experiments in abstraction were carried out away from general view and few, except a close friend like Howard Matthews, were aware of them.

Nolan's independent nature and desire to remain apart from the crowd was reflected in his attitude to employment. He was working for a manufacturer of men's hats, yet indulged in the ultimate protest of refusing to wear their product. He did carry a hat to and from work for fear of losing his job and the management finally insisted he wear it for at least the brief walk between the railway station and the factory. His career at Fayrfield Hats took on a new dimension, however, when, attracted by the promise of extra money, he agreed to become a model to promote the company's latest styles. The new role required him to dress up as a page boy, wearing a formal suit; and two outfits were specially made for him. He and an associate, Bernard Jones, who had wide experience of local social events, were expected to visit as representatives of Fayrfield the leading balls that took place around the suburbs during the winter months. The most prestigious on the calendar was the Lord Mayor's Ball at St Kilda's Palais de Danse, next to Luna Park. Nolan or Jones would join the welcoming line and reach the guest of honour, handing him a new hat, intoning the company's advertising slogan, 'Your hat, Sir'. At first, Nolan was worried about his ability to carry out this new role, fearing that nervousness would cause his stutter to reappear, but with fierce determination he gained confidence and began to enjoy the occasions so that the suburban balls became routine assignments of discovering the guest of honour's hat size beforehand and then making the presentation. There were special events that needed a different approach, such as in late October 1934 when the aviators C.W.A. Scott and T. Campbell Black flew out in the Melbourne Centenary England-Australia Air Race and landed at Essendon Aerodrome after a flight of almost seventy-one hours in their DH88 Comet *Grosvenor House* to win the event. There to greet them as they stepped from their plane were Nolan and Jones, immaculately dressed in their page boy uniforms and clutching the company's most exclusive models. They pushed through the crowds and thrust the impressive hat boxes towards the surprised Englishmen, while shouting out the familiar phrase, 'Your hat, Sir'. This dressing up lasted for a few months more until Nolan came to the conclusion he was becoming a slave to mere wages and, although he was meeting some interesting people, resented the idea of being used for a cause to which he was not committed.

Nolan had continued competition cycling with the Gardenvale Amateurs, regularly winning cups for races on handicap along two and five mile stretches of Dandenong Road. During the summer of 1936 while on a cycling journey to Sydney, Cliff Bayliss, who had just won the previous year's travelling art scholarship from the National Gallery School, and John Sinclair were resting beside the road near Goulburn in New South Wales when they noticed a lone rider approaching at considerable pace on a lightweight racer, wearing shorts and a cotton vest, his face, arms and legs peeling from sunburn. As he stopped to talk to the two northbound travellers it was obvious he was travelling light, with little else but a water bottle and a rolled-up waterproof sheet that he could put around his shoulders if it rained and which doubled as a blanket for sleeping beside the road at night. Nolan explained that he was returning to Melbourne and making good time, travelling up to 200 miles a day along the bitumen of the Hume Highway. He had heard of Bayliss and congratulated him on the scholarship, though privately he assumed it was the meticulously rigid quality of Bayliss's Leonardo-like drawings that had gained him the coveted award.

The large circuit of the city Nolan was making every day to and from work became quite exhausting: up early in the morning to get to Abbotsford; from there to the National Gallery School in the city and then home to St Kilda. Two of the full-time students at the Gallery School, John Sinclair and Laurence Pendlebury, together with an architecture student Gordon Daniels, decided to share a flat in the heart of the city within a few minutes walk of the National Gallery School. They had found a spartan place above a shop on the corner of Russell and Lonsdale Streets and, after the chance meeting on the Hume Highway, Sinclair invited Nolan to join them as the fourth member, sharing expenses and living a frantic round of parties in Melbourne's version of Bohemia. Nolan's home life had become increasingly frustrating for him because of the attention paid to the other growing children in the family and the exhausting effects of the long travel each day, although he could not face the thought of telling his parents that he had decided to leave. Instead, he put a few belongings into a haversack, tied up a pile of books with string and left St Kilda, saying he was going away for the weekend. It was a weekend that would stretch into years and upset Nolan's parents, although he assured them of regular visits and promised to keep his steady job, whatever the demands of Bohemia.

This first crack in the facade of family unity would soon be followed by another, indicating that the former carefree days were over. By the time he reached his forties, Nolan's father should have been ready for promotion to inspector, but his known activities as an SP bookmaker led to a difficult decision by the tribunal of the Tramways. When the employees were drivers, those sorts of activities were usually overlooked as being an extension of the men's social life. Inspectors, however, had to be seen as scrupulously honest, above suspicion of taking part in anything unlawful. Mr Nolan took it for granted that with his record on the trams he would receive promotion in due course, but the tribunal decided otherwise. Nolan accompanied his father to the Tramways offfices on the day the promotions were being announced and waited outside in the car for him as he was informed of the decision. He returned to his son, with tears streaming from his eyes and a look of disbelief on his face. He would continue working as a driver for a few years, but his heart was no longer in it.

CHAPTER TWO

The Bohemian Rebel

§

The city proved to have both advantages and drawbacks for Nolan who at first fitted awkwardly into the life of his flatmates while he continued at Fayrfield Hats. His display work was becoming increasingly routine and even the time he managed to filch from the company for reading and experiments with abstract imagery began to pall. Words seemed more important as he began to write poetry and was convinced this would lead to his writing a novel before long. Nolan had discovered that his first instinct when under pressure was to write. The group he associated with after his life veered from the athletic to the aesthetic thought of him as a would-be writer rather than a painter because in discussions his conversation was more often about books than art. Nolan continued his evening studies at the National Gallery School on a casual basis, rarely fired by anything he learned as the teaching was almost entirely academic, based on nineteenth-century French principles of drawing from plaster casts and, later, the nude where tone was all-important. The students progressed from the head of Homer to more complicated anatomical models and Nolan developed the greatest contempt for this study, although he admired the well-used casts themselves, particularly a representation of Ariadne, daughter of King Minos of Crete, which kindled in him an ambition to go to Europe and see the originals of these wonderful sculptures.

John Sinclair was surprised to see his flatmate going through the motions of being an art student and managing to survive without producing any notable work. Nolan's desire for knowledge was interesting to see, with frequent discussions with other students about painting and long hours spent in the Public Library where he devoured an amazing range of literature and studied all the reproductions he could find of paintings by Gauguin, Van Gogh, Matisse and Picasso.

Nolan's artistic sights were set on different horizons. He now had an interest in the works of the Mexican muralists, which he had also seen in reproduction, and thought their art, or something similar, could be valid in the Australian context. The political situations in Germany, Spain and China were constantly discussed in the cafes and Chinese restaurants of Melbourne and Nolan began wondering if art could participate in the revolutionary movements of nations, although he was careful to remain aloof from the hysteria and polarised attitudes in political discussions, and was not interested in any formal political process such as voting at elections. He began to meet a varied cross-section of Melbourne's radicals in the pubs and cafes, some of them self-confessed Fascists or Communists. He saw himself as a factory worker, but was being introduced to a broad range of philosophical ideas by academics and historians.

There were other meeting places in the city where the discussion concentrated on art matters. The Leonardo Bookshop, opened in 1930 by a genial Italian named Gino Nibbi, became the focal point for the local avant-garde, with a large stock of the latest books and modern reproductions from Europe. Nibbi had acquired some notoriety when the police regarded his prints of Modigliani nudes as obscene and mounted a raid to seize them. There was also the Primrose Pottery, an arts and crafts shop with etchings on the walls and the latest Danish furniture for sale. Its proprietor was a sophisticated dark-haired young woman named Cynthia Reed whom Nolan was too shy to engage in conversation. In fact, their only exchange was an accusation that he had stolen her watch which had been left on the counter. He had entered the Primrose Pottery wearing bicycle clips on his trousers and strongly resented the veiled suggestion from this overpoweringly fascinating woman that it was working-class people like himself who were always suspected of being thieves.

There came a time when, inevitably, the incessant theorising about art and politics became too oppressive for Nolan. He was frustrated by the fact that there was not enough money to escape overseas and find out what was happening in what he felt was the real world. One solution was to go bush, trying to eke out an existence while painting and experimenting, far from the pressures of the city. Nolan and Howard Matthews hatched a scheme to pool their cash resources — about £20 — and go to live in a remote weekender owned by one of Nolan's aunts near Selby, a couple of hours drive away beyond Ferntree Gully east of Melbourne. Their main expenses would be food and they decided to spend half their capital by following the advice of Matthews' sister who was a food faddist. She convinced them that a diet of pickled tripe would be nourishing and sustaining for long periods, and the two young men bought countless glass containers of this from a butcher's shop in North Melbourne. Most of the remainder of their money went on a supply of madeira wine in stoneware jars and these supplies, together with board, paints and sketch pads, were gathered in preparation for the trip.

Matthews was a close friend of Noel Blaubaum, a flamboyant fellow student at the Gallery School and the son of a fashionable Melbourne doctor.

Kiewa Valley, *1936*

Selby, *1937*

Unlike most of the others, Noel was far from penniless and some of his father's wealth was reflected in the open sports car driven everywhere, often at dangerously high speeds. Blaubaum had offered to take the two would-be recluses to the shack, setting out one Friday afternoon. The trip started badly at a cheap Italian restaurant in Exhibition Street where Nolan brandished a rifle they were taking to the country, pointing it at a waiter who had refused to give a table to the rough-looking and noisy trio. The police were called and some fast talking was required to avoid serious trouble.

After a meal elsewhere, they piled into the overloaded little car and set off in the chill of a winter's night for Selby. It was past midnight before they arrived at the township and had to rouse the owner of the general store who looked after the key of the cottage. The man was far from happy about being woken by this rowdy trio battering on his door. They had opened one of the jars of madeira during the journey, gulping it down as fortification against the cold night air, and it had gone to their heads. Nolan pulled out the rifle and shouted to the confused storeowner, 'You come down and give us that key, or take the consequences!' The sight of a firearm quickly convinced the man he should comply and he handed over the key.

Blaubaum returned to Melbourne with a hangover the next morning and Nolan and Matthews went along to patch up strained relations with the storekeeper and to buy some provisions. There followed a productive period of work with each taking one end of the cottage for studio space as they spent an uncom-

Nolan, aged 20 (Lorna Goslin)

24

fortable existence, stimulated by living close to nature but becoming increasingly depressed by the monotony of their diet. However, there was plenty of wood on the ground to keep a fire going to ward off dampness during the long winter evenings. The one kerosene lamp was too dim to work by, so they talked and read in front of the fire and then went to bed early so that the full hours of daylight could be used for drawing and painting, when Nolan produced a series of small conventional landscapes in contrast to his usual abstracts.

The weekends were punctuated by visits from Blaubaum and as many female art students as he could cram into his sports car. During one of these trips he said he would like to bring the celebrated old painter Rupert Bunny to stay on the following weekend and he left some money to buy extra provisions from the store at Selby to entertain their visitor in the best style they could manage. Bunny, born in St Kilda in 1864, was regarded by a handful of discerning critics and painters as one of Australia's finest artists, although his reputation among art lovers was tainted because he had spent the greater part of his career in France and much of his work was heavily influenced by French Impressionism. He was thus not part of the accepted tradition of Australian landscape. His wife had died in the early 1930s and he came home to live in Melbourne after an absence of nearly fifty years. Bunny was a rather lonely person in spite of exhibitions at Hogan's Art Gallery, where he showed his earlier mythological works, flower paintings, and scenes of the south of France painted in homage to Cézanne which the *Argus* critic dismissed as 'fuzzy and indeterminate'.

Nolan and Matthews eagerly waited for their guests to arrive on the following Friday evening, looking forward to stimulating conversations about life in Paris at the beginning of the century, descriptions of the French salons and reminiscences of meetings with famous artists. A casserole of lamb and potatoes had been prepared and it was hoped the dwindling supply of madeira would last for the weekend. By 9.30 nobody had appeared and, assuming the visitors were not coming that night, they were about to eat the food and go to bed, when Blaubaum and Bunny burst into the cottage, wet and exhausted. Apparently the old painter had fallen into the creek after getting out of the car and Blaubaum had fallen in as well while trying to drag him out. Bunny took off his sodden shirt and vest, and in the yellow light of the kerosene lamp looked white and gaunt and shaken from the experience, his teeth chattering. The visitors dried themselves in front of the smoky fire, then they ate the overcooked food and drank the wine as the conversation rambled over a wide range of subjects including politics and art until Blaubaum and Matthews violently disagreed on a point of aesthetics. The debate erupted into a noisy slanging match, disturbing their gentle guest by its ferocity, and Nolan tactfully suggested they should settle their differences outside. They took his advice and left the room while Nolan and Bunny settled down in front of the fire to talk about a painter's life in Europe.

Suddenly the still night was shattered by rifle shots which penetrated the iron chimney stack, hitting the fireplace and raising small puffs of ash in the hearth. Bunny slid to the floor for cover while Nolan nervously crawled to the door and peered out into the moonlight to discover what was happening. He could just make out the figure of Blaubaum taking pot-shots at the cottage while continuing his row with Matthews. Nolan screamed out for them to stop at once before somebody was killed and the two came to their senses and returned inside. At the doorway Blaubaum swung around, pointed the rifle and pulled the trigger to fire an angry final shot into the night. Striding back he had used the gun as a walking stick, jamming its barrel with mud so that when he pulled the trigger the weapon exploded in his face, blackening his cheek with powder but causing no injury. The realisation of what might have happened helped inflamed passions to cool and the four of them bunked down for the night, talking in the darkness until three in the morning and listening to Rupert Bunny's stories about his life in France. This lively conversation convinced Nolan and Matthews that exile in the bush was no solution to what they were seeking and it was with a feeling of relief that they packed up their equipment and returned to the city after a few weeks away, with the madeira finished but much of the vile pickled tripe untouched.

After the experiences at Selby, the thought uppermost in the minds of Nolan and Matthews was to get away from Australia to build their futures in Europe — or anywhere — because the act of leaving was symbolically important. To earn money for his fare Nolan worked for a short while in a gold-mining office at Ballarat in a job arranged by his girlfriend Elizabeth Paterson, whose father ran the business. But Ballarat was not for him and he returned to the city to face the chronic problem of insufficient money for overseas travel. Nolan and Matthews toyed with the idea of becoming missionaries in Tahiti, not for the joy of preaching the gospel, but to travel in the footsteps of one of their own gods, Paul Gauguin. The Missionary Society had a scheme which trained young men for a life of spreading the word of Christ throughout the Society Islands and, once accredited, their passage would be paid, provided that each new missionary could raise an initial £25 for living expenses. It was a large sum for both of them, but Matthews thought it just possible and was in the throes of negotiating to raise the money. Before this could be completed, however, an unexpected opportunity for getting to Europe presented itself.

Nolan and Matthews took the short train journey to Station Pier, Port Melbourne, one Saturday morning to farewell a friend who was leaving for Britain. They went aboard the liner carrying brown paper bags of beer bottles, found their friend, and settled down in the third-class saloon to some serious drinking. There was a brief interlude below deck to see his cabin, which proved to be a small airless box in the bowels of the ship, without natural light. It was, at £39 for the trip, the cheapest accommodation and would have to do as his home during the five-week voyage. Fortunately the ship was not full and there would be a little room to move as there were three spare bunks in the otherwise claustrophobic space intended for six passengers. They were returning to their beer in the saloon when the ship's siren sounded a loud blast and all visitors were requested to go ashore as the ship was about to depart. Howard Matthews thought it might be possible for Nolan and himself to use the empty bunks in their friend's cabin and thus remain on board without being detected, at least until leaving the Australian coast after Fremantle. By then, he reasoned, it would be impractical for the ship to turn back and they would have to be taken all the way to England. He told the others of his scheme and they agreed that it was a wonderful idea, although Nolan's senses were not too dulled by beer for a spark of responsibility. 'Well, if we're going to do it', he suggested, 'at least we ought to let our girls and parents know what we're up to'.

Brief farewell notes were hastily scrawled on the ship's stationery, explaining they had made a decision to embark on a great adventure into the international world of art. After reaching Europe, they would send money back to Australia as quickly as possible so their girlfriends from the National Gallery School, Elizabeth Paterson and Joan Currie, could join them. Nolan also wrote to his mother, asking her not to worry about him as he was fulfilling a life's ambition to reach the hub of art and culture, to return one day in triumph enriched by the experience. A visitor going ashore was persuaded to take the letters and post them while the three young men pushed their way to the ship's rail to watch streamers being thrown to shore. While watching this lively scene, Nolan idly put a hand in his trouser pocket and found six pound notes which he realised could be useful in an emergency, and to ensure their safety he stuffed the money into the sock of his right foot. As the last of the mooring lines was released and the tugs strained to pull the liner away from the pier, Nolan thought to himself, 'This is it. I've escaped at last!'

The moment of contemplation was broken when Matthews suggested they return to the saloon to finish off the beer and plan their strategy for survival. The tugs hooted a farewell as they left their charge to continue its journey down Port Phillip Bay under her own power, accompanied by the pilot boat from Queenscliff. As Nolan took one last look at the shore on the port side of the liner he could make out the St Kilda baths and the pier, and experienced a few twinges of conscience about what he was doing. Their fare-paying accomplice was beginning to wonder if he might get into trouble for harbouring stowaways. But the euphoria of the moment quickly dispelled such thoughts and Nolan and Matthews soon returned to their cavalier attitudes, elated by a sense of freedom.

The lunch gong sounded and the three young men bounded down to the third-class dining saloon and sat at the nearest table. As permanent places and sittings would be allocated to the passengers later, Nolan and Matthews knew they could not eat here again and would have to find food from a clandestine source. Eventually, they were brought some soup, a grey liquid with an indeterminate taste. Howard Matthews gingerly took a sip, spat it out and called imperiously for the head steward. Nolan was anxious to avoid undue attention but Matthews would not be silenced and continued his demands until the chief steward came to the table. Nolan and Matthews were unable to produce their tickets or cabin numbers and left the saloon unfed, agreeing to split up and hide until the ship reached the open sea.

The chief steward had become suspicious of their unruly behaviour and suggested the purser search the ship for stowaways. Nolan moved around the vessel for an hour, keeping close to groups of passengers, but then he got bored and sat down in a deck chair on the sheltered side of the ship and began to doze off in the warm sunshine. Suddenly he felt a hand on his shoulder and looked up to see an officer demanding to know his cabin number. With surprising agility, Nolan suddenly jumped out of his seat, scaled the adjacent rail and hung out over the sea, holding on by one hand and shouting, 'Another step and I'll let go!' It was an idle threat because if he had jumped, and not become tangled in the churning propellers, he would have been picked up almost immediately by the accompanying pilot boat. Two burly seamen pulled him down from the rail and marched him to a hatch cover forward where a dejected Howard Matthews was already sitting. The purser informed his captives they would be charged as stowaways, taken to Port Adelaide and handed over to the police the following day, but later it was decided they would be taken by the pilot boat to Queenscliff at the western entrance to the bay and handed over to the police. As the pilot boat pulled away from the ship, passengers lined the rails, waving and shouting catcalls as the stowaways were chilled by the sea spray and cool breeze into realising the seriousness of their position.

An uncomfortably long three hours was spent at the pilot station before a small boat was ready to take them into Queenscliff, where the police sergeant was peremptory in his reception and remarks, having faced this situation many times before. They would be charged as stowaways and held in custody pending any action the shipping company wished to take. The sergeant wanted to see the back of them as soon as possible, however, and so after taking their names and addresses, saying the police in Melbourne would be in touch if there were further developments, he told them to go.

The two deflated adventurers found themselves sitting in the gutter of the main street of Queenscliff pondering their next move. Nolan took off one of his shoes to ease an aching foot and found the money he had put in his sock. He pulled out the notes in triumph, and they were able to take the last local train to Geelong and then on to Melbourne, reliving the events of the day, more determined than ever to escape from Australia. On the Monday morning their escapade rather backfired when the letters they had written on the ship were delivered. The girlfriends and Mrs Nolan were shocked and it required some deft explanation to convince them it was meant only as a joke.

In Australia at this time contacts with the world at large in art, music, opera and ballet were very limited. Only popular plays and musicals whose success had been certified by the box office in London and New York were staged regularly and there was little local activity in the performing arts. But when the Russian ballet arrived in Melbourne the city became overwhelmed by the beauty of the performances and the seductive grace of the dancers. The man who called himself Colonel de Basil and claimed to be a former Russian cossack, together with René Blum, rescued the famous Ballets Russes from oblivion after the founder and guiding force, Serge Diaghilev, had died in 1929. Blum and de Basil took over much of the company's celebrated repertoire and engaged many of the choreographers and dancers, allowing a great tradition of ballet to survive. It was hard for de Basil to keep his forces together in the trying business of touring Europe from their base in Monte Carlo. Engagements were often difficult to book and were of short duration, necessitating constant travel. It was not until 1936, when a tour of Australia and New Zealand was arranged, that his company was able to experience the financial advantages of long seasons. Under the name of Colonel de Basil's Monte Carlo Russian Ballet they brought twenty works and a notable company of dancers headed by the Danish-born prima ballerina Helene Kirsova, spending from October 1936 until July the following year in Australasia, with the majority of performances being in Sydney and Melbourne. Following the success of this season, another tour was arranged and a company of more than one hundred brought new works and some old favourites to open at His Majesty's in Melbourne on 28 September 1938. The name was changed to the Covent Garden Russian Ballet because, it was rumoured, de Basil was avoiding his creditors in Europe. Once again the city took the ballet to its heart and many an eligible bachelor lusted after the charms of the young and glamorous ballerinas, Baronova, Riabouchinska and Toumanova. Their partners, David Lichine and Anton Dolin, brought a standard of male dancing never before seen in Australia.

Because of the publicity it was impossible to ignore the ballet's presence and Nolan longed to attend some performances, but there was never enough money for a ticket, and he came up with a scheme to break into the theatre by entering through the rooftop. Having absolutely no fear of heights, Nolan used to climb out onto the roof of his shared flat and walk a whole city block on the ledges and parapets of the buildings. Armed with a screwdriver and a pair of pliers he set out for His Majesty's with the intention of gaining entry by forcing a window on the roof and then finding an empty seat in the auditorium. He got as far as the skylight high above the stage when the orchestra began playing Handel's music for David Lichine's ballet *The Gods Go A-Begging*, but Nolan had to admit defeat because there was no way of gaining entry from the roof without plunging to the stage. He was able to buy the cheapest seats for a few of the performances, however, and managed to make his way backstage during the intervals to catch glimpses of the ballerinas. It was a European world that fascinated him, but one that seemed far removed from his own existence, although he did meet one of the leading dancers in a milkbar close to the theatre. She was Sono Osato, an American Japanese whose movements were seductively graceful. In works like *The Prodigal Son* her sinuous movements seemed to bring the subtlety of oriental dancing to western ballet. They talked about meeting again in the United States at the conclusion of the tour, but he had no money to travel and she returned to the theatre, leaving him with the lasting impression that ballet dancers are among the most beautiful creatures on earth.

After nearly six years in the art department of Fayrfield Hats, Nolan decided it was time to make a break. It was not a good year to find alternative employment, but as he approached the age of 21 the company indicated they were not prepared to pay an adult wage and planned to take on another youngster in his place. The only job Nolan could find had very little in its favour, except for the fact that he could walk there from his flat and did not have to worry about where his next meal was coming from. Hamburger Bill's was the first fast food outlet of its kind in Melbourne and, being situated in the busiest part of Swanston Street, quickly captured the public's imagination and developed an impressive trade. Nolan was forced to accept the serving job as a junior, take it or leave it, and had to sign a statement that he was under 18. In return he received 30 shillings a week and as many hamburgers as he wanted to eat. The proprietor really was named Bill, an American who had plans to establish a chain of his bars around Australia following the success of this first venture. One of its main attractions was that it stayed open until 4 o'clock in the morning, becoming a lively focus for the city's more adventurous night owls, who sometimes mixed with American stewards from the Matson Line passenger ships *Mariposa* and *Monterey*. Hamburger Bill's also became a convenient pick-up place for the local prostitutes, attracted to the American money that many of its late-night visitors had to spend. Business for the girls tended to be slower when the passenger ships were not in port but they still frequented the place, particularly after midnight, for 4d hamburgers and endless cups of coffee.

Times were difficult for staff and customers alike and when the boss was not looking it was customary for Nolan and his colleagues to help out by taking the money for a coffee and then serve eggs and bacon or a hamburger on the same chit. This deception was soon discovered by the owner, who made it clear to his

Colonel de Basil's Covent Garden Russian Ballet. From Le Spectre de la Rose *(left) and* Scuola di Ballo *(right) (Max Dupain)*

Ballerina Sono Osato, 1938

workers that any further discrepancies between money taken and food served would be dealt with in a dramatic way. To emphasise his point, he pulled out the revolver he always carried in a leather holster attached to his belt, pointing it at them in a threatening manner. This seemed an excessive reaction but there was little alternative work on offer and most of the staff were in desperate financial straits, many of them from country areas. He knew they did not worry any more about stealing from each other's lockers in the small changing room at the back of the premises than trying to defraud him.

On Friday 13 January 1939 the wind howled in from the north as if forced from an open oven. Temperatures soared over the century mark, the surrounding countryside sat tinder dry and fires which had been burning for days raced out of control. Melbourne became encircled by bushfires and in the late afternoon its surrounding hills were blotted out by flying ash while people fled for their lives as houses burned in the bush. The city became covered with a pall of smoke and the sun set unseen behind a western glow. The stifling heat in the city meant slack business at Hamburger Bill's and Nolan climbed out onto the verandah over the entrance to get a better view of the spectacle, unaware that seventy-one people were dead and the little town of Noojee destroyed. He was still in his chef's outfit and hat as he inhaled the acrid wood smoke and watched the eerie light over the city reflected from burning hills in the far distance. He became strangely elated by the experience and suddenly found himself performing handstands on the corrugated iron roof, which soon attracted a crowd to watch this surreal sight. The owner was horrified to see what was going on and demanded Nolan come down at once so he could be fired on the spot for causing such an embarrassing display that was obviously bad for business. Nolan tried, as usual, to have the last word, saying it would be foolish to dismiss him because he could make sure the police knew the extent of the prostitutes' pick-up activities and the authorities would probably close down the place. The owner knew he was cornered but countered by banishing Nolan behind the scenes to peel endless buckets of onions and regularly sweep out the bar. This job clearly had no future and Nolan was able to slink back to Fayrfield Hats where all he could expect now was the drudgery of a job in the factory itself, rolling hot felt. It was tiring, unpleasant labour and when his fellow workers decided to hold a protest strike, he was the one nominated to lead them. This put him in an invidious position, for he knew that his job would be on the line, but on the other hand he felt morally obliged to help. He telephoned the newspapers, reports appeared in the press and, predictably, the management demanded his resignation. Soon after he landed a job as a cleaner at Essendon Aerodrome and discovered that the skies must be very turbulent indeed, if the vomit-covered floors of the aircraft were any indication.

32

CHAPTER THREE

Gravitational Forces

§

There was an urgent need to earn money and Nolan realised he was lucky to have any sort of employment, but the demands of his cleaning job led to less time and inclination to study because the end of each working day now meant physical and mental exhaustion. One possible escape route was a scholarship offered by the National Gallery School providing travel to Europe and a generous living allowance. But there was intense competition for the travelling scholarship and with his dismal attendance record combined with his undistinguished work, there was no hope of winning it. A more promising prospect was one of the bursaries given by the urbane and powerful chairman of the Herald and Weekly Times publishing group, Sir Keith Murdoch, a visionary who was one of the few members of the Melbourne establishment to champion the cause of modern art. He subsidised a number of awards to lawyers, doctors and artists to foster a spirit of enterprise rather than the complacency he saw all around him. The problem in trying to win Murdoch's patronage was that all art applicants were recommended by William McInnes, principal of the Gallery School, who was unlikely to support such an errant student as Nolan.

The tantalising prospect of a weekly income of £6 for a period of three years meant complete freedom, and the fact that his flatmates Pendlebury and Sinclair were in the running for the awards spurred Nolan to action. He decided to bluff his way into getting a Murdoch scholarship. He had almost no art work to support an application but remedied that in a few nights of intense activity by doing a series of brush drawings on blotting and tissue paper. After the others had gone to bed, Nolan stripped off his clothes in front of an old mirrored wardrobe that stood in the corner of the kitchen. By the harsh glare of a naked light bulb he used himself as a model and composed a series of abstract figure studies which had something of the quality of Chinese calligraphy mixed with Paul Klee. He added a few other drawings from his limited collection and managed to piece together a respectable, if unconventional, portfolio by the time the milky light of dawn penetrated the small room. There was no time for sleep

33

on the appointed day because, having assembled the drawings for presentation, it was then necessary to plan a suitable wardrobe. Nolan had always been a neat dresser, a habit acquired from his mother, together with the more recent sartorial demands of the Fayrfield Hats promotions. Artists were not expected to look either neat or prosperous and Nolan knew it was essential to dress down for the encounters of the day ahead, putting on a pair of paint-spattered trousers, an old brown sweater with frayed sleeves and a pair of leather sandals, none of them part of his normal street wear. Looking every inch the Melbourne Bohemian he had never become, he set off from the flat with purposeful strides, portfolio under his arm, in the direction of the *Herald* offices, a ten-minute walk away.

It was precisely 9.30 when he walked into the reception area and jauntily addressed the woman sitting at the enquiry desk. He felt confident enough at the start of his deception. 'I've been recommended for an art scholarship by Mr McInnes at the National Gallery School who has arranged an appointment for me to see Sir Keith Murdoch.' The receptionist seemed to ignore what he was saying and instead stared at his outfit. Finally she looked down at an appointments sheet, shook her head, and then checked again to make sure that his name was not on it. He realised he would have to summon all his powers of persuasion or his plan to bulldoze his way into seeing Murdoch would fail right there. He remembered the cheeky stunts he had played in getting attention for Fayrfield Hats and knew something similar was needed now. He smiled sweetly at the receptionist who was impressed by his assurance and thought there might have been a mistake, picking up a telephone to check with Murdoch's office.

A few minutes later Nolan was led to the executive suite and found himself confronted by the formidable figure of Sir Keith's personal secretary who proved to be equally unmoved by his explanation. Having got this far, however, Nolan was not going to leave without one last supreme effort because on the other side of the panelled door was the person who held the power to change his life. The woman saw it was not going to be easy to get rid of this persistent young man and took the line of least resistance by informing the chairman of this curious situation. The next thing Nolan knew he was being ushered in to Murdoch's office. The spacious oak-panelled room had oil paintings on the walls and an extensive collection of Chinese porcelain arranged on stands. Murdoch was seated at a huge desk and seemed well disposed towards his unexpected visitor. He got up and shook Nolan's hand. At that moment the telephone rang and Murdoch became involved in a business conversation, motioning Nolan to sit down. The call seemed to divert his attention from the artist's unheralded appearance in his office, and he noticed his interest in the porcelain. Murdoch quickly warmed to the young man's charm and a conversation developed about the State Gallery's collection and how Murdoch, as one of the trustees, intended

Abstract, *1938*

to change its emphasis from the past to the present. Eventually he asked to look at the drawings Nolan had brought with him and, from the nods of apparent approval as he leafed through them, Nolan assumed his bluff had succeeded and he was within sight of a scholarship. Murdoch handed back the portfolio expressing interest in the work but saying that as a courtesy to the *Herald* art critic, Basil Burdett, Nolan should show him his work and then everything would be all right.

The secretary was instructed to take Nolan along the corridor to Burdett's office with an explanation that he was an applicant for a *Herald* scholarship. Here there were no conversational niceties and the critic, who was in the middle of writing an article, asked to see the collection straightaway. He had a reputation as the most cultured person on the local scene, not only in his knowledge of painting, but as a *bon viveur* who had travelled widely and could wear a black beret with nonchalance. He examined the flimsy abstracts with a look of growing dismay and finally exploded, 'No! No! You are approaching it from the wrong direction. You're putting the cart before the horse and not even Van Gogh did that. I'm afraid a lot more training is needed before you can hope to do what the modern masters are doing.' Nolan was angry at the Van Gogh reference and suddenly felt the quest for artistic freedom slipping away from his grasp as every flimsy sheet was examined by Burdett and then placed back, face down, in the portfolio. 'Where are your figure studies?' he demanded. 'Surely

McInnes suggested you include some in your presentation?' Nolan shook his head and made a helpless gesture of the arms. Burdett continued to demolish his hopes. 'You would need to have considerably more training before we could consider giving you a scholarship. You see, the modern masters are working from a knowledge of past art; they certainly didn't start off in this fashion.' He pointed accusingly to one of the calligraphic sketches, then handed back the portfolio and led Nolan to the door. Almost as an afterthought, in his only display of encouragement for the young artist, Burdett suggested that he should show his work to George Bell at his art school or, failing that, to a solicitor named John Reed who had an interest in art.

Nolan's dreams of a scholarship had suddenly evaporated; the only possibility lay in following the advice of the *Herald*'s art critic who was, after all, reputed to be the most influential voice in Melbourne's art world and a member of Murdoch's social circle. Nolan dismissed thoughts of his abortive attempt to gain a scholarship and carried his portfolio along to the corner of Bourke and Queen Streets where the Bell-Shore School was housed. It had been in existence for six years and gained the reputation in that short time of being one of the few forward-thinking art schools in Australia. Arnold Shore had a deep commitment to colour and form, being a great admirer of Van Gogh's work, although his approach to modernism could hardly be described as anything more than tentative. His colleague, George Bell, was the dominant force, whose presence gave the establishment its personality and sustained its reputation. Bell had spent time travelling in Europe followed by study at the Westminster School in London, whose principles he brought back to Melbourne, attracting a lively group of students who found his life classes and painting tuition exhilarating after the dull academic principles of the National Gallery School. There was another gulf between the two institutions, apart from their difference in size: the scale of fees charged by the Bell-Shore School meant that only students with reasonable financial resources, such as Russell Drysdale, David Strachan, Sali Herman and Maie Ryan, could afford to attend.

Nolan climbed up the creaky wooden stairs to the studio and peered inside through a half-open door to watch the students painting at easels with an attractive female model sitting on a box, while the appealing smell of oil paints permeated the warm air. He thought Bell would be impressed with the contents of his portfolio because of Bell's reputation among young painters as a kind of revolutionary. Instead of offering praise, however, Bell took immediate offence when he saw some of the minimal images. He told Nolan to concentrate for the present on simple, straightforward illustration and learn to draw a table or a chair properly, with the various perspectives correct. Nolan's heart sank at such basic advice, although he made a show of heeding Bell's words by nodding in apparent agreement. Bell was adamant that Nolan's work was not good enough to gain him a place in the school, even if he could manage the fees. He suggested that Nolan work as a commercial artist, unaware that he had earned a living in this way for several years. As Nolan left, he mentioned that he intended to visit John Reed, not knowing that Bell and Reed were engaged in a long and bitter argument about principles of art and culture, a continuing feud where it seemed there could be no capitulation from either side. Bell looked horrified. 'My God', he exclaimed. 'Well there's no telling what could happen! I wish you success.'

It was now early afternoon as Nolan plodded on in his sandals, paint-spotted trousers and increasingly itchy sweater and found Reed's small office in Collins Street. Sitting at a desk reading Wilenski's *The Modern Movement in Art* was a dark, good looking man. The book was open at a reproduction of Rousseau's *The Wedding of Apollinaire* and immediately Nolan felt at home in an atmosphere that seemed anything but a solicitor's office. He introduced himself and explained he had come not for legal advice but on the recommendation of Basil Burdett. Reed pushed the book to one side and seemed relieved that he did not have to discuss legal matters with a client. Nolan's confidence was on the wane after the previous encounters and for a moment he almost gave up trying to sell himself but he rallied and decided to stake everything on a final effort. 'Before I show you my work', he tried to explain forcibly, but stumbled over his words, 'I want to make my position absolutely clear. I believe I'm cut out to be an artist, whatever other people think. And that is what I am going to be. I've got my life's work here', he tapped the green cardboard folder under his arm. 'I want £50 for it and then I can go off to Paris.' Reed was amused by this forthright approach, admiring the wild-cat spirit of the young man. He opened the covers and took his time with the contents, turning over page after page and examining each sheet carefully. Nolan waited, expecting to hear the reaction that had become standard during the day. Finally Reed said, 'Interesting. Very interesting indeed. But I have to tell you that neither I nor any of my friends could see their way to raising the sort of money you want for a trip to Paris.' The words were friendly but firm. In the next breath he added disarmingly, 'Perhaps you'd like to come to my place for dinner?' Nolan was surprised but stammered a vague acceptance, thinking a good meal would be a relief after such a frustrating time. After telephoning his wife, Sunday, Reed suggested Nolan would want to go home and change before they met at Flinders Street Railway Station for the journey to Heidelberg.

Heidelberg was in the country, beside the willow-fringed Yarra wending its way through lush river flats with gentle hills rising on either side. The township appeared out of the trees above the northern bank, bearing no physical resemblance to the German university city after which it was named. There was a mere strip of a community with a few shops and facilities to serve the scattered population around the upper reaches of the Yarra and throughout the surrounding

Heide (Barrett Reid)

hills. The city was within easy commuting distance by the regular train service, but Heidelberg was unquestionably rural.

The Reeds had known and loved the area from the time before their marriage in 1932, when Sunday Baillieu, a strikingly attractive divorcee from one of Melbourne's leading business families, and John Reed, a Cambridge-educated lawyer with a Tasmanian pastoralist background, both in their early thirties, motored through the area with its small farming properties and orchards. They heard about a dairy farm with an old weatherboard house on fifteen acres which was owned by an elderly widow who was past caring for the property, and they went to see it. There were a few straggly trees around the house and everything was in a sorry state, but its location was attractive and Sunday saw its potential. The Reeds were able to purchase the house and land in 1934 and moved there in the autumn of the following year, when they began a planting programme in the grounds, adding as many trees as they could manage to water, while supervising the remodelling of the house, installing a modern bathroom and kitchen and adding extensive bookshelves. Under Sunday's patient care a kitchen garden was planted and flower beds were developed with the assistance of Neil Douglas. They bought a cow which kept the household supplied with fresh milk and cream for the constant visitors and longer-term guests. The handsome young couple seemed to have acquired the best of all worlds, with their family backgrounds, good education and an adequate income that allowed them freedom to indulge in their love of art and literature. But there was a hidden side to this apparently ideal marriage which centred on Sunday's inability to bear children and the subsequent drift into casual relationships that developed within their circle.

The area had a long tradition of association with painters, ever since the so-called Australian impressionists had established summer camps along this stretch of the Yarra and begun painting in the open air. In the late 1880s, around the time of the centenary of European settlement, Arthur Streeton, Tom Roberts, Frederick McCubbin and Charles Conder spent weeks in the district with their girlfriends and cronies leading an idyllic existence, producing small, rapidly-executed oil sketches that nobody wanted to buy, but developing a freshness of style that would become known, imprecisely, as the Heidelberg School. By the 1930s, when Melbourne's growing suburbs were encroaching on the countryside, permanent artists' colonies were established, with Justus Jorgensen building Montsalvat, a two-storey chateau-style dwelling at Eltham, and Danila Vassilieff, the Russian-born painter, later constructing a great fortress called Stonygrad. Adrian Lawlor, leader of the modernist movement, half-a-dozen other artists and a handful of educationalists with advanced ideas also lived in the area. They knew each other in a common cultural bond, although their aesthetics and opinions were often so polarised that meetings ended in violent arguments. The Jorgensens, for instance, regarded themselves as the arbiters of the only way to paint, their theories based on Max Meldrum's scheme of tonal divisions; if the tones were right, a painting would succeed. Nolan was appalled that a whole generation of Australian painters was emerging from the Meldrum school, carrying on those rigid principles, which made the Reeds' own circle seem like an enlightened Bloomsbury of the bush.

The train pulled in at Heidelberg station after a journey of fifty minutes. Nolan followed his host up a curved path from the station to where a car was parked and they drove down the hill, across a bridge over the Yarra River and then up the other side to a ridge where the Reeds' converted farmhouse named Heide sat overlooking the river flats and the small community in the distance. It was a glorious summer's evening with the setting sun casting a yellow light on the paddocks and the white weatherboards of the old house surrounded by its neat picket fence. They were greeted at the door by Sunday, who then disappeared into the kitchen to prepare their meal. The two men sat down in the library in easy chairs before the empty fireplace with large glasses of whisky. Nolan was known to be a hearty beer drinker among his friends but this was the first time he had ever tasted Scotch. He sipped the fiery liquid with some apprehension, while noticing a number of interesting modern pictures. John Reed slowly sipped his drink and observed that his guest was becoming quite lightheaded. 'Why do you think D.H. Lawrence had such an interest in sex?' he asked. Nolan had never considered the question and found the whisky answering for him, rather inanely, 'Perhaps it was because he'd been in a number of hot countries, including Australia'. Reed took the comment seriously. 'No, I don't think that necessarily follows. I'm quite certain the climate had nothing to do with it.' Nolan was always ready for a discussion and entered into the spirit, agreeing with his host. 'I can understand that it probably wouldn't since there are plenty of Eskimo children, but Middleton Murry says . . .' Reed interrupted him. 'Ah, you mention Middleton Murry . . .' But before he could find his copy of *Son of Woman*, the story of D.H. Lawrence that was somewhere on the bookshelves, Sunday arrived at the door and announced that dinner was ready.

During the meal Nolan's head was spinning from the effects of drinking whisky and then wine on a previously empty stomach, combined with the effects of lack of sleep and an excessive amount of talking during the day. He listened and observed as much as he could, noting that Murdoch, Burdett, Bell and Reed had engaged him in straightforward conversations, masculine and direct, whereas Sunday's talk was intensely feminine, complicated and strangely disturbing. He was intrigued by this relaxed atmosphere where frank discussion was not necessarily the springboard to intense argument. The Reeds showed a lively interest in what he thought and where he imagined he was headed. It was a bemused Nolan who returned to Melbourne that night on the last train. He felt curiously elated, although he had achieved nothing of what he had intended, and there was no way of knowing it was a turning point in his life which, after this encounter with the Reeds, would never be the same again.

The exhilaration of finding himself accepted as a creative individual after meeting the Reeds was offset by Nolan's growing affection for Elizabeth Paterson. He knew that the Reeds, and Sunday in particular, had no interest in his girlfriend and he had to develop a defensive stance between the sophistication of Heide and his other world with Elizabeth and her friends. She was the granddaughter of John Ford Paterson, a Scottish-born painter who had lived and worked in Melbourne for much of his life, becoming a friend of Streeton and one of the originators of what was jokingly called 'the whisky haze' of the Australian bush which characterised nationalist painting during the 1880s and 1890s. Paterson died in 1912 leaving a modest art dynasty with his nieces Esther and Betty as well as his granddaughter being promising painters.

Elizabeth was in love with her fascinating art student and keen to get married as soon as possible because the mounting interest in him at Heide seemed to be threatening their relationship. Nolan was virtually without income and in no position to support himself, let alone a wife, but Elizabeth was persistent and he promised to do something about the situation. He was passing the Dutch Reformed Church in City Road, South Melbourne one morning and on the spur of the moment decided to find out how quickly they could be married. The pastor said he could perform the ceremony as soon as Nolan brought his

Sir Sidney and Lady Nolan on their property at Bundanon, New South Wales

Abstract, *1940*

Roof tiles, *1940*

Luna Park, *1941*

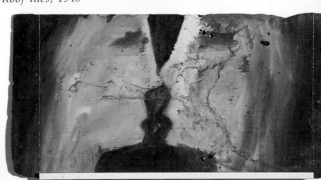

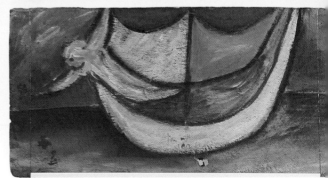

intended wife along to the church and paid for two witnesses who could probably be found on the street outside. And so in the simplest of ceremonies Sidney and Elizabeth became Mr and Mrs Nolan. Before departing for Ocean Grove where they had been offered a house rent-free for a year, the 21-year-old groom returned to his parents' house where he had been living again because of his lack of income. He wanted to tell his mother of his marriage, and explain why a traditional ceremony had not been arranged. Nolan walked into the dining room, took off his coat and hung it over a chair while he went to his bedroom to look for some books. He did not notice that the marriage certificate had fallen out of his pocket and when he returned he found his mother sobbing in the kitchen. She had picked up the paper from the floor before there was an opportunity to tell her of the marriage.

Living at Ocean Grove, 75 miles from Melbourne, was pleasant and inexpensive for the newlyweds and their cocker spaniel named August. At this time of the year the grassy slopes were dotted with field mushrooms every morning, basic foods from the local store were cheap enough, and there was no rent to pay. In between periods of painting Nolan was able to earn a few shillings by cycling into nearby Geelong carrying out messages for a neighbour, a cripple named Martin who bred spaniels. Like most people in the district during these times of depression, Martin was constantly short of money, particularly to purchase food for the ever-hungry dogs, and he enlisted Nolan's help in shooting a decrepit old horse which he had bought cheaply for dog meat. After the beast had been felled with a single shot through the brain, a strange ritual took place on a hillside overlooking Bass Strait. Martin sat in his wheelchair and watched as a quartet of men, including Nolan and a visiting painter named Gray Smith, hacked the carcass apart with axes, staining the grass with blood. This violent scene, which might have come from a painting by Hieronymus Bosch, was followed by the men cutting every last remnant of edible flesh and gristle from the bones with sharp knives.

Ocean Grove had the right combination of soil and climate for growing excellent asparagus and there were several farms in the area offering casual work for pickers during the short season. Nolan was able to land one of these jobs which entailed shuffling along the rows of ridged earth in a stooped position looking for delicate green tips just breaking the surface. A long knife was inserted in the soil and the young spears of asparagus cut off and extracted. He was not very proficient at this backbreaking toil and, being piece work, the rewards were minuscule. During lunch breaks the workers discussed their conditions and decided to approach the farmer for a pay increase. Once again, Nolan found himself drawn into a dispute as group spokesman and was asked to draw up their demands in the form of a manifesto to present to the owner of the farm. He was reluctant to let his fellow workers down by failing to display

41

solidarity with the cause, but he also knew he might be victimised, if previous experience was any indication. These reservations proved well-founded; the farmer demanded to know who had compiled the men's demands and when Nolan owned up, he was promptly sacked, although the owner did agree to negotiate with the others, because with the delicate asparagus ready for cutting he would find it very difficult to assemble another gang at short notice.

Nolan's leadership role was not wasted this time as the farmer was quick to realise that if the young man was bright enough to write a manifesto, he could operate one of the washing machines. Managing the semi-automatic device for cleaning the asparagus spears was far less demanding than the toil of the fields and, for once, Nolan found himself on the winning side. In fact, he proved such a willing worker that when the short picking season closed, he was offered further work helping to spread the paddocks with a blood and bone mixture to fertilise the soil for its next crop. It was hot and uncomfortable work with the fine dust being blown everywhere by the sea breezes, clogging the pores and penetrating the skin with its repulsive smell.

The couple continued to work at their art and Nolan went about his painting with a single-minded purpose that tended to ignore the fact that Elizabeth was a good artist as well, attempting to develop her own style. He appropriated the sunny end of the room they used as a joint studio and this domination inevitably led to growing strains and disagreements. Nolan seemed to be hell-bent on his own theories which increasingly embraced Rimbaud and much revolutionary French culture. He had a conviction, as he put it, that in art 'the screw has to be turned ever further, that one has to be more violent, more avant-garde, more abstract'. He remained a loner, standing apart from official groupings, although the influence of John and Sunday Reed was growing more powerful and extended as far as Ocean Grove, where they became regular visitors. Nolan was persuaded by them to become a foundation member of the Contemporary Art Society, and to contribute a painting to the first group exhibition held at the National Gallery. There was a small representation of work from the Reeds' favoured circle of painters among a wide selection of more conventional material from Melbourne's self-styled modern artists. Nolan's entry, *Head of Rimbaud*, stood out as a striking revolutionary statement, looking a little like an abstract three-tiered cake, painted on cardboard with a background rendered in Kiwi boot polish, an innovative device that gave the effect of a rich stain when rubbed into the surface.

Head of Rimbaud attracted little attention from the hundreds of people who visited the exhibition, except for Adrian Lawlor, a talented painter himself. During Lawlor's own one-man show, Nolan had stood before some of the paintings, sketching little abstracts from Lawlor's imagery, analysing the geometry of his construction and attempting to look at the structure behind the

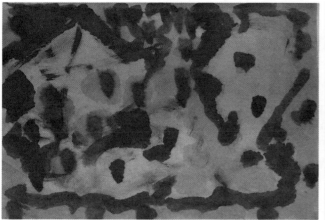

Abstract, *1939*

Head of Rimbaud, *1939*
(Heide Park and Art Gallery)

surface of the paintings. Lawlor happened to visit the gallery at the same time and took exception to what Nolan was doing. He thought the young man was trying to steal his painting ideas and now he was able to get his own back at the CAS exhibition. He stopped at the Rimbaud head, noting the title and name of the artist, and gazed at the work for a couple of minutes in silence. Nolan was hovering nearby and Lawlor beckoned him over to the painting. 'Tell me, Mr Nolan', he asked with more than a hint of sarcasm in his voice, 'What exactly is a rimbaud? A French cheese?'

Melbourne's artists during the 1930s generally had been a depressed bunch, coming together in small cliques for a sense of solidarity; poor, with uncertain futures, they were beset by economic insecurities and questions about their place in society and the nature of society itself. It was a time of transition in many walks of life, with a drifting away from the values and traditions of earlier decades. There were writers and poets, craftsmen and academics, painters and commercial artists, but a woefully small market for their products and ideas. The horizons for these radical thinkers were physically confined to their home city of Melbourne but at the same time were limitless in embracing culture and politics from Europe and, to a lesser extent, the United States. When the self-styled reformers were noticed at all by the community it was as irritants and threats to artistic values that had changed little for more than half a century, since the golden age of pastoral landscape that had become the textbook style for generations to follow.

With the economy recovering from the worst effects of the depression, the dichotomy between radicals and conservatives had been brought into sharp focus by the establishment in Canberra of the Australian Academy of Art, modelled on the principles of Britain's Royal Academy. Some artists thought it had happened fifty years too late, while conservative painters welcomed it. Its champion was Robert Gordon Menzies, a consummate politician, lover of traditional art and a fervent admirer of the British way of life. As the federal attorney-general, he sounded out the possibility in London of the Australian Academy gaining a royal charter and the indications were favourable. Menzies' intention was for the Academy to administer federal funding for the arts and to establish a national gallery in Canberra. There were many reservations among artists about the potential imperialism of an Academy, but most of the long-established art societies were in favour because there was strength in numbers and, if the traditional rivalries between Sydney and Melbourne could be overcome, there was the prospect of increasing the appreciation of good art, and its market. Menzies was able to gain the support of establishment figures in the art world as well as Sydney's Society of Artists and wooed the Victorian Artists Society with the promise that modernism would receive short shrift from the Academy. There was a surge of resentment from painters and teachers who supported modern art and it resulted in the formation of the Contemporary Art Society, a breakaway group from the Victorian Artists Society, headed by George Bell with John Reed as its first lay president.

Ocean Grove was mostly a pleasant interlude for Sidney and Elizabeth Nolan. There were the continuing problems of lack of money combined with personal tensions, but the spring and summer weather was bracing and healthy and they both continued with their painting. Friends came to visit at weekends, including the parents on both sides of the family as well as the Reeds, who continued to monitor Nolan's development and cause continuing unease to Elizabeth because of the way they seemed to monopolise her husband, raising the emotional temperature each time they visited.

The young couple's own trips to Melbourne were less frequent but there was one occasion from which nothing could keep them: an exhibition of British and French painting at the Melbourne Town Hall. One of the problems for artists in Australia was their isolation from great works of art. The National Gallery of Victoria was the best endowed in the country but its collection could hardly claim to be representative of past movements, let alone display vital aspects of the twentieth century. During the 1930s there had been only a couple of touring shows from abroad that allowed a glimpse of what was going on in the outside world, and they had been devoted mostly to British works, although as long ago as 1931 Keith Murdoch had sponsored an exhibition of modern European works owned by private collectors in Australia, including Modigliani, Matisse, Utrillo and Dufy, and showed it in the *Herald* building. The present exhibition came about because Murdoch felt committed to introducing the Australian public to some of the finest art of their own time. He agreed to sponsor a major touring exhibition organised by his friend and adviser, the *Herald*'s art critic Basil Burdett, who visited Europe and America to arrange for the individual loans.

Burdett's personal kudos diminished, however, after he contracted jaundice during the sea journey back to Australia and was confined to bed while a favourite of the Heide set, Peter Bellew, took over management of the exhibition and received much of the credit for its considerable success. The show's list of artists was dazzling: seven Cézannes, nine Picassos, four Braques, works by Van Gogh, Gauguin, Matisse, Seurat, Dali, Modigliani, Léger, Gris and Vlaminck, together with a British representation from Sickert, Wilson Steer, Tonks, Augustus John and Graham Sutherland. They came as a revelation to the people who flocked to the show in the Lower Town Hall, opened on 16 October 1939 by the French consul-general soon after the outbreak of war, prompting his remark that what was seen hanging on the walls was remarkably good propaganda for the Allied cause.

The Nolans made their pilgrimage from Ocean Grove a few days after the official opening. Sidney had no suitable clothing for the city, not even his 'artist's outfit' had survived, and all he could find to wear on his feet was a pair of rubber milking boots. Melbourne was experiencing a foretaste of summer and his legs soon began to ache from the tight, sweaty rubber, but it was a small price to pay for the joy of seeing so many original paintings by such important artists. Peter Bellew, who was a close friend of Sunday Reed, showed a sure hand in publicising the show, engaging Adrian Lawlor as a sort of combined ringmaster and lecturer with a rostrum on wheels which could be moved around the hall and placed in front of paintings while he addressed the patrons. Nolan heard him saying, 'Dali is the greatest thing since Beethoven's late string quartets', and going off at a tangent about the musical glories of Beethoven before realising he had digressed. He then jumped off his chariot and pushed it along to the Cézannes where he would start all over again.

Nolan met the energetic Peter Bellew, some five years his senior, for the first time and Sunday Reed also introduced him to a young painter named Joy Hester, whom Nolan had seen at the National Gallery School and who was the girlfriend of another artist, Albert Tucker. The show had a deep effect on Nolan, confirming what he had learned after many years of looking at reproductions, although it would not change his approach to painting in any dramatic way. It did provide the motivation to move back to the city, however, because only here were essential stimulations like this exhibition and people such as the Reeds, Peter Bellew and Adrian Lawlor. Furthermore, Ocean Grove was no place to have the baby they were now expecting and, as their year was nearly up, it was time to move back and face an uncertain future in wartime Melbourne.

Rooms were hard to find in the city and Elizabeth went to live with her parents until suitable accommodation could be arranged. The best that could be found was a pie shop in Lonsdale Street with combined living and studio space above. Nolan borrowed £50 from his father and found himself as a business-man-artist, a role he felt totally unequipped to play. Planning the daily lunch-time demand became a trial and he and Elizabeth would wake up in their sparsely furnished room above the shop and drink several bottles of Coca-Cola to make them sufficiently conscious to decide how many pies and sausage rolls to order from the baker as he made early morning rounds with his cart. It was a boring existence which earned little money for them except on the day the Australian 7th Division went off to war and marched down Lonsdale Street to the cheers of the crowds lining the route.

Nolan began to spend more time with the Reeds, to the increasing annoyance of Elizabeth, talking art and art politics with John and Sunday and their passing parade of interesting friends and visitors. He was still not convinced, however, that his energies would be devoted to painting. Access to the extensive library at Heide saw Nolan devouring Faulkner and Joyce, Lawrence and Blake, Verlaine and Rimbaud, and he began to write more poetry himself. His art up to this time had been highly individual and often symbolic, linked to the exploitation of materials and the exploration of techniques, with Paul Klee as perhaps the dominant influence, together with Miró, Masson and Ernst. One of these paintings was a tent-like abstract, vaguely in the shape of the big dipper at Luna Park, that Peter Bellew liked and had taken with him to Sydney. It was one of several pictures Nolan composed on Luna Park themes linked to lines from a poem by William Blake and influenced in style by Picasso's studies for *Guernica*.

Bellew, who had founded a branch of the Contemporary Art Society in Sydney where he was editing *Art in Australia* and acting as art critic for the *Sydney Morning Herald*, contacted the Reeds and asked them to pass on a message inviting Nolan to prepare some designs for Serge Lifar because the choreographer and leading dancer with the de Basil company had seen the tent painting and liked it. The company had returned late in 1939 for a third tour and Lifar was preparing a new version of the one-act ballet *Icare* for a premiere during February 1940 in Sydney. Nolan, excited at the possibility of working with the company, immediately began to think about his approach, unaware that the brilliant young stage designer and painter Loudon Sainthill already had been commissioned by Colonel de Basil for the same production, but had been edged out by Lifar and Bellew. Nolan knew nothing about stage techniques, although he had read about Russian constructivist design for the theatre, and his first idea was to create a cubist construction based on the tent motif, extending it in three-dimensional terms from the backdrop to the wings and onto the dancing

46

surface. The rendering was intended to be mainly in black and white so that from the auditorium it would be difficult to determine whether a lit area was a flat surface or part of a cube; the eye would be dazzled by the design, its lighting and the movement of the dancers. Nolan also set to work on some ambitious costume sketches with a zig-zag motif which he thought would combine effectively with the stage design he was creating. Lifar, as the principal dancer in the role of Icarus, would be dressed in a zebra-like costume in front of a striped background, merging to become part of the entire concept. Nolan's approach was adventurous and well-planned within the theories of Russian constructivism, which had strong links with twentieth century art movements in Europe. The initial designs were sent to Peter Bellew in Sydney and a few days later Nolan received word that Lifar liked them.

Tent, *1940*

This was an opportunity that could not be ignored; in fact, it was the greatest recognition of Nolan's talents so far. It also solved the problem of the unsuccessful pie shop and Elizabeth agreed that they close it down and that she would follow Nolan to Sydney shortly. He had no illusions about what was at stake, being fully aware that Lifar and the traditions of the de Basil ballets were part of a vital thread of European culture and that it was an unusual chance for an Australian to participate creatively in their work. Nolan met Serge Lifar backstage during the rehearsals at the Theatre Royal in Sydney and at first found it difficult to communicate because of the Russian's heavily accented broken English, but he was obviously a man of taste, slim with long dark hair, black eyes and a certain insolent manner combined with panther-like movements. Nolan was fascinated by this man who, at 35, was approaching the end of his dancing career, which had first achieved international prominence in 1923 with the Ballets Russes. After Diaghilev had died six years later in Venice, Lifar was appointed ballet master and *premier danseur* at the Paris Opera Ballet where he also created many new works before joining de Basil's company. Nolan was particularly impressed by his association with Jean Cocteau and Pablo Picasso and he listened to some scandalous stories about them. But when they came to discuss the new ballet Nolan learned that Lifar had changed his mind and was no longer interested in the designs sent from Melbourne. In fact, he became quite angry, claiming that Nolan's costumes and set destroyed the line of the ballet.

The opening was looming and new designs were needed quickly. Nolan spent a couple of sleepless nights at Peter Bellew's flat, re-working *Icare* with a conventional backcloth having flats at the side and leaving an unobstructed stage for the dancing. Nolan's inspiration again came from memories of St Kilda, although this time it was not the soaring structures of Luna Park, but the contours of the long, wooden pier which had played a prominent part in his early days. He evolved a linear abstract incorporating a rainbow with the image of Icarus transfixed on it. Nolan was sorry his original ideas incorporating Russian stage theories had been rejected, but he now returned to convention making sure the results would be decorative, if somewhat ambiguous. Then the costumes became the cause of another misunderstanding. Nolan had decided to give them a flowing, weightless effect and knew that silk was the only material for this, hoping to use a local designer, Mavis Rippon, to make the garments. That idea was vetoed by de Basil who decreed they should be made by the company's own wardrobe staff from much cheaper fabrics. Nolan was not prepared to compromise and this led to a violent row the day before the dress rehearsal, with Colonel de Basil berating him for his cheek and Nolan demanding his name be removed from the programme. Finally, Peter Bellew had to mediate in this impasse of inflamed passions and wounded egos.

48

Nolan working on the design of Icare, *watched by Lifar and de Basil*

Serge Lifar in his ballet, Icare *(The Australian Archives of Dance)*

Nolan had to admit that the modified costumes worked quite well and the backcloths, which he painted with the help of Sydney artist Frank Hinder, gave a timeless quality to the production. Before he left Melbourne he had borrowed a dress suit from Vernon Jones at Fayrfield Hats to wear for the opening night on Friday 16 February 1940. The Reeds were in the audience together with Elizabeth, who applauded heartily as her husband was called to the stage after many curtain calls. He shuffled towards the footlights in his ill-fitting white tie and tails, blinded by the brilliance of the strong lights, only to be upstaged by Lifar who was not going to let anyone steal his acclaim. The dancer nimbly stepped in front of his designer and monopolised the applause, then turned to Nolan, giving him an elegant embrace with kisses on both cheeks.

Notwithstanding his major credit for decor and costumes of *Icare*, Nolan realised that during Australia's increasing involvement with the war there could be no hope of capitalising on his success in Europe, or even at home, in the foreseeable future. While he was studying the pictures in the *Herald* exhibition, he had begun to experience a kind of kinship with the European painters; it was a feeling he had not experienced with any local art. He decided that this was the sort of company he wanted to be among, although he would have to suffer the Melbourne scene until he could get away to the real world of culture after the war. Seeing at first hand the work of Van Gogh and Cézanne and Gauguin confirmed for Nolan that his work was on the right track. The difficulties he had experienced with unsympathetic colleagues, the claustrophobic art scene in Melbourne and the delicate balance of his increasingly confused relationship with Elizabeth and the Reeds, culminated in a desire to hold a one-man exhibition.

This was not easy to organise because the handful of commercial galleries would never accept his work and there were few other exhibition outlets for an unknown artist. Nolan had taken a studio in condemned premises in Russell Street, directly opposite the Museum at the back of the National Gallery and State Library that stretched for a whole block from Swanston Street. This area, above a greengrocer's shop, with rickety wooden floors and leaky roof, had previously been used by Howard Matthews and Noel Blaubaum who had attempted to make the tenament more cheerful by painting the walls shocking pink. There were several other artists in the building who paid a small rent to its Chinese owner. Noel Counihan had the space below, although he was recovering from tuberculosis at the time and needed to take long rests. In fact, 320 Russell Street was a warren of hopeful young painters working away in a variety of incompatible styles; they rarely met each other and Nolan preferred it that way. He came to the conclusion that his pink studio was as good a space as any for a show, but it was only the first hurdle to overcome; there was also the pressing question of materials. He had so little money that canvas and board were prohibitively expensive and another, cheaper, medium was required. There were several slates that had fallen off the roof lying in the courtyard and Nolan began experimenting with these, discovering that the application of Ripolin enamel to the absorbent matt grey surface gave pleasing effects. He climbed up into the rafters to gather more supplies, creating a few more gaps in the roof for rain to come through.

Nolan's first one-man show was ready for its opening in these unusual surroundings by June 1940 as the chills of a Melbourne winter penetrated the draughty building. An old iron stove had been found which devoured wood at a great rate in the hopeless task of trying to keep warm the exhibition area, which extended to several small rooms. With a theatrical flourish, Nolan decorated his studio like a stage set in the style he imagined French artists would have adopted in Paris, transforming it into a little salon with lengths of discarded furnishing material hiding the bare boards, together with some borrowed tables and chairs, and books scattered everywhere. There were almost two hundred pictures on the walls: abstract paintings, calligraphic drawings, collages and tiles with strong Miró and Klee influences which had been mounted by Nolan himself with assistance from Martin Smith.

It was unrealistic for anyone to expect much attention for an art exhibition by an unknown painter when the morning's newspaper headlines told of the

German advance on France reaching the Seine at Rouen with Parisians preparing to defend their city. So it was all the more surprising to read a constructive review of Nolan's exhibition in the *Sun* by George Bell, the man who had ridiculed his early efforts to obtain recognition. 'One sees the efforts of a young artist to explore the possibilities of his medium', Bell wrote.

> He is striving, as many are overseas, at an absolutely pure art — an art in which representation of objects has no place at all. In these examples, which are entirely abstract, he is seen experimenting with line, colour, mass and surface texture, significant in themselves as elements of a design discarding all extraneous association of ideas. Preserving his flat surface, he uses arabesque rather than form, pattern rather than volume and colour in its own right and different paint textures rather than imitative textural effects.

Bell was obviously a good analyst of a painter's techniques, although he might have been highly critical of Nolan's abstracts, particularly as his teaching was committed to a solid grounding in drawing and the tonal aspects of painting. The 'cart before the horse' approach of Nolan's was foreign to him, although his review did not reflect this and was quite positive: 'His results are extremely interesting and stimulating, his line is intriguing and his colour is rich and sometimes rare in quality. Whether or not this aim at the absolute in art will be found wanting eventually in its relation to life, these experiments in the bare elements of painting will lay a foundation for the future of this young artist which will be invaluable.' Basil Burdett in his notice dismissed the show as 'highly esoteric'.

The selling prices of the pictures ranged from 30 shillings for the small decorated slates to six guineas for the largest work on board, but there was no interest in buying from the few adventurous souls who managed to find their way up to the chilly atelier. One day when Nolan was out at lunch, somebody found a can of paint in a corner and in a prankish comment daubed one of the brush drawings with green paint, adding a couple of eyes. The newspapers were far more interested in incidents like this because they reflected a community conviction that abstract art was to be ridiculed, and a highly exaggerated report appeared of paint being flung at Nolan's pictures.

Undaunted by the lack of customers, Nolan continued to produce more paintings, including one that would soon achieve considerable notoriety when entered in the second show of the Contemporary Art Society. The idea had come from a visit to St Kilda one memorable evening with John Sinclair, when he saw his friend silhouetted against a full moon rising out of the bay. Nolan painted the scene in its most minimal form, a large yellow disc representing the head with a small stalk of a neck against a blue-black background. He set out to compose a simplified image with flat yellow paint on an equally flat dark blue background, trying to make it appear animated, having the idea that the bold shape and the interplay of two colours would give an impression of volume, assuming a spherical form. Nolan imagined he had solved one of the great problems of painting: how to make a two-dimensional object appear three-dimensional. This modest experiment first was named *Portrait of John Sinclair at St Kilda*, although somebody soon called it *Moonboy* and Nolan accepted the new title.

Adrian Lawlor took violent exception to the work when it was hung, moving it from a prominent position to an unseen corner. Nolan promptly put it back. He was surprised at this behaviour, in spite of their earlier clashes, because he still regarded Lawlor as the most forward-thinking person in Melbourne art. In fact, at the opening of the exhibition Lawlor took down his own works and started off down the stairs with them as a mark of protest against Nolan's *Moonboy*. Nolan tried to mollify him and John Reed hurried to assist, but they were unsuccessful in persuading Lawlor to return his works. Instead, Reed suggested the three of them should stroll over to Lawlor's studio and attempt a reconciliation by talking about the incident away from the crowds. They sat down and discussed the matter in a desultory fashion for fifteen minutes but the disgruntled artist refused to accept that this foolish squabble was likely to harm the cause of modern art. 'My daughter of six could do better than that', were his final words on the matter. *Moonboy* remained hanging and was to signal the end of Nolan's abstract phase, although the image would re-appear in several other forms and circumstances in the future.

Some male members of the Heide circle made every effort to avoid the call-up and detested the thought of becoming 'chocos' — chocolate soldiers — as conscripts were known, to differentiate between them and the more honourable volunteers of the Australian Imperial Forces. Nolan waited with apprehension and a sense of helplessness in the face of many pressures. His relationship with Elizabeth was becoming increasingly distant and although he was delighted at the birth of their daughter, Amelda, he was an increasingly errant husband and father. The war, combined with his domestic and financial situation, had forced him to abandon any thoughts of getting away to Europe. And then, as a substitute for that dream, his thoughts in relation to his art began to turn more to Australia and its landscape, although that was a subject he had never seriously considered.

Sunday owned a fine landscape by the young Arthur Streeton from the time when the Heidelberg painters were in the first flush of enthusiasm. Taking this as an example, she began talking about evolving a contemporary response to landscape in the way the young radicals of the 1880s had approached it on their terms fifty years before. Nolan at first was adamant that it was impossible, certainly for him. Nonetheless, he was intrigued by her suggestion and happy to accept a challenge in the spirit of experiment. The Streeton was a delicate

52

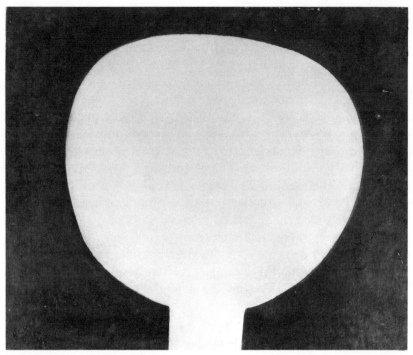

Boy with the Moon c. *1940; also known as* Moonboy *(Australian National Gallery, Canberra)*

twilight pastoral with distant figures bathing in a pool surrounded by the river flats of the Yarra against a background of trees lit by the pink glow of a summer evening. Titled *Yarra Valley at Heidelberg*, it bore none of the nationalistic overtones of Streeton's later work, a point the Reeds had found attractive when they bought the painting on moving to Heide in 1935. It became a focus for countless discussions about the possibility of interpreting the Australian landscape in 1940s terms. Sunday was persistent in her belief that the challenge could be met and that Nolan was the person to achieve it, as his recent pictures of Heidelberg and St Kilda had elements of landscape in them. He knew his affair with abstraction had run its course and that Sunday's persuasiveness was difficult to resist, although it was an uncomfortable position for any artist close to the Reeds because they represented themselves as spearheading the thrust of the avant-garde and landscape was not supposed to be one of the weapons. Returning to the cradle of Australian art by regression to the land itself seemed a little like betraying a cause.

By the time of the third show of the Contemporary Art Society, the director of the National Gallery was not prepared to accept any more radical works on his walls and an alternative venue had to be found. The splendid new Hotel Australia in Collins Street was taken as a gallery and provided a glamorous setting for the 310 works to be displayed, including five by Nolan as well as a piece of sculpture by him titled *Woman and Bird*. An added attraction was two concerts, one of jazz presented by Don Banks and Graeme Bell, and the other a classical evening. The cover design for the show's catalogue was designed by Nolan as a kind of Garden of Eden theme incorporating a tree laden with fruit and Eve to one side with a striped snake below.

The exhibition took place at a time when opposition to the idea of Robert Menzies' Australian Academy of Art was at its peak and the CAS, the Academy's sworn enemy, decided to gather signatures protesting against the attempt to establish an official art. The patrons were asked to sign a petition at the jazz concert on the night of 28 October 1941 where, according to a report in the Melbourne *Truth*, the city saw one of its strangest gatherings for a long time. The paper recorded 'Long-haired intellectuals, swing fiends, hot mommas and truckin' jazz boys rubbing shoulders on friendly terms'. The report stated the music reached its crescendo as 'swingsters hollered "Go to town" and jittered in the aisles', while the 'intelligentsia' was said to have 'learnedly discussed differences between rhythms of hot jazz and pigments of Picasso'.

The petition, aimed directly at the trustees of the National Gallery of Victoria for ignoring modern movements in art and refusing to hold this current exhibition of the Contemporary Art Society, was intended to be presented to the chief secretary of Victoria. Writer Michael Keon, one of the Reeds' circle, was appointed as master of the rolls and cut an impressive figure with his long flowing hair and bright yellow tie as he went around collecting signatures. Most members of the audience were happy to sign, but two naval officers strongly objected to the petition, snatched the paper away, rushed into the men's room and began stuffing the sheets down a toilet.

A fight ensued with the naval men shouting threats about the consequences of besmirching the king's uniform. The police were called and a scene that would not have disgraced one of Hollywood's best silent comedies was played out with people jumping over partitions and in and out of the cubicles attempting to rescue the increasingly soggy sheets of signatures. It was a good story for the newspaper reporters present and Michael Keon was quoted as saying, 'This puerile, barbaric and intolerant destruction of the petition is typical of just that attitude we are trying to control'. 'Art Jitterbugs Het-Up' was a headline in Melbourne *Truth* a few days later which drew attention to the exhibition at which the influence of the CAS was greatly extended and would persuade Adelaide and Sydney branches to affiliate with Melbourne.

His association with the Reeds imposed a huge strain on Nolan's loyalties, and relations ebbed and flowed depending on the pressures from Heidelberg. Sunday had made a suggestion that he move there *en famille*, where she would enjoy the baby's presence, but Elizabeth would not consider the idea. Although now

Figure and Tree, *1941*

living apart from his wife and their baby daughter, he was reluctant to make a formal move to break up their marriage because of the disappointment it would bring to both their families. The situation reached a crisis point when he was invited to spend the Easter holidays with the Reeds and another couple on a travelling holiday to the Wyperfeld Park in the northern Mallee district of Victoria. Elizabeth issued an ultimatum, requesting Nolan to make a break from Heide so they could reassess their relationship on a new footing. It was an invidious position for her with a small child, having to rely on family support, and Nolan agreed to the request, deciding instead to go in the opposite direction to sort out his thoughts by taking a lone cycling trip to Tasmania. He imagined a change of scene would clear the air for everyone, although it proved to be a lonely and expensive time for him. He had to sell a camera to buy food and pay for cheap accommodation and the weather turned unseasonably cold so that his light clothing was inadequate for keeping warm.

He returned in high spirits and anticipation only to discover that Elizabeth suspected his trip had been engineered by the Reeds and paid for by them as a way of fooling her. She found it hard to regard it as a genuine gesture on her husband's behalf towards a reconciliation. Nolan was devastated; not only had the Tasmanian journey been a waste of time, it had also consumed most of his ready cash. Elizabeth told him that while he was away John Reed had contacted her, suggesting she go and see him at his Collins Street office in a couple of weeks' time with a view to his helping her to solve their problems. Things seemed to improve a little from this moment and Nolan began regular visits to his wife and baby at their house in St Kilda, travelling there on his bicycle before going off to work in the mornings. There were many conversations through a flyscreen door and over window sills, although he never ventured inside to see their baby daughter. Then, soon after Elizabeth's meeting with John Reed, Nolan received a letter from her stating she would have to terminate the relationship and he must regard their marriage as over. Nolan blamed the change of heart on his father-in-law who had always seemed antagonistic towards him, particularly during the short time he had worked on his gold mining claim. He was sure that Mr Paterson had put pressure on his daughter to make the split and he was at a loss to know how to circumvent this influence and handle the situation. He showed Elizabeth's letter to his mother and she was able to offer maternal sympathy but no explanation. Nolan's call-up papers for army service arrived and one of his first actions as a conscripted soldier was to sign over his pay of six shillings a week to Elizabeth as a final helpless gesture. He felt himself powerless to do anything about his failed marriage in the face of the increasingly powerful gravitational force the Reeds now exerted on their protégé. Divorce would be the only way out.

Dream of the Latrine Sitters, *1942*

Lagoon Wimmera, *1943 (Ripolin enamel on composition board, 63.5 × 75.9 cm., National Gallery of Victoria. Presented by Sir Sidney and Lady Nolan, 1983)*

Under the Pier, *1945 (Nolan Gallery, Lanyon, ACT)*

Catani Gardens, *1945 (Nolan Gallery, Lanyon, ACT)*

Ferris Wheel, *1944—45 (Heide Park and Art Gallery, bequest of John and Sunday Reed)*

Rosa Mutabilis, 1945 (private collection)

CHAPTER FOUR

War in the Wimmera

§

Nolan was ordered to report to an induction camp on 15 April 1942, a tented area established on the Caulfield racecourse in Melbourne's eastern suburbs. The call-up was later than most of his friends and colleagues because he had a wife and child to support and he was trying with the help of John Reed to establish non-combatant status by being appointed an official war artist. Every time he was called to account for himself among the milling throng of new conscripts he would try to explain that he had a special category, which he thought was good reason to avoid being sent to Port Melbourne for loading ammunition onto supply ships. Nolan had no document to support his claim, however, and most days during the first confusing fortnight of his army service saw him labouring on the wharves, until it became obvious he was not to become a war artist yet and was available to be drafted anywhere. Nolan made it known he was not prepared to shoot a rifle and was told to join a motley group of thirty tough-looking individuals who had been branded as unco-operative. After a long wait in the hot sun, a sergeant informed them that they would either be sent up to New Guinea or to Dimboola in the west of the State. Private Nolan, bearing army number V206559, opted to join a small platoon for training at a camp near Seymour with the 3rd Supply and Personnel Company before taking up labouring and guard duties.

Following training, there were a few days' leave before being posted to a group of supply depots around Dimboola. He had been dismayed at the cattle-like conditions at Seymour, but with a new landscape opening up in front of him as the men were driven west in a noisy truck, his spirits began to improve. Previously he had travelled widely in the eastern parts of the State and visited Sydney twice, but this was different territory, new and fascinating, unlike anything he had experienced before. These first impressions were vivid and lasting. The distant line of blue mountains known as the Grampians gave way to the flat, almost featureless plains of the Wimmera, a vast area of wheatlands, brown and dusty at this time of the year, stretching to the infinity of a heat haze, dotted by clumps of trees which seemed to float like a mirage above the surface. Nolan was exhilarated by what he saw and intrigued by the challenge of interpreting the scene. He had brought sketching materials and paints along, hoping to put any spare moments to good use.

The town of Horsham was reached in the late afternoon and following a short stop they travelled on a further sixteen miles to Dimboola just as the sun was setting. Captain Bilby, the English officer in charge, stood before his ragged platoon and addressed them in a clipped military style, outlining their duties. All Nolan could think of was how beautiful the little town of Dimboola looked under its limpid sky. They were quartered in a hotel, one of two in the town, and that evening over pots of beer in the bar, long after it had closed to the public, Nolan learned a little about his captain, the only person in the group to interest him.

There were subtle things happening in this landscape with its shape and colour constantly changing according to the angle of the sun and the presence of clouds in the vast, uninterrupted expanse of sky. There was no opportunity for Nolan to paint in the open air while on duty but he stored up his impressions for later translation into paint, although he knew he would experience a conflict in coming to grips with this country. Its flatness beneath a limitless sky was dazzlingly bright, shimmering with light, and he thought his heroes might see it through different eyes. Nolan imagined Rousseau, Cézanne, Matisse and Picasso being happy in this environment, but he doubted their ability to capture its essence with their European vision. At the same time he wondered if he had a native ability to express it. He described his impressions of the mood of this country in a letter to Sunday: 'I wished you could have seen this morning the sun when it first came through. The air was clear and distinct but the sky seemed a soft mist almost as if there was an ordinary morning mist, but one that stopped a few feet away and the air between belonging altogether to another day.'

Army rations were stored around Victoria as security against attack from the Japanese. In the event of invasion a government contingency plan known as the Brisbane Line would allow the enemy to penetrate the northern part of Australia, but a line forming a crescent from Brisbane, north of Sydney, Melbourne and Adelaide across the continent to Perth on the Indian Ocean, where the vast majority of the population lived, would be defended. The stores were strategically placed to supply the troops if they were forced back to defend the imaginary line. Nolan's soldiers learned that just one of the anonymous sheds they were guarding contained enough food to provide a million meals. They speculated about the Japanese making a landing in the north and moving rapidly south so that Dimboola and Nhill, Horsham and Wail, would come to play a frontline role, but most of it was pub gossip and Nolan gave little thought to the possibility of an invasion.

58

Following the posting at Dimboola and a brief stint in Horsham, Nolan was transferred for a month in July 1942 to a training camp at Hurstbridge, conveniently close to Heidelberg, before returning to Dimboola. This allowed him to spend more time with the Reeds at Heide during weekends. In an atmosphere of encouragement that was steering his painting, at Sunday's instigation and with John's approval, away from abstraction into landscape, he would spend the weekend painting rapidly on board placed on the floor of the dining room. On the wall above him was one of the most striking Australian paintings of the 1930s, an adventurous abstract, inspired by the music of Bach, called *Organised Line to Yellow* by one of the Reeds' first protégés, Sam Atyeo, who had left for France before the war to further his career. Nolan worked away at a furious pace, oblivious of his surroundings and of visitors such as H.V. Evatt and his wife Mary Alice, Gordon and Kate Thompson, Jack and Molly Bellew, all of whom watched through the door. He continued to be fascinated by every conceivable technique, sometimes toying with luminous paint on brightly-coloured paper propellers spinning on sticks stuck into a scarecrow in the paddock or placed on the top branches of the leafless almond and cherry trees. The pumpkins in the well-stocked vegetable garden would acquire painted purple trousers and red eyes after a late evening visit by the artist. When he slept, Nolan's dreams matched his conscious imagination; often colourful, vivid, full of incidents and imagery.

He remained pleased with his *Moonboy* painting and decided to use the corrugated iron roof at Heide to expand the image to a size about ten feet square in the spirit of the Mexican muralists. The original idea was to treat the whole roof as protection against rust but the prominent symbol appeared in white paint on part of the structure, looking a little like the Japanese rising sun, and it did not take long for the pilots of training aircraft flying over the district to notice it. Heide was soon visited by two Intelligence officers from the Royal Australian Air Force who pointed out that the device, whatever it was, could be interpreted by invading Japanese as a navigation sign pointing to Melbourne and they ordered it to be removed. Nolan arrogantly said that he was not in the habit of destroying his paintings for anyone and that if the Japanese were really coming to attack, the officers might like to get up on the roof themselves and do the job. They explained that the penalties for collaborating with the enemy were severe and could lead to a long gaol term if the owner of the property did not comply with their orders. Reluctantly, he painted over the roof and *Moonboy* disappeared, but he was determined to make an even larger version one day.

Captain Bilby was impressed by Nolan's intelligence, seeing him as one of the few conscripts he could engage in a decent conversation, and he recommended Nolan for promotion. When congratulating Corporal Nolan, Bilby told him he could become an officer. Nolan was flattered, thinking of it as an extension of the page boy stunts he had perpetrated with Fayrfield Hats. Dressing up in a splendid military uniform seemed attractive, and for a while he imagined that being an officer was his rightful destiny, and it would certainly please his mother. But then as he considered his present situation with the freedom to paint, solitary walks around town, swimming in the river and generally leading his own life, the idea of a commission became much less attractive. Nolan realised he would have to join the A I F and almost certainly go overseas to fight. Coming to grips with the local landscape was the only battle Nolan wanted to fight at the moment and being accepted for officer training would mean the end of his artistic aspirations.

Within a few weeks of coming to the Wimmera area Nolan had sensed it was possible to forge a new imagery from the unpromising countryside and proceeded to go through the painful experience of dismembering his former cubist approach to art, flattening the perception of what he was seeing to embrace the character of the area with its broad wheatland plains dotted by the tall, monument-like structures of the wheat silos all sharpened by an extraordinarily transparent light. He was attempting to transform his previous broken imagery into a flowing, coherent statement about this environment. He was helped by the notorious *Moonboy* in solving the challenge of depicting a flat landscape, which was achieved, not in the traditional manner of the Dutch old masters with a low horizon line, but by tilting the picture plane and providing a high horizon. The solution was derived from a mixture of direct observation and adaptation of Cézanne's use of distorted planes and tilted perspective.

From this period came a series of landscapes, portrait heads of the men in his platoon and some self-portraits. Often these were distorted, psychotic representations, reflecting Nolan's own inner turmoil. He had thought of himself as something of a revolutionary before the war but after settling down to this strange military life he became a different person and felt more relaxed. He was reminded of a comment made by W.B. Yeats when asked about his attitude to war. 'I wouldn't take it too seriously', was the reply and Nolan agreed as he dreamt his way through the months, drifting on the emotional currents and eddies that washed around him.

In the country, the only contact with the harsh reality of the times was loading supplies onto railway wagons and knowing that after some mysterious journey they would reach the Australians fighting the Japanese in New Guinea. Some of the men at the battlefront were his friends and occasionally he received letters from them, although the rigid censorship did not allow descriptions of the horrors of jungle warfare, which made his situation in the Wimmera seem even more remote. Nolan was in a kind of rural vacuum, and any talk about a second front, the Russian situation or political manoeuvres that previously interested him, had little effect on him now. He had entered the army as an abstract

Head of Soldier, *1942*
(Australian National Gallery, Canberra)

Self-portrait, *1943*

painter with his thoughts and influences based on Paris, but exposure to the Wimmera and the serenity of country life gradually changed his feelings and he forgot about Picasso, Klee and Lifar and became attached to this landscape and its vibrancy of light.

With Nolan's sights still set on becoming a war artist, he and John Reed sent a formal application to the officer-in-charge of the army's Military History Section, Lieutenant Colonel J.S. Treloar. He was responsible for the selection of artists in association with the Commonwealth Art Advisory Board and, although the events of the war were moving rapidly, the appointment of official artists was extremely slow, with intense competition from traditional painters. A note attached to Nolan's application described him as 'an extremist of the modern school', which was unlikely to expedite anything. In fact, he had little time to complete many paintings during his first few months in the army, but managed to do a number of chalk sketches which, he told Sunday, 'keep me honest I think and help bigger paintings when they come'. These rapid drawings of the Grampians, the Wimmera River and Little Desert were sent back to Heide where Sunday had the idea of exhibiting them locally. The ideal place was Sheffield's Newsagency, one of a cluster of shops near the top of the hill, and John Reed persuaded the owner to let him have his large window for an exhibition of

Nolan's first Wimmera landscape impressions, together with some drawings of faces, expressionistic and quickly-sketched. A catalogue sheet was typed with prices kept to a minimum, the highest being three guineas. It was a great opportunity for perceptive local buyers, but none was attracted and Nolan's second one-man show remained without a sale.

Nolan's main military efforts were now concentrated on convincing Captain Bilby that he was not such good officer material after all. He began to slacken his previous efficiency as a corporal in charge of a squad of ten men. This odd bunch of men thrown together by the vagaries of war became the lords of Dimboola. Discipline in Nolan's platoon became poor, with fireplaces left uncleared and minor looting of stores; some of the men even wore slippers on duty. Weekends were the time for dances and, with the local young men all away fighting, some of the soldiers formed close attachments to the local girls. The only regular commitment, apart from guard duties, was to smarten up the platoon and cover up for pilfered stores when the official visit came around each week.

Nolan's war began to produce an impressive flow of painting in spite of frequent shifts of duty between the towns of Dimboola, Nhill, Horsham and Ballarat. Only the latter provided a hindrance because it was the site of a large army camp and while there he had to dress properly, take part in parades and carry out regular duties under constant supervision. Nevertheless, Nolan managed to keep a room which served as a studio for the time he could take off.

Exhibition at Sheffield's Newsagency, 1942 (Barrett Reid)

Wherever he was stationed, the Reeds continued to provide canvases for him and he sent back completed paintings or carried them himself on the frequent weekend leave passes. Dimboola was too far away for short visits, but Nolan could be at Heide every other weekend from Ballarat. This apparent freedom to come and go as he pleased was resented by some of the men under his command and they would sometimes take leave without authority. On one occasion this came to the attention of a group of officers and there were some serious questions to answer, but with his usual facility, Nolan was able to talk himself out of trouble and continue the life of a painter, affected only marginally by the war.

During 1942 he painted two pictures at Dimboola with the same title, *Going to School*, in which an incident was presented from different perspectives. The apparently peaceful town is seen in the first, painted on a steel sheet because he had run out of canvases, with a cloudless blue sky overhead giving warning of a hot November's day. The scene is dominated by a yellow training aircraft overhead looking like a hovering angel. Nolan started to put a watching schoolgirl in the foreground but was unhappy with the composition and afterwards painted out her head, leaving vestigial lines of a blue-striped school uniform on the bottom edge. In a letter to Sunday, he described how he had yelled at the image, willing it into the right shape, 'and when it goes dead I could kick a hole in it and hold my fist through the back just to feel there was something real'.

The schoolgirl also appeared in the second painting, done on tissue paper stuck to pulpboard. She watches the crash of one of the trainers onto her school building where she would have been if it had occurred later. It was based on an incident Nolan had experienced at first hand in the open country near Dimboola when his squad was sent to the site to collect the wreckage after an aircraft developed engine trouble and had crashed and burned, with its trainee pilot parachuting to safety. Nolan recorded the scene in a series of rapid sketches and from them he developed a painting with an angular, cubist-like composition embracing wheat silos, the angles of house roofs, jumbles of telegraph poles and intersecting railway lines, against the green of the surrounding wheatfields. He was trying to come to grips with composition, but was not happy with the results. 'Things kept stumbling over themselves', he wrote in frustration, 'and I ended up feeling I had used a lot of paint and a lot of hard work doing it'. He admitted, however, that such an exercise got rid of 'junk thoughts' and when he returned to the subject in the afternoon it brought better results. This was an exacting business for him, described as 'a trial and error method' in which he sometimes approached painting like a bullock. The next day Nolan added the head and shoulders of the girl in the foreground, her back to the viewer. She gazes at the crashed aeroplane which looks like a grounded, broken bird

Going to School, *1942*   Going to School, *1942*

wrenched from its natural environment, its yellow plumage scorched and blackened, leaving a scar on the earth with tilted telegraph poles to mark its final
resting place.

The two paintings were sent to Melbourne and entered by John Reed in the
Anti-Fascist exhibition held at the Athenaeum Gallery during December 1942
and opened by the State secretary of the Communist Party. They, together with
another work, *Dream of the Latrine Sitter*, were included on the assumption
that they illustrated facets of Australia at war. Reaction to the exhibition as a
whole, as Reed observed, was indifference from public and painters alike. The
artists' protest against the horrors of war in general and Fascism in particular
had as its blueprint the Artists International Association in Britain during the
early 1930s, which had been revived during the war with an impressive list of
supporters including Henry Moore, Paul Nash, Vanessa Bell, Augustus John,
Lucien Pissarro and Kenneth Clark. A similar group was organised in
Melbourne by Noel Counihan and following Pearl Harbour a congress of artists
met in the Town Hall. It attracted, and for once united, a surprisingly broad
spectrum of political sympathies and painting philosophies and a manifesto to
oppose Fascism was drawn up. There were fifty signatories, but not even this
show of solidarity could persuade Albert Tucker and Sidney Nolan to add their
names to the document.

Art as propaganda came to be regarded by many people as unconvincing
because, in looking for political or humanitarian statements, it was felt the
painters overlooked artistic content. John Reed did not agree with this view,

however, believing that art needed to express the reality of a situation as a legitimate response to the events that dominated the world. He thought that the artist's job in such a situation was to 'record, accept, endure'. This attitude generated so much disagreement within the Contemporary Art Society that the resulting arguments began to rival the heat of anti-Fascist sentiments in the general community. The Contemporary Art Society had helped to make the early 1940s one of the most vital periods in the history of the arts in Australia, and now it was assisted by the literary and art magazine *Angry Penguins*. The journal, whose influence was much greater than its circulation figures would suggest, expressed the opinions of the more radical members of the Melbourne branch of the CAS and provided a platform for wide intellectual discussion and for the preferred art of the Heide circle.

Angry Penguins was started by a precocious young man in Adelaide, Max Harris. He had been educated at one of the city's best schools, St Peter's College, became a copy boy on the evening newspaper, the *News*, and then read for a degree in English and economics at the University of Adelaide. The mercurial Harris with dark curly hair, penetrating eyes, and a great intellectual curiosity, held left-wing political opinions and soon made his presence felt in the rather arid literary scene of South Australia. His first poetry was published in 1939 at the age of 18 and a collection of verse under the title *The Gift of Blood* followed a year later. He was obsessive about Australian culture, convinced that it must spring from indigenous values and not attempt to be an imitation of trends from abroad. Harris' efforts in Adelaide paralleled those of John Reed in Melbourne and, although their territories were separated by 500 miles, it seemed inevitable they would join forces. The first issue of *Angry Penguins* had appeared in 1940 as 'an act of defiance', with academic backing from the University of Adelaide and jointly edited by Harris and Donald Bevis Kerr, who was to be killed on active duty in New Guinea two years later.

At first there was only modest support for the journal but it was admired by John Reed, and before its second issue appeared he asked Max Harris to come to Melbourne to discuss the possibility of enlarging the format and expanding its content if the Reeds subsidised the venture. During that visit Harris met Nolan and saw some of his work with the result that he included a reproduction of *Woman and Tree* in the second edition of the magazine together with a perceptive note:

> Very few sincere and interested people will deny that among Australian artists, Sidney Nolan is undoubtedly to be numbered. Immersed in the creative tradition of the last fifty years, and in particular in the symbolic and gigantic figure of Picasso, he yet reacts to his environment, not in the terms of those who have gone before him, but in terms which he has made his own, and which our sensibility demands we should accept.

A note about the Contemporary Art Society stated, 'Already the forces of reaction are feeling keenly the impact of this organisation, and while on the one hand it increasingly attacks their strongholds, of even more importance is the active creative spirit within its ranks ...' By the fourth edition, in early 1943, *Angry Penguins* became a joint Reed and Harris production edited from Melbourne, devoted to the spiritual and political aims of the CAS and championing the cause of surrealism in the written word and the painted image as 'a forum for the highest literary and art level energy for this country'. Nolan became associated with the publication by assisting in its layout and design, even though he was away for much of the time fighting his war in the Wimmera. On visits back to Melbourne he was drawn into the decision making, the plotting and planning, and sometimes made written contributions of his own including a piece about Rimbaud.

Nolan's work was not entirely devoted to Wimmera subjects. On weekend visits to Heide he would often reminisce about growing up in St Kilda, and he worked at several paintings using nostalgic memories of happy days at Luna Park or on the beach. One of the themes was St Kilda pier, a central feature of the beach, stretching far out into the bay, with its boardwalk and white railings terminating at a quaint kiosk. The Reeds and their visitors watched Nolan's impression emerge of children standing stark and dream-like holding spinning paper propellers, like the ones he sometimes placed in the trees outside. These suburban innocents stood exposed and suspended in time upon the pier above a dark blue sea. He had explained his approach in one of his regular letters to Sunday, 'Memory is, I am sure, one of the main factors in my particular way of looking at things. In some ways it seems to sharpen the image in a way that cannot be achieved by other or more direct means.'

Nolan exhibited a sinewy elation in his work, painting away at the board with a stubby brush and laughing as the imagery began to work. Sunday was always fascinated to peep in and watch him at work, with shirt-sleeves rolled up for action and one of her kitchen aprons around his waist to protect his trousers. He mixed paints with an intense fervour as if anxious to get them onto the picture in a race to keep ahead of his thoughts. 'Look at *this*!' he exclaimed to himself or to anyone who happened to be watching, pleased with the way the composition was developing. He would build on his St Kilda reminiscences later, describing his boyhood stamping ground as 'a kitsch heaven'. It had also been his cathedral, although there was nothing sacred about the completed paintings; they would become scuffed and knocked as everyone handled them, passed them around, and discussed the content and technique.

Heide in the summertime was synonymous with fresh food: hot scones, rum babas, omelettes from freshly-laid eggs, warm milk from Summer the cow, named by Nolan. Sweet unsalted butter melted deliciously over the bountiful produce of the vegetable garden, particularly tender young peas, baby carrots and new potatoes. It was a congenial atmosphere with flowers in all the rooms, a sense of commitment to principles, new rows to fight over, Graeme Bell playing jazz in the tin shed, and the destinies of the Contemporary Art Society to be guided in what would be seen in retrospect as a vital and formative period of Australian arts and letters. Nolan was now happy to be ensnared in a most intimate union with the Reeds and their close friends which allowed him to embrace a wide range of new experiences. The French would describe the relationship as a *ménage à trois*, although it was much less formal, having a freedom where all kinds of permissiveness were accepted as part of a total physical and intellectual experience. Outsiders regarded the Heide circle as a lively cultural and political group because most other activities were kept discreet, although several people on the periphery were aware of the true situation.

Sunday Reed at Heide. Top right, with John Reed at window, Barrett Reid and Laurence Hope on steps (Barrett Reid)

The Reeds kept a holiday house at Point Lonsdale, not far from Ocean Grove, where they invited their friends to join them during the holiday period over Christmas and New Year. It was a good place for long walks along the beach or into the nearby scrub. Nolan managed to take a few days leave with them, finding the shoreline interesting with its wiry vegetation clinging tenaciously to the sand dunes. He had acquired a social fluency with his good looks, pleasant personality and sly humour that allowed him to alternate easily between the rough country pubs of the Wimmera and the Baillieu and Myer summer houses at Sorrento. He was able to look at the local scenery with a fresh vision, almost as if he were experiencing a new continent as D.H. Lawrence had when looking over the landscape at Darlington near Perth in the early 1920s. While admiring the wonderful clarity of sky and air, Lawrence saw the land beneath as dry and hoary, like a sleeping princess on whom the dust of ages had settled. He thought that the bush stretching out over the hills looked as if dark gods possessed it, and he sensed the alienation and isolation; twin forces to which most Australians succumbed at some time. In his painted impressions at Point Lonsdale, Nolan was uncorrupted by traditional European views of the Australian bush. He looked at the nondescript seaside scrub and responded with an apparent chaos of line and colour within a treatment that was surprising in its fidelity.

In spite of happy times by the sea, at Heidelberg and with his dream-like existence in the army, Nolan remained confused about the break-up of his marriage and often wondered about the circumstances that had brought it to finality. Another brief visit to Melbourne provided the answer. One evening he was travelling in uniform in the centre compartment of a tram heading along St Kilda Road to the city, when he noticed Elizabeth's mother sitting inside. He made to greet her but she saw him first and pulled the stop cord, causing the vehicle to make a screeching halt just before the traffic lights at Domain Road. Mrs Paterson jumped off, quickly followed by Nolan, who was mystified by her behaviour. The passengers stared out at them as he rushed to engage her in conversation under the yellow light of a street lamp. Mrs Paterson was distraught and would not stop, shouting over her shoulder, 'Go away, I hate you!' She took a dozen more paces and then added, 'How could you possibly have let that man say such terrible things to my daughter?' It transpired that when Elizabeth had gone to see John Reed with the intention of trying to find a solution to her marriage problems, Reed had told her she was ruining Nolan's life and that he could never become a proper painter while they were married. Mrs Paterson was disappearing into the darkness as she uttered one final comment, 'How could you tell him to say those dreadful things?' There was nothing more for Nolan to say; he walked back to the tram stop thinking, 'So that's the name of the game, that's how it was fixed!'

The most extensive selection of Nolan's Wimmera paintings, comprising seventeen works including landscapes, portrait heads and various Wimmera town activities, went on show in the Contemporary Art Society's studio at 527 Collins Street in Melbourne during August 1943. The exhibition was arranged by John Reed whose catalogue introduction stated, 'Drawing, perhaps for the first time here on the real sources of the Australian visual image he is, first of all, a painter who paints what he sees in the world about him, revealing to us with remarkable integration and lovely clarity the essential heart of his experience'. Albert Tucker, who was now the society's president, reviewed this show together with another by Vassilieff. He wrote in *Angry Penguins*:

> His long immersion in radical modernism, prolific, with magnificent trivialities, has paid high dividends in the development of an individual perception of a very high order, and in the steady growth of a rare, lyrical talent, maturing in his Nhill and Dimboola landscapes. Here, as with Vassilieff, we glimpse for the first time since Roberts, McCubbin and the early Streeton, the return of an authentic national vision on a higher and more independent level.

Railway Yards Dimboola, *1943*

Flour Lumper, *1943*

As *Moonboy* had completed one phase of Nolan's painting, so he felt that in finishing the 1943 landscape titled *Kiata*, with the perspective lines of road and railway tracks leading to wheat silos and a farm cart, he had solved the problems posed by the Wimmera landscape. The critic Paul Haefliger had already noticed this work in the annual CAS show and wrote in the *Sydney Morning Herald*, '*Kiata* is one of the most original abstracts conceived by an Australian'. Nolan had written to Sunday, 'Sometimes the silos look so powerful here, that seen from a distance standing up from the trees you could imagine them as made by the Aztecs for no other reason than to worship the sun'.

Nolan had received no reply to his request to be considered as a war artist, but was determined not to give up. He invited Lieutenant Colonel Treloar to see the exhibition of Wimmera paintings with the explanation, 'I feel more than ever I could play a larger and more realistic part dealing with my own activities as a painter, rather than in the capacity I am presently serving in the army.' Treloar visited the show, made no comment, and declined to act on Corporal Nolan's application.

Nolan's life was about to plunge into disarray again. Back in Ballarat he was supervising the transfer of supplies from a horse-drawn dray into a railway wagon and was standing absent-mindedly with a hand resting on the open doorway when the animal shied at the noise of an aircraft flying low overhead. The dray was suddenly forced back against the steel loading door which closed on Nolan's left hand, slicing off the tops of two fingers. Nolan watched the accident happen as if in slow motion, thinking to himself, 'I had that coming to me!' He watched the severed fingers arc their way into the dust and then he felt a searing pain and slumped to the ground. He was lifted onto the dray, rags were wrapped around his hand to staunch the flow of blood, and the two dusty finger tops retrieved. He was taken to the army hospital at the Ballarat Showgrounds and admitted to a ward full of Americans suffering various war wounds — both mental and physical. It was winter, with the temperature dropping to below freezing during the night, and inadequate heating in the wards made sleep difficult. Nolan's lacerated fingers were extremely painful and when it was made clear there was no possibility of rejoining the severed sections, he consoled himself with the fact that the damage was not to his painting hand. His condition was certainly much better than many of those around him. In the next bed was a young man who, with five others, had been shot up by fellow Americans in the open sea after their aeroplane was forced to ditch into the Pacific. He and his friends seemed to be recovering from the harrowing ordeal; each day they did the crossword in the morning newspaper and became so proficient that it took as little as six minutes to complete. The first to finish would throw up his hands in triumph and they compared times and notes with each other. But after that, introversion crept into their thoughts as they began to relive the horror of the attack.

Nolan had happier memories of exploring Ballarat with Sunday a couple of years before, strolling through the quiet streets of the once-rich gold mining town with the cast-iron verandahs and elegant awnings supported on slim columns. A few streets away were the tailings from the mines, looking almost like threatening mountains behind the workers' cottages. He soon regained the facility to paint after his accident and produced in a rented studio some pictures of the town — spare, elevated views using the considerable techniques he had been developing over the past few years.

He spent a month back in the Wimmera at the beginning of 1944, just long enough to paint a final group of pictures unlike anything he had done previously. The countryside had undergone a dramatic change and was now in the grip of one of the worst droughts on record. During December and January the land became bare like a desert with hot gusty winds sweeping in from the west and north raising choking dust storms across the area. They stifled the normal life of the towns and whipped up fierce scrub fires that often spread to blacken the remaining stubble of the wheatlands. It was a heartbreaking time for the farmers, although it contained elements of visual drama for Nolan to incorporate in his paintings. He recorded the scene in quick sketches when the troops were called in to assist the farmers in saving what little remained of their fodder crops. At night the sky bore a red glow across the horizon as distant fires burned out of control. Nolan was following in the footsteps of Eugen von Guérard who ninety years before had painted idealised views of bushfires, emphasising their grandeur.

Ballarat, *1943*

71

Nolan's approach was entirely different, both technically and emotionally. He depicted the aftermath of the flames, fascinated by the way the land seemed to want to conceal what had happened. His landscape was still recognisably the Wimmera, but now there were black patches etched into it where the fires had been, although they seemed to be only transitory, waiting for change to erase them. He continued to see the influence of Cézanne in many of the scenes he painted, sometimes lying flat on his back watching the gum trees shimmer in the breeze beside the Wimmera River, imagining how Cézanne would have loved these moments with their ever-changing patterns of vibrant light and deep purple shade. This series of paintings bore some resemblance to the master's constant re-working on the Mont Saint-Victoire theme, although they showed little of the meticulous refinement of his approach. 'Rough as bags' was how Nolan described his own work, but when he had to leave the area for the last time in February 1944 to return to Melbourne, he had unknowingly forged a new vision of Australian landscape.

Nolan was drawn increasingly into the activities of *Angry Penguins* and he became part of the editorial team that produced a special issue during the early part of 1944 which covered three major cultural events: the publication of Max Harris' novel *The Vegetative Eye* with a cover design by Nolan, who also provided a review; the controversy in Sydney over William Dobell winning the Archibald Prize for portraiture; and the first publication of the complete works of an unknown poet named Ern Malley. A few months earlier, at the end of October 1943, Harris had received a letter addressed to him at the *Angry Penguins* office in Adelaide. It was hand-written and signed by one Ethel Malley, who said she lived in an outer suburb of Sydney. Its regular, confident script revealed surprising information about her brother who, she explained, had written some poetry and left it among his belongings when he died recently.

Angry Penguins *cover, May 1944, showing Nolan's* The Sole Arabian Tree

Ethel Malley said she had shown the poems to a friend who suggested they were good enough for publication. 'On this advice', the letter read, 'I am sending you some of the poems for an opinion'. Apparently Ern had been a loner, never revealing his literary skills and, according to Ethel, 'He was very ill in the months before his death last July and it may have affected his outlook'. A postage stamp was enclosed for a reply. One of the shorter poems was titled 'Dürer: Innsbruck, 1495' and Harris read it with growing excitement:

> I had often, cowled in the slumberous heavy air,
> Closed my inanimate lids to find it real,
> As I knew it would be, the colourful spires
> And painted roofs, the high snows glimpsed at the back,
> All reversed in the quiet reflecting waters —
> Not knowing then that Dürer perceived it too.
> Now I find that once more I have shrunk
> To an interloper, robber of dead men's dream,
> I had read in books that art is not easy
> But no one warned that the mind repeats
> In its ignorance the vision of others. I am still
> The black swan of trespass on alien waters.

Harris was convinced that he had stumbled across a major talent and that *Angry Penguins* had the rare opportunity to reveal it. He replied to Ethel Malley's letter, seeking further examples of her late brother's work and requesting additional personal information about him. This duly arrived; a collection of poetry and a concise biographical statement in 700 words. It described how the young Ern had arrived in Australia as a baby after his English father had died from war wounds in 1920. The family lived in the Sydney suburb of Petersham where the boy first had gone to primary school followed by the Summer Hill Intermediate where his academic record was undistinguished and he left before gaining the intermediate certificate. Ern took a job as a garage mechanic and then at the age of 17 went to Melbourne where eventually he sold insurance policies for the National Mutual company.

John Reed's initial response was of disbelief and, therefore, rejection. He thought such a chance discovery was most unlikely, although he did not believe they were fabricated poems. Nolan read all the verse carefully and thought it might be a pastiche of overseas influences because it did not sound like Australian language or thought to him. He was suspicious of the way in which the poems had come to light but in the heady atmosphere of discovery, combined with Harris' infectious enthusiasm, said nothing except to express the opinion that they were not local. In fact, Nolan found 'Dürer: Innsbruck, 1495' very interesting, particularly in its rhyming structure which he noted was elaborate and consistent. Another poem titled 'Boult to Marina' he thought erotically beautiful:

Only a part of me shall triumph in this
(I am not Pericles)
Though I have your silken eyes to kiss
And maiden-knees
Part of me remains, wench, Boult-upright
The rest of me drops off into the night.

They all agreed, however, that the complete works, together with Ern Malley's story, must be published and Max Harris began to compose a florid introduction while Nolan painted a cover illustration for the magazine inspired by a line from another of the poems called 'Petit Testament':

Dear we shall never be that verb
Perched on the sole Arabian tree.

The special edition was published and made a good impression on its readers, although there were some reservations about the authenticity of the Ern Malley poems and it was not long before Dr Brian Elliott, who lectured in Australian literature at the University of Adelaide, suggested they were a hoax and composed a poem of thirteen lines whose first letters read vertically 'MAX HARRIS HOAX'. This was followed shortly afterwards by the publication in a supplement to the Sydney *Sun* of a statement by two young poets that they had assembled the Ern Malley poems as part of a serious literary experiment, without any personal malice against Max Harris. James McAuley and Harold Stewart, who were both in the army, said they had regarded with distaste the gradual erosion of meaning and craftsmanship in contemporary verse, particularly 'an Australian outcrop of a literary fashion which has become prominent in England and America'. The two perpetrators had thought that if Harris showed enough discrimination to reject their poems, then he and the *Angry Penguins* group could not be accused of running a mutual admiration society of would-be intellectuals. The only way of settling the matter, they believed, was by 'experiment' to discover if those who wrote and praised that type of writing could tell the real product from 'consciously and deliberately concocted nonsense'. Accordingly, McAuley and Stewart gave birth to Ern Malley and his equally fictitious sister Ethel. They claimed to have written the poems during one lazy afternoon at Victoria Barracks with the aid of a collection of books that happened to be on their desks at the time, including the *Concise Oxford Dictionary*, a collected Shakespeare and a dictionary of quotations. These were opened at random, with words and phrases chosen haphazardly and woven into nonsensical sequences. They deliberately misquoted, made false allusions and selected awkward rhymes. The first three lines of 'Culture as Exhibit', for instance, were taken directly from an American report on draining the breeding grounds of mosquitos:

Swamps, marshes, borrow-pits and other
Areas of stagnant water serve
As breeding grounds . . .

The Australian popular press seized upon the incident and featured it prominently on the news pages; the London *Times* reported the event and *Time* magazine ran a story about the brilliant hoax. *Angry Penguins* suddenly found itself famous after years of struggling to sell a thousand copies an issue and being constantly in debt. Max Harris was understandably furious that McAuley and Stewart had revealed their deception to a popular newspaper, which effectively forestalled any serious discussions. The outcome was that the public had its laugh, the cause of modern culture in Australia took a battering, and the *Angry Penguins* group received more than their fair share of ridicule. Somebody said tauntingly to Nolan, 'I suppose the next thing you'll be doing is to paint Ned Kelly!', while Australia's intellectuals took sides on the issue.

Ern Malley entered the annals of Australian literature, achieving immortality without being born, and the affair became a turning point for each of the *Angry Penguins* editorial staff. Max Harris adopted an unrepentant attitude, although Nolan thought he would be affected by it for the rest of his life. John Reed would have to decide how long he and Sunday could continue to support the magazine now its credibility was in question, and Nolan thought that they all deserved what they got, including himself. He maintained that Stewart had displayed a good ear for rhyme, McAuley demonstrated a fine intellect and, considering they had been lifting whole lines from Shakespeare, it was little wonder that some of the poetry read well.

With the disruption of this cultural maelstrom, the cause of modern art seemed to have been forgotten, but Nolan had several paintings in the 1944 CAS exhibition, including a fine landscape of Heidelberg, and they were noticed by the most astute of Australia's art writers, the Swiss-born Paul Haefliger. He had already written about Nolan's participation in this show when it was seen during June in Sydney. Readers of the *Sydney Morning Herald* learned that this Melbourne painter's 'decorations are many, his loyalties few, and unpredictable. He is the *enfant terrible* of Australian art.' Now Haefliger contributed a piece about the exhibition for *Angry Penguins*, containing some prophetic thoughts:

Quite unpredictable are the paintings of S. Nolan with their splendid feeling for spacing and their happy colour combinations. He is a gay adventurer, and lives, in these paintings, entirely upon his sensations. He can be very good and also the reverse. He plagiarises when he follows too closely in the steps of Picasso, and he is trite when he uses, for instance, a Picasso profile head, which has through constant recurrence, entirely lost its meaning. But he is also, on occasion, most original and certain of his passages are of rare subtlety. He appears possessed of a rare lightheartedness which seems to deny real seriousness, but follows the way of his whimsical nature. It scarcely matters, his lyrical impulse, his natural talent assures moments of realisation which are as spontaneous a delight as anything in Australian art. This is a period of transition, we are at the beginning of a new cycle, and ours is a new spring.

The burgeoning book publishing activities of Reed and Harris were outlined in this latest issue of the magazine. They included a novel, titled *Lucky Alphonse*, by John Reed's sister, Cynthia. Nolan was interested to read this semi-autobiographical work based on the experiences of an Australian girl training as a nurse in hospitals in Chicago, London and New York. It gave an insight into the background of an intriguing woman he had met once before the war and whose brief presence at Heide had left a deep impression on him.

There was a strong probability that Nolan would be sent to the bitter fighting in New Guinea at this critical time in the Pacific war and he knew he would have to pull strings to avoid that. His first move was to get admitted to hospital at Watsonia Barracks near Heidelberg, which was easily achieved by claiming stomach pains through dyspepsia. His aim was to be classified as B class, which meant he should escape being drafted overseas, but he was not successful because it was pointed out that once the dyspepsia was cured he would be perfectly fit to go off to fight. Security was lax and Nolan found it a simple matter to arrange a couple of pillows in his bed to resemble the shape of a sleeping figure and to spend the night at nearby Heide before returning to the hospital the next morning. These escapades only lasted for a short time, however, because the nurses began to joke about their disappearing patient, the officers got to hear of it, and Nolan was confined to barracks.

The only person with whom he discussed his dilemma was a conscientious objector named Douglas Cairns, a friend of John Sinclair, who was working in the hospital as a male nurse. Nolan found him a gentle, good-hearted person who advised against desertion, suspecting the consequences would be disastrous for Nolan's future. Cairns had a solitary, almost religious nature, keeping very much to himself, but Nolan learned that before the war he had specialised in singing songs by the Elizabethan composer John Dowland. Cairns had auditioned for the ABC but few people were familiar with the works of Dowland and he had failed to get on the air. He leased a small warehouse at Parkville, just north of the city, and suggested that if Nolan were determined to get out of the army, by whatever means, he could use this building because few knew of its existence and it could double as both a studio and a hideout.

Arthur Boyd was in the hospital at the same time and he and Nolan played cards with the other inmates of ward 13, although it was a harrowing experience because many of the men were receiving insulin treatment for combat shock and they might be able to play quite happily one day and the next time be incapable of any concentration. Nolan tried to extend his dyspeptic state until he was ordered to go to Heidelberg Hospital for an interview with an army psychiatrist named Captain Brown. The meeting started badly when Nolan told him he thought any analysis was pointless, and received the blunt reply that he was probably well adjusted. Nolan came straight to the point. 'Well, I'm going to desert if I don't get a B grading, because my mental and physical state are not stable enough for me to be sent overseas.' Brown told Nolan that if he deserted he would be arrested and have to face the consequences.

Nolan left this meeting with the intention of getting an introduction from John Reed to one of Melbourne's leading medical men whom Nolan felt would back his claim for special consideration. He had a small yellow fleck in one eye and thought this might be a way out. A consultation with an eminent eye specialist was arranged and Nolan went along and sat in the waiting room, surprised to see a small late-period Streeton on the wall. 'An indifferent painting', he thought to himself. Noting his patient's interest in the picture, the specialist told him it had been done when Streeton was blind in one eye. Nolan explained that he had just developed a worrying yellow speck in his eye, which he feared might affect his sight if he were put under any strain, such as being sent to a combat zone. The specialist, who had been unsympathetic to this point, now became positively hostile. 'You were born with that slight stain in your eye, and you know it. It has absolutely no effect on your sight and I'm insulted that you've come here to deceive me.' Nolan tried to contradict him, but soon realised there was no use in persisting with this man and found himself bustled out of the surgery.

There were other abortive visits to doctors and then John Reed suggested he should see Dr Reg Ellery, writer, contributor to *Angry Penguins* and fervent socialist, who had done much to humanise the science of psychiatry. He was a close friend of the Reeds and took a particular interest in the behaviour of soldiers under the stress of combat. Nolan made no attempt to cover up his purpose this time, coming straight to the point. He now had a genuine fear of a mental breakdown if he continued in this aimless way for much longer. Ellery had been briefed by John Reed and this time Nolan was successful. After a fortnight's absence he returned to Heidelberg Hospital with his signed certificate from Ellery, as important a piece of paper as he had ever possessed. Captain Brown gave it a cursory glance and then looked back at his visitor. After fully a minute he remarked, 'Well, he's the best psychiatrist in Melbourne'. He told Nolan to take the certificate and an accompanying note to his captain immediately. Nolan accepted the papers and made for the door, feeling as if an overpowering weight had suddenly lifted from his shoulders. Just before he left

Dr Reg Ellery (Barrett Reid)

the office Brown called after him, 'Take this straight to your unit, won't you?' The emphasis seemed unnecessary and Nolan was immediately suspicious of Brown's motives, particularly when he came to the door and shouted after Nolan, 'Just take it the way it is and give it to the officer'.

He took the envelope to the hospital kitchen, boiled a kettle and, without being seen, steamed open the flap. Brown's note read, 'Corporal Nolan has an overwhelming ambition, such as I have rarely struck before, to avoid front-line duty. He is in my opinion physically and mentally equipped for combat duties.' Nolan sat looking at the note, trying to decide what to do next. At dusk he scaled the hospital fence and walked along the road to the nearest public telephone and called Sunday. 'I've deserted', he announced. There was a shocked silence at the other end and then she asked, 'Do you think that's wise?' Her voice was full of concern and Nolan was suddenly gripped by doubts. 'My God!', he thought, 'What have I done? I'm on the run like an outlaw'.

CHAPTER FIVE

Artful Folklore

§

At first, both John and Sunday Reed regarded Nolan's desertion with dismay. They found it difficult to accept such a renegade step, particularly as many of Sunday's relatives were serving in the armed forces. But after a while, when it seemed reasonably safe to assume that he would not be arrested, they started to accept it as a brave deed. By contrast, Nolan's father was horrified to hear of his son's behaviour. He had been a military policeman during the First World War and could never condone this action. When Martin Smith returned to Melbourne from New Guinea where he had been a stretcher bearer, he described his personal terror of the Kokoda Trail and wondered if he had the will to face further action; Nolan's reaction to his friend's stories was that whatever the conditions up there, they were probably preferable to the strain of being a deserter on the run in Melbourne. He tried to explain the hollow feeling of guilt, of letting the side down and the rejection by society of those who acted in this way, deciding it would be wise to adopt an alias with false papers arranged by John Reed. Nolan took on the identity of Robin Murray, even going to the extent of sewing name tags on all his clothes while living in Douglas Cairns' Parkville studio between visits to Heide.

The theme of the next edition of *Angry Penguins* was planned as a kind of symposium for sympathetic contributors in the defence of modern poetry, but in early September 1944 there came an enforced halt to any published discussion of the hoax when Max Harris was charged by the South Australian police with having published 'indecent advertisements', seven of them identified from the sequence of Ern Malley poems. The police alleged they were 'indecent, immoral or obscene' under the legal definition of the terms which came from various precedents, mostly from a time when the social climate was vastly different; the test for obscenity, for instance, being based on a case in 1868.

The prosecution was carried out with determination and thoroughness by the authorities, with Max Harris finding himself ranged against a magistrate, prosecutor and a formidable witness for the prosecution, Detective Vogelsang. In

Nolan in his Parkville studio, 1944

defence, John Reed had arranged a group of experts including Dr Reg Ellery, Professor J.I.M. Stewart and Brian Elliott. The case was perceived by the press as good entertainment with salacious overtones and the unlikely star turn of the proceedings proved to be the taciturn Detective Vogelsang, on whom the prosecution's case rested. He presented his evidence in the form of written statements alleging that various words and passages in the Ern Malley poems violated community standards. The quality of his testimony was demonstrated in a statement made about the word 'incestuous': 'I don't know what incestuous means', he admitted, 'but I think there is a suggestion of indecency in it'.

When it was time for cross-examination by the prosecution there was more emphasis on Harris' literary record than the offending poetry. The opening question, 'Do you consider yourself one of the greatest Australian writers?' set the tone for what followed. The expert witnesses for the defence were called and given a difficult time by the Crown with constant interruptions through objection. Dr Ellery was halted ten times during his testimony and seven objections were lodged against him. The same happened to Stewart and Elliott with the result that the defence became disjointed and unconvincing. The judgement of Mr L.E. Clarke SM was tediously long, but thorough, ending with: 'In the result I find that none of the matters complained of are immoral or obscene, but that the passages to which I have referred are indecent'. Given the verdict he had little choice than to find the defendant guilty, ordering him to pay £5 with the alternative of twelve weeks jail. The publishing firm of Reed and Harris accepted the fine.

Nolan began to feel uneasy about his role in the running of *Angry Penguins*. He had enjoyed such tasks as setting type, reading proofs, arranging colour blocks, devising covers, and supervising the layout, and he retained an artisan's pride in his work, regarding himself as a process worker, factory-trained and used to pragmatic solutions to problems. He attended editorial meetings but tended to remain quiet because he was sure the journal's policy had lost its focus. Two Communist sympathisers, the painter Noel Counihan and writer George Farwell, were particularly scathing about the Ern Malley incident. Counihan, writing in the Communist weekly the *Guardian* in July 1944, had confirmed the left-wing view that 'the publication reflected the complete cultural bankruptcy of the decadent right wing of the Contemporary Art Society, hopelessly devoid of all critical values'. He made reference to 'wealthy' John Reed who was, significantly, married to a Baillieu; to the 'primitive' painter Sidney Nolan; and the 'red-baiting political theoretician' Albert Tucker.

The effects of being a deserter combined with the events surrounding the Ern Malley affair meant that Nolan's art went through a fallow period after he left the Wimmera. It was not until the second half of 1944 that he was able to resume regular painting in the security of the Parkville studio, where, with a picture of Dimboola, he took one last retrospective look at the wheatlands which had given him so much visual stimulation over the past couple of years. The painting is a night scene and seems to be a farewell to that phase of his life. A full moon hangs in a velvety sky illuminating the ghostly silos which tower as dominant as the Parthenon in the centre of the composition. The surrounding countryside is dark green and merges with the smoke from a passing train. Two forlorn figures stand facing the viewer: a man wearing strange attire as if from another time and place, and a woman in a conventional cotton dress who clearly belongs to the town. The distancing from each other suggests their tryst is transitory, or perhaps it never took place.

By the end of the year Nolan's life had slipped back into a routine of living at Parkville and Heidelberg and working in the city where he felt safe. In fact, the only close call he experienced was when travelling by train to Adelaide to stay with Max Harris. There were civilian and military police at the stations to check papers and his identity of Robin Murray was accepted without question. On the way back, however, a railway inspector discovered he was travelling without a ticket and handed him over to the military police on arrival at Spencer Street station in Melbourne. Once again, he had to call on all his acting resources to avoid arrest.

A happy interlude at this time was the wedding of the painter John Perceval, who was 21, and 16-year-old Mary Boyd — both regular visitors to Heide — in the Brown Room of the Boyd family home at Murrumbeena, with Nolan as one of the witnesses at a ceremony dominated by the family patriarch, Merric, who

Dimboola, *1944*   Giggle Palace, *1945*

was embracing religion with a passionate fervour. As a young man he had
studied at theological college, although his life was based on a fine reputation for
art pottery with a genuinely Australian style. Merric had remained a practising
potter until ill health had forced him into the less strenuous pursuit of drawing.
At the informal wedding ceremony he made a long utterance about the love of
God and described how, blessed in this way, he and his wife Doris had been able
to experience life as a long honeymoon. He finally exhorted the guests to join
him in kneeling in prayer and everyone, including the official celebrant,
complied. The only change in the domestic arrangements was that Perceval
could now move into the household to sleep in Mary's room. John Reed was
amused to see them both retire there after the ceremony, although it proved too
much for old Merric who, forgetting about the wedding, demanded to know
what that man was doing in his daughter's bedroom.

   A radio in the Parkville studio kept Nolan in touch with the rapidly
accelerating developments on the war front as well as providing background
music for painting. The end of the fighting in Europe was announced in early
May 1945 and a public holiday was proclaimed for 9 May. Under a warm sun
the day began soberly and reverently with a solemn ceremony at the Shrine of
Remembrance in St Kilda Road. The mood changed in the afternoon with a
human chain of thousands of merrymakers parading down Swanston Street and
spilling over Prince's Bridge to fill the parks and gardens on the other side of the
Yarra. They waved flags and cheered as fifteen RAAF fighter aircraft flew low

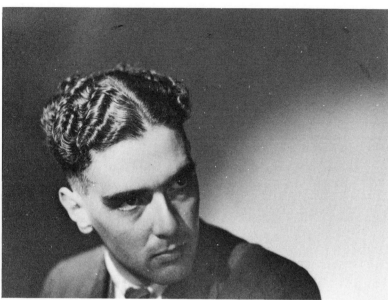

John Perceval (Barrett Reid)   *Max Harris (Barrett Reid)*

over the city where Chinatown was holding its own celebrations with Chinese Nationalist flags fluttering from every doorway along narrow Little Bourke Street. That night the Melbourne sky glowed from the flames of bonfires lit in suburban gardens and the central streets were crowded with young people. Nolan watched as a fire was lit on the verandah of a store on the corner of Flinders Lane and Swanston Street and firemen had to break down the door to gain access, to the wild cheers of the onlookers.

As the Pacific war was moving to its conclusion, the Nolan family was shocked to learn that their younger son, Raymond, serving with one of the army's small ships companies in the Pacific, had been killed, not in action, but through what sounded like a senseless accident. The official report of his death stated that a group had gone ashore at Cooktown on the far north coast of Australia where a lively party had ensued. As they were preparing to return to their ship, they clambered over a rickety wooden landing stage in the darkness and Raymond Nolan had trodden on some rotten planks and fallen into the water. It was high tide and he drowned before being rescued. Mr and Mrs Nolan thought this an unlikely story because their son had not been a drinker before going into the army and, furthermore, was an excellent swimmer.

Nolan and Max Harris often discussed ideas for *Angry Penguins* and one of their recurring themes was the mystique of Ned Kelly. Harris considered the outlaw's effect on Australian culture worth investigating and Nolan, remembering the remark during the Ern Malley hoax about painting Ned Kelly, thought it could be a suitable theme for him. With this in mind, the two of them decided to find out more about the Kellys and their surroundings. Nolan already knew a good deal about the outlaw because of his family connections with northern Victoria. He had read the voluminous report of a Royal Commission into the state of the police force after Kelly had been convicted of murder and hanged at the old Melbourne gaol on 11 November 1880, and found it an absorbing document, particularly its descriptions of the people and conditions in what had been frontier territory, an Australian wild west. He remembered the stories of his grandfather who had been stationed as a police officer at Beechworth and had many tales of brushes with the notorious gang. There was also a well-known publication by J.J. Kenneally called *The Complete Inner History of the Kelly Gang and Their Pursuers*, full of information and having on its cover a commercial art representation of Ned's iron helmet, with two eyes staring out of a rectangular-shaped slit, which had long appealed to Nolan as a potent symbol of defiance. This was not a fashionable subject in Melbourne social and intellectual circles where Kelly was usually regarded as a thug and scoundrel whose status as a folk hero among the working class was unfortunate.

Harris and Nolan hastily threw some clothes into a couple of bags and took the train north, heading for the centre of Kelly country, the township of Glenrowan where, on a cold June night in 1880, armed police had surrounded the hotel, wounding Ned in his suit of home-made armour, capturing Dan Kelly, and killing two other members of the gang. The travellers planned to be away for a couple of weeks exploring the sites of the Kellys' exploits across a wide area of northern Victoria. Their first call was to the Glenrowan Hotel, which looked very much as it had for the past sixty years when it was rebuilt after being destroyed by fire at the time of the celebrated shootout. It remained small and smoky with few modern conveniences, except refrigeration to keep the beer cold. They swept into the bar during the early evening with Harris announcing, 'It's drinks on the house for anyone who'll tell us about Ned Kelly'. This unexpected intrusion was greeted by stony silence and the visitors had to stand sheepishly at the bar ordering beers for themselves. There was a number of distant Kelly relatives still living in the area, but they were hostile, even belligerent, to strangers coming into the district and prying into their family affairs, particularly those who offered them free drinks to blab about their hero. As the evening progressed this mood of antagonism began to soften a little as Nolan played up his Irish connections, claiming a strong family affinity with this part of Victoria.

The next morning, nursing hangovers and following an uncomfortable night on makeshift beds, unable to sleep for the buzz of mosquitoes, they shuffled along the road to the police station to ask about any surviving Kelly records. The sergeant greeted them coolly and seemed to be more protective of the town

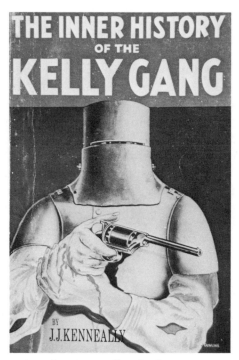

Jacket of J.J. Kenneally's book

than Ned Kelly's reputation. He said he did not want Glenrowan written about
or investigated because it might attract crowds of visitors and he preferred a
quiet, uncomplicated life among the people he understood. The policeman
revealed that he regarded Kelly as little more than a criminal, and he suggested
Nolan and Harris leave the township immediately.

One piece of information which they gleaned from the previous night was
that the youngest member of the Kelly family, Ned's brother Jim, was still alive
and living nearby. They decided to go in search of him and eventually found an
old man, alone and reclusive, sitting in the shade of the verandah of a
tumbledown weatherboard cottage. Nolan thrust out his hand in greeting, but
old Jim Kelly would have nothing to do with strangers and refused to shake. He
remained silent about his famous brother and refused to say much about the rest
of the family. Harris and Nolan were bitterly disappointed at the reception and
they reluctantly took their leave to pay a visit to the races where Steve Hart, a
member of the gang, had once disguised himself as Kate Kelly by wearing a
dress and riding side-saddle in the women's event. The two travellers joined the
crowds at the racecourse with its old-fashioned atmosphere giving a taste of
what the district had been like at the time of the Kellys. In between events a
man came around selling raffle tickets for a saddle and Nolan put his hand in his

pocket for some small change and discovered he was wearing the wrong coat. He had intended to change before leaving Heidelberg and money for the trip had been left at home in another jacket. He was furious because he was beginning to enjoy himself, recalling a way of life he had experienced as a boy when taking holidays with relatives in the nearby Goulburn Valley.

Max Harris was not so content; he found the heat, the flies, the dust and country towns not to his liking and, in their financial circumstances, thought the best thing was to return home immediately. Nolan had to agree that the tour must be terminated because there was little hope of getting cash from Melbourne and none of the locals would trust them with credit. They hitched a ride from a passing motorist along the Hume Highway to Wangaratta where they spent the night in a cheap hotel. The only room they could afford contained six beds with a drunk stretched out across two of them, causing sleepless hours with his stentorian snoring. There was just enough money for the train fare back to Melbourne, although nothing left over for food on the journey.

As he began to immerse himself in the Kelly theme, Nolan saw that what he had experienced in the Wimmera paintings could be an integral part of a new series: the light, the landscape and the rural reality. Against that background, he could play out the narrative drama of the Kelly gang, with its central figure, Ned, being presented in a style he had learned during his spray-painting days at Fayrfield Hats, those experiments with Moholy-Nagy images and, in particular, a black square. He realised he had noticed the shape cropping up in a surprising variety of ways, but principally in the work of the Russian constructivists, such as Malevich, which had influenced his initial designs for Lifar's *Icare*. Nolan went through the process of combining disparate aspects of his experience into an entirely new expression. The vision of landscape he had evolved during army service would provide the background for the story of Ned Kelly, whose iron armour, fashioned from the mould boards of ploughs, with blue quilting sewn inside the helmet, would be represented by the omnipresent black square.

Nolan used Ripolin and hardboard, painting his new works on the refectory table in the dining room at Heide, but there were many interruptions because he was busier than ever with the layout and design of the various Reed and Harris magazines and books in their expanding publishing programme. When he had time to work on the Kellys each painting only took about two days to finish but the prospect of completing the series stretched into the far distance. There were few studies for individual works, although Nolan had made a considerable number of preliminary paintings on strawboard after returning from the Kelly country, and there was a confusing number of sketches in crayon and pencil, although many of these were drawn after paintings were completed and could not be regarded as studies or preliminary designs. Nolan's mind continued to be

Kelly in the Bush, *1945*

in turmoil because he felt powerless to resist being drawn more tightly than ever to the Reeds' influence and he was still technically on the run as a deserter. Up in the ceiling above the dining table were his army rifle and uniform carefully wrapped in newspapers and hessian bags as a constant reminder that, like Kelly, he remained an outlaw.

The end of the war was the only topic of conversation in Melbourne by the beginning of August 1945 when a great air armada was reported to be massing for the final assault on Japan and victory was predicted within a month. But then on Monday 6 August, Tokyo Radio announced that Super Fortresses had caused considerable damage in raids on Hiroshima with a new type of bomb. When this was heard over the Australian radio and appeared in the press, conjecture began about the destruction of all life by this harnessing of atomic energy. It was seen as both a global catastrophe and a triumph of science and, before the effects could be fully reported or assessed, hopes were being expressed that after the war scientists could channel their efforts to the service of mankind.

By Thursday of that week the full horror of Hiroshima was revealed with a graphic illustration of atomic devastation on the front page of the *Argus*, showing a street plan of central Melbourne similar in size to the area obliterated in the Japanese city. It stretched from Victoria Parade in the north to Albert

Park Lake in the south, from Spencer Street railway station in the west to Punt Road in the east. But this was quickly forgotten when the news finally arrived of Japan's capitulation on Wednesday 15 August. It was the cue to throw off wartime restraints and go wild with celebration.

The morning had dawned cold and grey with a fine drizzle in the air, but nothing could dampen the enthusiasm as many thousands of workers left their offices and factories to journey by train, tram, bus and on foot to the central city. They were greeted by snowfalls of confetti made from torn-up telephone directories, filing cards, ledgers and newspapers, drifting down from the buildings. In Elizabeth Street a sack of brightly-coloured feathers was emptied onto the tram tracks and they flew up in a Technicolour blizzard every time traffic passed. Most of the city stores closed as soon as the news was announced, their staff spilling into the streets, joining hands, forming long crocodiles and singing loudly. Flag-bedecked cars, many of them trailing old buckets and tin cans, travelled along the roads, adding to the festive din. Horse-drawn lorries and carts overflowing with passengers headed for the city and the police were forced to impose boundary limits for vehicles. Out in the suburbs, housewives had been unprepared for the news and they rushed to food shops where nearly all supplies were soon sold out. No bread was baked, most cafes and restaurants remained closed, and even some hotels had to shut their doors because they had not yet received the special three-day supply of beer to celebrate victory. At night the city was ablaze with light and many children stared wide-eyed at illuminated shop windows for the first time, floodlights were turned on and neon signs flashed their multicoloured messages after being dark for so many years.

After much soul searching, Nolan, at 28, finally accepted that the life he was leading was contrary to his working-class ethics. Moreover, there were now violent scenes at Heide when tempers would flare and frequent emotional storms that threatened to tear their relationships apart. Steeled by the experience of being on the run, he came to the decision to leave Heidelberg, the Reeds and Melbourne. However, Nolan found it difficult to contemplate completing the Kelly series without the assistance of his patrons and so for the time being he kept on painting.

Certainly, living in a *ménage à trois* had rarely been dull, although it left him open to the jibes of outsiders who would accuse him of being a kept man. Sunday Reed cast an immensely attractive spell on those she favoured. Apart from her physical beauty, people were also attracted by her character, which held deep currents of incomprehensibility in many of her thoughts and actions. She was sensitive to most situations, but after a certain point her brain seemed to go into a strange, private spiral with heightened clairvoyant abilities. Nolan's close relationship with her and the equally attractive John Reed involved an

Steve Hart dressed as a girl, 1947 (enamel on composition board, 91 × 121.5 cm., Australian National Gallery, Canberra)

Constable Fitzpatrick and Kate Kelly, 1946 (enamel on composition board, 91 × 121.5 cm., Australian National Gallery, Canberra)

Dog and Duck Hotel, *1948*

Pretty Polly Mine, *1948 (synthetic enamel on hardboard, 91 × 122.2 cm., Art Gallery of New South Wales)*

artistic endeavour and purpose that was unusual in Australia at the time. Others saw it as an aesthetic association, as if Heide were some sort of antipodean Bloomsbury. But Nolan could never regard it that way although there was one common bond: Bloomsbury and Heide both revolved around intimate association and a single-minded belief that creativity was the most important thing in the world.

While he worked away, Nolan kept thinking about a visitor to Heide during his early years. He had met John Reed's sister Cynthia, a dark, elegant woman with an aura of mystery surrounding her, on only a handful of occasions well before the war when she attracted a lively circle of artists and friends to her arts and crafts shop in Flinders Lane, before she went overseas. After considerable travelling she had married in England but soon after, her husband joined a British intelligence unit and was killed in Romania early in the war.

When Cynthia Hansen had arrived pregnant at Heide at the end of 1940 she was the most sophisticated member of the group. Good-looking, intelligent and charming, it seemed she would add brilliance to the household, with recent experience of life in Vienna, Paris, London, Los Angeles and Chicago. Her presence, however, was an obvious challenge to Sunday's dominance and she was determined to be rid of her sister-in-law. Cynthia soon learned about Nolan's relationship with the Reeds. He was painting in the dining room one day, on leave from the army, when she entered and without any preliminaries asked, 'Why don't you get out of this situation?' There was no formal salutation, just the blunt question. Nolan was taken aback by this directness and could only manage a rather lame response: 'Is that the way you usually greet strangers?' Cynthia's reply was even more abrupt: 'Just get out and go away from here'. He was due to return to his unit in the Wimmera the next day and was destined to see her only once again when a similar exchange took place, ending with the advice, 'If you've got any sense, you'll get out, or you'll be lost as a painter and as a person'. Soon after this Cynthia moved to Sydney and they lost touch, although John Reed occasionally showed him photographs of his young niece named Jinx. Nolan had remembered Cynthia's words and continued to be intrigued by this beautiful, strong-willed woman. He had the curious conviction that their paths would cross again.

He continued his Kelly pictures and gradually progressed to what was intended to be the centrepiece of the entire work, the fire at the Glenrowan Hotel. It did not remain that way for long, however, because he and Jack Bellew, who was editing the Reed and Harris journal *Tomorrow*, got drunk together one night at Heide and Bellew suggested that Nolan cut the painting in half because 'the workers don't want paintings as big as that'. Nolan promptly sawed the large panel into two which then conformed in size to the rapidly-growing number of completed pictures.

The general reaction to the artful folklore of the Kelly series from those who saw the work progressing was favourable and there was discussion about how they might best be exhibited. One suggestion came from Dr H.V. Evatt, who was one of the driving forces behind the establishment of the new United Nations Organisation. He had discussed with his close friend John Reed the possibility of appointing him Australia's ambassador to the Soviet Union and, if that eventuated, he thought Moscow would provide an ideal venue for the first showing of these inherently socialist works. Nolan sensed what he described as a 'dottiness' about these discussions at Heide and put little faith in the many schemes that were proposed. Max Harris thought the paintings interesting, particularly because of his association with the artist on their brief foray into the Kelly country a couple of years before. Albert Tucker, who now dubbed Nolan 'Ned', remarked, 'Even if you never do anything else, Ned, this will serve as your statement'. With the future of the series still in doubt, Nolan stacked the paintings against the dining room wall at Heide, wrote down the names and appropriate quotations for each panel and numbered them from 1 to 27.

Nolan's talent remained the jewel in the Reeds' crown, but he had become an increasingly rough diamond, fitting uncomfortably into its setting, and they began discussing his future, what he should do and where he might go, because it was evident that if Nolan stayed with them at Heide for much longer, the mounting tensions would lead to disaster. One of the suggestions was for him to visit Macquarie Island, far to the south, where a weather station was being established halfway between Australia and the Antarctic. John Reed made the appropriate enquiries and prospects looked favourable for Nolan's attachment to the expedition for a year during which he could paint the rugged scenery and make a study of the island's prolific bird life. However, the warmth of Queensland beckoned instead of the chills of the Southern Ocean.

Now that the war was over, Nolan told the Reeds that he must visit north Queensland to find out for himself the real circumstances of his brother's mysterious death. While away he planned to look for new painting subjects but there was no talk of a complete separation. However, Sunday noticed him packing a suit and she began to weep, recalling Nolan's statement that suits were for funerals or job interviews. He denied he was leaving Heide permanently as he packed his yellow-banded suitcase, but with a woman's intuition of impending crisis she continued to cry.

In July 1947 the Reeds drove Nolan to Essendon aerodrome where he was to board his first ever flight which would take him to Sydney on the journey north. His thoughts dwelt for a moment on the gloomy days when the only job he could find was as a cleaner at this airfield. His mother and father were also there to see him off, and Sunday waved with a shadow of apprehension on her face as the motors roared and the DC3 gathered speed down the runway. Nolan

The Trial, *from 1946—47 Kelly series*

felt a finality about the farewells, but as the plane took off and began to gain height his attention was caught by the patterns of cow tracks across green fields glimpsed through the windows and then the great bulk of Mount Macedon loomed up in the hazy blue distance. He suddenly felt weightless and elated, as he had five years before when first catching sight of the Grampians from the back of the army truck on its way to the Wimmera. Gone was the constriction of being a deserter, to be replaced by a freewheeling, almost dizzy, sense of freedom and anticipation.

CHAPTER SIX

In Search of Cynthia

§

A member of the Heide circle helped to make Nolan's journey easier and was the means of introducing him to a wide range of new experiences. During the early 1940s a circle of young poets and writers living in Brisbane became interested in the activities of the *Angry Penguins* group and several of them paid visits to Melbourne, staying with the Reeds. One of them was a promising young poet named Barrett Reid who now offered Nolan accommodation at his father's house outside Brisbane.

One of Nolan's first trips was to Fraser Island, the largest sand island in the world, just off the Queensland coast, which he had heard about from Tom Harrisson, a former major in the British army, who had been sent out to Australia during the war to train commandos. Much of the instruction had taken place on Fraser Island, with its rough terrain thickly covered by trees and undergrowth making it ideal as a jungle classroom. Nolan had been impressed with Harrisson on meeting him at Heide, finding him a cultured man, a keen ornithologist and an interesting writer, whose *Savage Civilisation* was published by Gollancz in 1937. He also had a keen eye for art and became the second person to buy a Nolan painting when he acquired one of the Wimmera landscapes. During long conversations Harrisson had enthused about the beauties of Fraser Island, which he enjoyed as a natural paradise and an excellent place to study bird life.

Nolan had also heard about the colourful episode of Mrs Fraser, the wife of a Scottish sea captain who in 1836 survived a shipwreck and managed to get ashore only to discover that her sole white companion among a tribe of hostile Aborigines was to be an escaped convict named Bracefell. He agreed to help her back to civilisation if she would plead for his pardon. After a time during which the two of them lived together they were discovered by a rescue party, but Mrs Fraser, ashamed of her close relations with Bracefell and unwilling to face censure because of them, betrayed him at the last moment, although he was able to avoid capture and escape into the bush. Nolan would soon discover that the island bearing the lady's name was everything that Harrisson had described and he imagined its terrain, combined with the intriguing story, could make an excellent setting for another series of narrative paintings.

At the picturesque little port of Maryborough Nolan and Reid managed to obtain permission to go out to the forestry reserve and got a passage on an old sea-going barge that had seen better days and probably a more efficient crew, because this one, to a man, soon suffered from seasickness after leaving the flat water of the river and meeting the choppy seas of Hervey Bay. During the afternoon the continual lurching of the vessel caused a retaining stay to snap with a loud report like a rifle shot and there was a danger of the two stubby masts being shaken loose if the cable was not quickly re-connected. Barrie Reid had found a sheltered spot and sat consoling himself with a book and a bottle of Beenleigh rum while the captain, also swigging the local rum, looked around for an able-bodied man to fix the stay. Nolan appeared to be the only one capable of doing it and to everyone's amazement he happily agreed to shin up one of the rocking masts and make a temporary repair.

It was a slow journey but as the boat approached the island in the late afternoon, Nolan and Reid could make out a featureless profile rising to perhaps 800 feet at the highest point, part of the great east coast sand dunes formed during the last ice age. It was an apparent wilderness little changed from when James Cook charted it from the other side more than 170 years before. The area was now mainly a forestry reserve with no wharf facilities; timber was loaded from a small creek where workers disembarked and received their occasional supplies. It was too late for Nolan and Reid to land that day, however, because of the rapidly failing light, and they spent an uncomfortable night offshore until the barge could be negotiated into the creek the following morning, to be greeted by a band of ferocious looking men. They were bearded and dark-complexioned, although surprisingly some wore bunches of wildflowers in their hatbands. These forestry workers were headed by their foreman, a large man named Norm, who had lived on the island for several years with his wife and daughter, the only women for miles on this part of the coast. Nolan and Reid soon found themselves enchanted by the surrounding natural beauty which had not been obvious from a distance. Great stands of trees formed a lush green canopy against the sky, throwing deep purple shadows on the sandy soil below. There were little streams of pure, fresh water trickling lazily to the sea and in the south of the island a series of fresh-water lakes, the home for hundreds of seabirds. Fishermen occasionally appeared on the surf beaches to net large schools of mullet and tailor moving up the coast during the late winter and early spring.

Not long after he had left Heide, Nolan began to experience periods of loneliness and severe depression, turning over in his mind what might have happened had he not met John Reed on that fateful day almost a decade ago and begun an association that not only changed his life dramatically but dominated it for eight years. He supposed he would still be married to Elizabeth and, perhaps, have more children which would have kept them poor and committed to remaining in Melbourne. Getting to Europe would have been pushed into the background until the incentive and determination was lost through lack of encouragement. However, Nolan did not regard living at Heide as patronage; he had worked hard enough for board and lodging in the garden and with household chores and had also contributed much to the production of *Angry Penguins* and the other Reed and Harris publishing activities. What had tied him to the Reeds for such a long time was an interdependent relationship that existed on every level and was intensely stimulating and fulfilling. That was now finished.

In Queensland, Nolan was able to journey further afield by joining an expedition on a trip to the Carnarvon Ranges in search of dinosaur bones and a blind fish that was known to inhabit underground rivers. There was a surveyor in the party who was mapping part of the mountains as a future national park. It was a rough and uncomfortable journey, but constantly fascinating to inquiring eyes that had never before seen the colours and the majesty of Australia's outback, the deep blue of the skies contrasting with the vivid ochre landforms to introduce an optical illusion of a thin yellow dividing line. Nolan was thrilled by the quality of the light which seemed to confuse his previous concepts of distance that he had last grappled with in coming to terms with the Wimmera landscape. He suspected that this new landscape could be another fertile field for his painting. But as pleasant as these diversions were proving to be, there was the personal pressure to move on to the far north coast as quickly as possible where his odyssey would become a pilgrimage to the little port of Cooktown to seek the truth about his brother's death.

Nolan eventually arrived at his destination after a launch trip through a choppy turquoise sea from Cairns between the rugged coastline and the almost continuous line of shoals forming the northern part of the Great Barrier Reef. Cooktown is the last port on Australia's east coast before the remote northern extremity of Cape York. The place had seen bursts of action and fluctuating populations since it was established in 1873 to serve the rich gold strikes of the nearby Palmer River which attracted an initial rush of 35,000 men. Cooktown's fortunes had ebbed and flowed with depressions, booms and war and now, in late 1947, the tide of prosperity had turned once again and it had become a sleepy little community of a couple of hundred souls, dozing in the glare of the tropics, cut off from the rest of the world except by sea. With its mangrove-choked foreshores skirting the estuary of the Endeavour River, it had changed little since Captain Cook, continuing the first-known survey of Australia's Pacific

94

Fraser Island, *1947*

coastline in 1770, had steered his damaged barque into this haven after striking a submerged coral reef offshore and nearly foundering.

Nolan's first visit was to the police station where the sergeant in charge reluctantly confirmed from his records the navy's version of Raymond John Nolan's demise a few days before his 21st birthday on 25 July 1945. The police report stated that Raymond was drowned when he fell overboard from a refuelling tender of the 15th Small Ships Company, Royal Australian Engineers, servicing American warships in the Pacific. There was a suggestion that he and a number of American sailors had been drinking heavily in the Cooktown pubs and, on returning to their ship, Raymond had fallen overboard from the tender or through the planking of the jetty and drowned before he could be rescued. The Nolan family had attempted to get more information in Melbourne but there was some confusion because the young man, although enlisted in the army, had been seconded to the Australian navy and was working for the Americans at the time of his death. Nolan took some photographs of the rickety pier where his brother might have fallen into the water, but there was little else he could do.

This outpost seemed to be a living museum of nineteenth-century colonial Australia. Nolan was suffering pangs of personal guilt, agonising over leaving Melbourne, missing the support of the Reeds and knowing how disappointed his parents would be that he had failed to clarify the facts about Raymond's death.

But there was the exhilarating antidote of the light, the fierce heat, tropical fruits, quaint balconied hotels facing a straggling main street, an overwhelming sense of decay and colourful characters straight out of Joseph Conrad. Cooktown was a torpid paradise for dropouts and beachcombers and Nolan began to be drawn into their company, adopting the local lifestyle, sometimes drinking until four in the morning and then sleeping through the blaze of a tropical dawn where he had collapsed, on the grass verge opposite the hotel, in an overgrown park or fanned by gentle sea breezes along the gritty strip of foreshore. This way of life lasted for a few days, until he realised his limited funds were being drunk away and the police began to take more than a passing interest in this new arrival.

The days at Cooktown drifted by, stretching into weeks and then more than a month until he realised that Christmas was approaching and he had better wrench himself away if he was not to join the permanent band of local eccentrics, drinking their lives away and surviving on dreams and fantasies. He got a lift on a fishing boat to Cairns, planning to take the railway south to Townsville to visit his brother's grave and then return to stay with Barrie Reid in Brisbane. It was the holiday season, however, and almost impossible to get a seat on the trains. Finally, he did manage to cram himself into a compartment with a large Italian family, who fed him on bananas and bread and offered countless glasses of rough red wine from an apparently inexhaustible supply of glass flagons they carried with them. The result was that he fell fast asleep, missing the stop at Townsville, and woke up after many hours with a throbbing hangover, well on the way to Brisbane.

Nolan stayed for a brief time in the Queensland capital gathering his thoughts about the series of paintings he wanted to complete on the Mrs Fraser theme for an exhibition that had been arranged for him at the Moreton Galleries in Brisbane from the middle of February. He said goodbye to Barrie Reid, who assumed he was returning to Heide, and arrived in Sydney where he was determined to stay. An art student friend he had known in Melbourne, Alannah Coleman, lent him her studio apartment near Kings Cross while he found his feet and pondered how to carry out his next move, which he had planned while his aeroplane was leaving Melbourne several months before.

The sculptor Oliffe Richmond had the downstairs studio and often worked outside in the small garden. He was shortly to leave for London for study at the Royal College of Art before becoming an assistant to Henry Moore. The Sydney art scene was in a constant and confident state of flux. Nolan thought it related more to the city's hedonistic tendencies rather than the political ferment that had obsessed him and his fellow Melbourne painters from Heidelberg to St Kilda. There seemed to be an absence of innovation here — with the exception of Russell Drysdale — as William Dobell, Donald Friend, Jean Bellette, Francis

Lymburner and Justin O'Brien produced decoratively urbane pictures, a world away from Tucker, Boyd, Perceval and Vassilieff. Nolan regarded this sunnier and more relaxed approach — whose executants were convinced was the best in Australia — as excellently suited to art exhibitions which became social events, where paintings were to be glimpsed between flowered hats during animated conversations. Melbourne art was earnest and meaningful; in Sydney it tended to be gracious.

In this rather foreign atmosphere, Nolan was relieved to find a number of fellow artists he had known in Melbourne now living nearby and he joined a group of them, including Joan Currie, Alannah Coleman, Gray Smith and Joy Hester, at a New Year swimming party to welcome 1948. It was not an altogether happy occasion, however, because Joy had recently learned that she was suffering from the incurable Hodgkin's disease. Nolan saw her and Gray Smith frequently during his first fortnight in Sydney and their talk often turned to their mutual difficulties in extricating themselves from the influence of the Reeds.

After these conversations, which began to depress him, Nolan decided it was high time to seek out Cynthia. He had her address from John Reed and one sunny morning set off by train for the long journey to the northern suburb of Wahroonga. On approaching Cynthia's house he had second thoughts about his motives, suddenly losing his nerve, and walked back to the small shopping centre in search of a malted milkshake to boost his stamina, as he had done before bicycle races in his youth. It was the middle of a sultry afternoon by the time Nolan strode up to the front door of the house and found it open but guarded by a latched flyscreen. He rang the bell to no avail then tried again. A sleepy voice wafted out of the darkened interior, 'Who is it?' Nolan did not reply, but vigorously twisted the bell again. A dishevelled Cynthia came to the doorway, wearing a light cotton gown, still groggy from this sudden awakening from her afternoon nap. She ran fingers through her dark hair and squinted against the exterior glare, freezing suddenly when she realised who was standing there. Instead of the greeting Nolan anticipated, she stood behind the flyscreen scowling and snapped, as if it were a continuation of their earlier conversations in Melbourne, 'Go away. Go away!' He had not made this effort to be repulsed yet again, so he stood his ground and said nothing.

'What do you want, Sidney?' Cynthia demanded. 'Who sent you? Please go away. I don't want to see you, as I'm sure you understood before.' Nolan attempted a wan smile and remained mute, which had the effect of making Cynthia talk nervously. 'Have John and Sunday sent you to see me? What do they want?' She was peppering him with questions and revealing her suspicions. Nolan knew that whatever he said must be inconsequential, even frivolous, if this delicate moment was not to crumble into disaster. 'Well, at least you could

Cynthia's house in Wahroonga, Sydney, 1986

offer me a cup of tea', he chided. 'A cup of tea and a biscuit for the traveller who's come all this way to see you from sunny Queensland.' She replied, 'But I don't want to see you and the sun shines quite nicely here, thank you'. He countered, 'What, no biscuits? Nothing for the stranger just returned from the desert?' This banter continued for a few minutes and Cynthia finally relented, letting him into the house and then preparing tea while Nolan told her what he had been doing over the past few months. She began to relax when she learned he had left Heide and that his visit had nothing to do with her sister-in-law. The relationship blossomed and within a few days Nolan had packed up his belongings at Kings Cross and transferred them to Wahroonga where he began working on the panels of the Mrs Fraser paintings in an atmosphere of harmony and peace that he had forgotten could exist.

He started to enjoy the simple domesticity of suburban life, often cooking the dinner and getting to know Cynthia's lively six-year-old daughter, Jinx. The atmosphere became so congenial, however, that Cynthia wondered about the dramatic turn of events, her equilibrium upset by this attractive man entering her life. He seemed relaxed and creative in the company of Jinx and herself. Cynthia, two years his senior, enjoyed Nolan's presence and thought his work had elements of genius, which she was certain would lead to his acceptance and success, but she worried that their affair seemed to be going too well and could not bear the thought of her shattered state if it collapsed.

One evening after dinner Cynthia surprised Nolan by saying things were getting too close between them and she thought he should leave. For a moment he believed she was joking but the steely look in her big eyes soon told him that

Cynthia's daughter, Jinx (Barrett Reid)

the words were to be taken literally. He was utterly dismayed and hurriedly suggested that he could sleep in the garden shed he had requisitioned as a studio while they worked out their differences. Cynthia responded bluntly that he would have to go considerably further than that, preferably away from Sydney altogether. 'Well', he said, 'I haven't even got the fare to get as far as Gosford, so there's no question of that'. Cynthia picked up her handbag, took out a purse, and counted out all the bank notes it held. 'There's £14', she said, thrusting the money at him. 'Take it and go back to Queensland.' Nolan realised that given her mood he had better get away for a short time so that they could both think about the future, although he remained convinced that their lives would be spent together.

He took the money, packed a small bag and the next day boarded a train from Sydney's Central Railway to Bourke in the far west of New South Wales. Nolan had no idea what he would find there but the well-known expression 'back o' Bourke' suggested space and distance and remoteness to him which he found an attractive prospect in these emotional circumstances. He arrived at his destination after an impossibly long and uncomfortable journey to find the town a disappointing place, dusty and rundown, with no decent accommodation and a general hostility to strangers. It had little to excite the senses after his rich experiences in Queensland.

While he was away, Nolan's Mrs Fraser pictures, twelve of them painted in Ripolin on hardboard and each measuring four feet by three, went on exhibition at the Moreton Galleries in Brisbane, one of the most staid cities of Australia, and were greeted as grotesque curiosities. In spite of a catalogue introduction by Clive Turnbull describing Nolan as 'one of the most interesting of the younger Australian painters' and pointing out that 'many overseas visitors have found him the most interesting of all', a local daily newspaper mounted a scathing attack, describing the works as 'monstrous daubings' and the use of the hardboard, which was a commercial product known as Masonite used for lining walls and ceilings, as 'deliberate maltreatment of so much useful and hard-to-come-by building materials'. The review was followed over the next few days by letters to the editor of the *Courier-Mail* complaining of this outrage to the well-ordered sensibilities of Brisbane's art lovers. A rare defence came from the poet Judith Wright, who wrote to the newspaper saying that the attacks showed 'a disgraceful provincialism'. The paintings were priced at 25 guineas each and only two were sold, but the allure of Mrs Fraser would become a continuing theme in Nolan's work.

He survived for three nights at Bourke and then decided that he either keep going overland to Darwin to find a ship heading for China or go back to Sydney to square things off with Cynthia. China would have to wait, although his reception back at Wahroonga proved to be a repetition of a few weeks before. There was the almost ritual ringing of the doorbell, the rejection from Cynthia and the pleading from Nolan, but this time he knew he had to be firm with her. 'You don't know what life's about', he accused, raising his voice. 'You could be making a new start with me and it could be happy and exciting'. Cynthia did not find this a particularly persuasive argument, although she reconsidered her stand and, after talking it over with close friends, accepted that they should be together. They married soon after on 25 March 1948.

In 1948 John Reed arranged for the Kelly series to be exhibited for the first time at the Velasquez Galleries in Melbourne. It received little critical attention and only one sale — to the art critic and writer Clive Turnbull. The Reeds were obviously still proud of their protégé, with John describing the works as 'the most sensitive and profound harmony between symbol, legend and visual impact. That this has been accomplished in language of the utmost simplicity is itself an indication of the strength of the artist's vision and discipline.'

Most of Nolan's residual guilt about deserting from the army had evaporated with his new-found domesticity, but it was jolted back into sharp focus when he learned of an amnesty for deserters, announced by the government. If he reported to a military garrison with uniform and rifle, a dishonourable discharge would be issued and no further legal obligation would apply. As far as Nolan knew, his army issue were still safely in the ceiling at Heide. Much of the discipline and what he regarded as aimless military procedures had escaped him, but it had been drilled into every man to look after his rifle and make sure it was always clean and at the ready. Consequently, he had smothered the weapon with Vaseline, wrapped the parts in an oily rag and put them in a hessian bag together with his uniform, carefully placing the package on two cross beams with a space underneath to allow the air to circulate. Nolan now requested John Reed to send the package to Sydney and on receipt took it along, unopened, to Victoria Barracks in Paddington. He timidly approached the sergeant at a reception desk, watched disapprovingly by three soldiers hovering in the background. He stated his name, army rank and number, explaining that he was declaring his desertion and returning property under the terms of the government's amnesty. The hessian bag was securely tied with strong twine and one of the soldiers used a bayonet to open it. Both the uniform and the rifle were in very poor condition, the uniform full of moth holes and the rifle a mass of rust, but Nolan finally received the piece of paper documenting his dishonourable discharge and an uncomfortable phase of his life was behind him.

Not long after news of their marriage had reached Heide, the Nolans were telephoned by John Reed to say that Sunday was ill and her doctor had suggested it would help the situation if Nolan went to see her. He refused to go alone and Cynthia was understandably reluctant to accompany him, but Nolan was able to persuade her and they flew to Melbourne together. On reaching Heide, he went straight to Sunday's room where she was lying propped up in bed, looking very pale. Cynthia stayed in the sitting room talking to her brother and Joy Hester, who was also visiting from Sydney, while Gray Smith prowled the passage in an agitated mood that threatened to develop into one of his epileptic fits. Sunday's first words to Nolan, whom she had not seen for nearly a year, referred to Smith. 'Doesn't he have a beautiful profile? It's a classical Greek face. You know, I wouldn't mind at all if he had one of his fits on the end of my bed.' This conversation was enough to confirm for Nolan that he was back in what he had described to Cynthia as 'cuckoo land', with Smith pacing up and down outside and Sunday playing the part of an eighteenth-century consumptive heroine making oblique remarks. He listened reluctantly as she intoned a long meaningless monologue, with the occasional sentence breaking through the torrent of disconnected words.

She continued without a pause until Nolan could stand it no longer. He looked at her and stated quietly, to emphasise his new status, which she already knew, 'I'm married'. Sunday stopped abruptly and called out for John, who dashed into the room and sat next to her on the bed as she repeated what had just been said. 'He's married'. There was a long silence and then Sunday added, 'He's changed, Johnny, hasn't he?' Reed replied impersonally, 'Yes, he's changed'. 'His eyes are different', she added and he repeated the words as if a litany, 'Yes, his eyes are different'. Nolan thought to himself, 'Well, it's back to square one again, to the old familiar triangle'. He knew it was futile to attempt reason at a time like this and all he could think about was to rejoin Cynthia and get away from Heide as soon as possible, realising it had been a mistake to have returned.

At that moment Cynthia burst through the door, ignoring her sister-in-law, and with typical tempestuousness announced to her husband, 'I'm off! You can either come with me or stay in this madhouse.' Nolan rose to follow her but was restrained by John Reed while Sunday, with a burst of energy, leapt from the bed in the direction of a cupboard where Nolan thought she kept a pistol as protection against intruders when John was away. She tripped on the sheet and fell to the floor with a little scream of rage.

Gray Smith was now standing at the doorway watching the disarray and breathing heavily. John Reed remained sitting on the bed and Sunday looked as if she might head for the cupboard at any moment. But then, with an intuitive sense of impending danger, she screamed out 'Let him go, Johnny! Let him go!' Their eyes met for a last moment, and Nolan realised that she now accepted he was indeed a different person. He rushed out of the front door and into the driveway, grabbing Cynthia's arm, and they strode away together watched by a sullen Joy Hester, while John Reed and Gray Smith ran to catch up with them. They had a final confrontation by the picket gate under the pine trees. There was nothing more to be said between brother and sister and Nolan had the final word. 'Well, John, the rest of your life is looking after Sunday, so you'd better go back inside and start doing it.' They moved away without looking back, striding down the hill in the soft afternoon light, over the bridge spanning the Yarra and up the hill on the other side towards Heidelberg station.

In the calmer air of Sydney, Nolan worked hard on paintings prompted by his experiences in outback Queensland and met new friends, many of them part of Cynthia's circle of influential people in the arts. He returned briefly to the theatre, designing a production of Cocteau's *Orphée*, produced by Sam Hughes for Sydney University Dramatic Society as part of a double bill with *Pericles, Prince of Tyre*, attributed to Shakespeare, whose decor was designed by Jean Bellette. Nolan painted his own sets, assisted by Margaret Olley, and he also compiled the complete theatre programme, even the advertisements, illustrated with his drawings. He felt that Sydney now harboured the liveliest cultural scene in Australia, unencumbered by the dogma and bitchiness of Melbourne, although it could still be agonisingly parochial. Any arts personality arriving

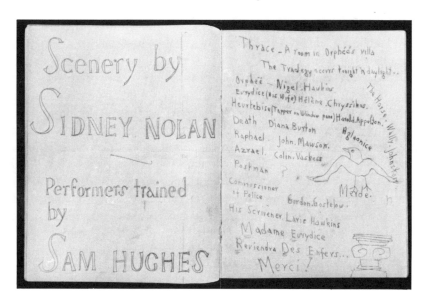

Nolan's programme for Orphée, 1948

from overseas was certain to be lionised and, if famous enough, likely to be hailed as a messiah.

Such a visitor was Kenneth Clark who travelled to Australia in early 1949, principally to visit the National Gallery of Victoria for whom he was adviser to their Felton Bequest, which over the years acquired a great number of works, making the Melbourne gallery's collection the richest in the nation. Clark had found the trustees' recent requests somewhat erratic and, although he was able to negotiate a number of important works for them at reasonable prices, he remained confused about the buying policies, which seemed to follow the whims of fashionable art magazines and were, therefore, unreasonably expensive. Clark's reputation was built on an energetic and influential directorship of the National Gallery in London and, at the time of his arrival, he held the post of Slade Professor at Oxford University. He was also well known as an author and his series of Slade lectures on response to landscape had attracted huge student audiences and produced a best-selling book, *Landscape into Art*.

Clark's ship arrived first in Sydney for a few days' stay and he was immediately attracted to the raffish harbour city, dominated by the span of its great steel bridge. He enjoyed meeting Australians whom he considered the only true democratic and non-hypocritical people in the world, concerned less with wealth than with leading a relaxed lifestyle in delightful surroundings. He liked the unselfconscious lack of sophistication, but was appalled by the pretentious behaviour at a dinner party given by eastern suburbs socialites. Kenneth Clark paid a courtesy visit to the National Art Gallery of New South Wales where he was saddened to note from the best part of the collection how the promise of the so-called Heidelberg School of painters in the late nineteenth century had not been sustained in twentieth-century art. He was heartened, however, to see some of the latest work entered in the annual Wynne Prize for Australian landscape and as he was leaving he caught sight of a picture that stood out from the others with its daring composition and the bold use of colour.

The gallery director did not know the artist's name but Clark consulted his catalogue and discovered the painting was *Abandoned Mine* by Sidney Nolan. The director had to admit he knew little about Nolan when Clark requested his address. He contacted Nolan to ask if he and a colleague might visit to see more of his work, nominating a time the following afternoon. Nolan knew of Clark's reputation and was delighted to confirm the appointment, although Cynthia was strangely antagonistic about the arrangement, becoming unduly possessive about the house and her husband, and regarding such intrusion as a threat to the stability of their marriage. Nolan arranged his paintings around the walls of the small front room of the house and the appointed time came and went with Cynthia getting increasingly agitated, suggesting they forget the arrangement, lock the front door and ignore any visitors. Nolan was able to calm her and then, an hour late, a taxi pulled up and two well-dressed men got out to be greeted by the artist, who was wearing his warm weather painting outfit of khaki shorts, sandals and a brightly-coloured shirt to match the bird pictures which were his current work. It was an urbane meeting at the front gate with profuse apologies for their late arrival from Clark and his companion, Joseph Burke, another Englishman who had recently taken up the *Herald* Chair of Fine Arts at the University of Melbourne.

Nolan ushered them into the front room to look at the paintings and Clark was immediately impressed. It was warm inside the house and as he studied the paintings he slipped off his coat and placed it neatly on a chair, revealing his striped shirt and bright red braces. Cynthia had been hovering nervously in the background and seemed to be waiting for a moment like this. 'Do you usually carry on in such a fashion at other people's homes?' she demanded icily. Clark, thinking she must be making a joke, diverted his attention from the pictures and asked, 'Do what?' 'Take off your coat before you're invited', was her blunt response. Nolan stood there in his shorts and shirt trying to make light of the situation while Clark realised that this awkward woman was serious. He gathered up his coat with a gracious flourish, saying, 'I am very sorry to have left my jacket on your chair without permission. As an Englishman I find it a rather warm afternoon and I wonder if you would be so kind as to arrange another place where it might hang?' Cynthia took the offending garment with little grace while Clark asked Nolan if he could take one of the paintings outside to inspect it in the daylight. He studied several other works in silence, fascinated

Death of Captain Fraser, *1948 (Nolan Gallery, Lanyon, ACT)*

The Traps, *1949 (left) and* Flower Study, *1949 (right), both painted on glass*

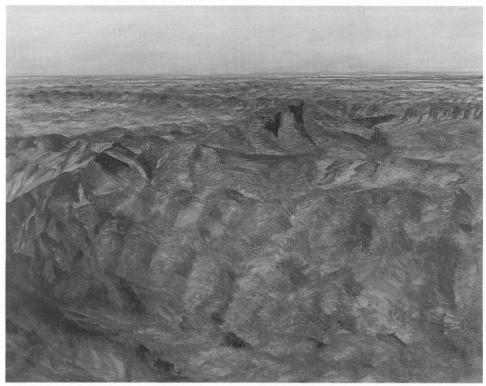

Central Australia, *1950 (Nolan Gallery, Lanyon, ACT)*

Carcass, *1953*

Burke and Wills, *1950*

Greek Cove, *1959*

by the strong element of fantasy and impressed by the sure touch of paint and tone combining in a style unlike that of any other artist. He then turned to Nolan, who feared that the visit was becoming an unmitigated disaster, and told him he could either stay in Australia and continue painting its sights and its birds, or he could go abroad. He offered to arrange an exhibition for Nolan in London, warning that once he went to England he would not go back to Australia, in the sense that there would be a complete change in his work.

Clark decided to buy one of the paintings to go with his Drysdale and picked out a large Queensland outback picture, four feet by three titled *Little Dog Mine*, which Nolan sold him for £30. As they were preparing to leave Nolan asked Clark for his advice on what he should do but Clark told him he would have to work that out for himself. Nolan pressed the point, 'Supposing you were a painter, what would you do then?' 'But Nolan, I am not a painter', he interrupted with an enigmatic smile. 'Painters do things that are incomprehensible. And nobody knows why they do them, least of all me.' He left his card, however, and reiterated his promise to organise something for Nolan at the Leicester Galleries.

Meeting Kenneth Clark had left a deep impression on Nolan but he remained confused by the oblique remarks about his career. Superficially, he had thought both Clark and Burke were almost caricature Englishmen with their well-tailored suits, exquisite manners and grooming, and accents which led to a common language becoming almost a foreign tongue, with schoolboy-like jargon peppered with an excess of 'jolly goods'. But the visit had stirred something in him, emphasised by the way Clark looked at paintings with the practised eye of authority. He had never seen anyone appraise works of art with such conviction, certainly not John and Sunday Reed. The meeting with Clark had convinced Nolan that he must now make the effort to get to Europe, otherwise he would never know his potential, and he wanted to prove that he was more than just an Australian landscape and bird painter.

Nolan was committed to a spell of hard work for the next few weeks, a time of energetic productivity and selection that would pave the way for exhibitions to follow in quick succession. The first of them, in the art gallery of the large David Jones department store, was opened by Maie Casey — the former Melbourne art student Maie Ryan — at the beginning of March 1949 and proved to be an artistic and financial success, although it required considerable work behind the scenes. Cynthia telephoned her various collector friends in an effort to persuade them to attend the show. Many got as far as the door of the gallery then began to abuse her, asking why she was wasting their time with these frightful daubs of paint, and she felt she would scream if another person told her that any child could do as well. But she was also fascinated by the unexpected visitors to the exhibition, sometimes bringing their sandwiches to eat while looking at the outback landscapes. She was surprised to see Nolan's barber come into the gallery one day and stand absorbing the work with obvious pleasure. Cynthia went over to greet him, saying how nice it was for him to make the effort. 'What do you mean, nice of me to come?' he asked. 'I come every single day. This is something for me as an Australian; it's never been stated before.' There was a similar reaction from a typist who lived opposite the Nolans at Wahroonga. Her comment was, 'Isn't it marvellous! These are the things I've seen around Bourke.' As Cynthia explained to Nolan, 'The people who really understand your work are those who have fresh, untouched minds. They probably haven't seen paintings in a gallery before and so they're not afraid to say what they think. Unfortunately, it's the people who think they know a great deal who are confused.' It confirmed their own convictions that the appreciation of art was an instinct and available to everybody.

For the first time in his life, approaching the age of 32, Nolan received a decent return from his work and a wide public could see his paintings and discover for themselves aspects of Australia that not many had ever seen and few artists had depicted before. Sydney's two leading critics were almost ecstatic in their reviews and employed literary and philosophical references to put Nolan's twenty-seven Queensland outback pictures into a frame of reference. Paul Haefliger, who was no stranger to the artist's work, having admired it in several CAS shows, wrote:

> The world, which he so gaily displays . . . is so obvious that really the child alone perceives it. 'To know how cherries and strawberries taste, ask children and birds', said Goethe to Eckermann. But it is the artist who can hold for eternity the transient sensation of the child. Nolan observes what others take for granted. His very pure but trembling line is eager to embrace those strange shapes and harmonies which are constantly before our eyes and which surprise us in their bareness through their force of reality. The elementary is always a little startling.

The outback scenes of unfamiliar birds poised in pink skies, a convict escaping into desolation, and a lonely old man sitting dreaming in the harsh sunlight, caught the imagination of the Sydney art public. The ancient landscape seen through fresh eyes revealed scenes of mining operations, outback pubs and wide brown horizons with a sense of vast space: still, silent and eternal. They were images in bright primary colours to imprint themselves on the viewer's memory and haunt the imagination.

Buyers came out in force, including the National Art Gallery of New South Wales which led the way with two major purchases, *Carron Plains* and *Pretty Polly Mine*. Harry Tatlock Miller ended his comprehensive review of the show for the *Sun* with a prophecy by courtesy of André Gide: '"Be faithful", said Gide to the artist, "to that which exists nowhere but in yourself, and thus make

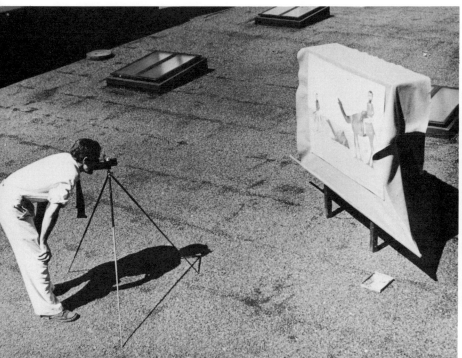

Nolan photographing Burke and Wills Expedition, *1948*

A corner of Nolan's studio at Wahroonga, 1949

Royal Hotel, *1948*

yourself indispensable. What another would have done as well as you do, do not do it." Already seeming aware of this, Nolan may well prove himself indispensable to the art of this country.'

Nolan capitalised on this success by accepting another exhibition within three months because he felt a growing sense of urgency about getting to Europe and following up Kenneth Clark's promises. It would take too long to organise a further group of large pictures and he had to think of a subject and treatment that could be produced quickly and at the same time would appeal to the clientele of the Macquarie Galleries, which, since his arrival in Sydney, had included Nolans as part of group shows. He turned again to Australian history, re-reading Raffaello Carboni's *The Eureka Stockade*, first published in 1855, and began painting his version of Eureka, the uprising on the goldfields of Ballarat in Victoria that crystallised early hopes for Australian nationalism. The sixty-six works were brushed, drawn and doodled onto glass panes to produce a lively parade of goldfields life, centred on the town of Ballarat as the backdrop for this minor epic of armed conflict between rebellious miners burdened by excessive licence fees, and the Victorian police. Nolan's painted narrative was rather like a series of still frames from a silent screen dramatisation of the events, each scene rich and raw, recorded with the asperity of a war artist on the spot. He called them 'one-off snapshots of each episode and of the dramatis personae'.

Eureka was a subject, along with the Kelly story, that had also been favoured by the Australian cinema. There had been a successful silent movie version as far back as 1907 and, only the year before Nolan's show, Ealing Studios revived the theme in a major production starring Chips Rafferty as Peter Lalor. The child-like quality of Nolan's art was mentioned again by Paul Haefliger in his review of the exhibition, although he pointed out:

> Children's works, however, are usually repetitive and too confined. They do not have the invention or the stamina so consistently displayed by Nolan. Nolan takes the best of child art, the innocent vision which looks upon the world with astonishment as well as an inherent sense of patternmaking; the rest belongs to maturity. Perhaps, intellectually, one may not believe in this cavalcade of history, but Nolan's conception has the quality of persuasion which appeals to the senses. For the moment, this is the Eureka Stockade.

Harry Tatlock Miller — equally enthusiastic — stated, 'Sometimes Nolan is too child absorbed in his own play, and we become bored with the bushy eyebrows and the beards. But, after all, the game is his, and is it not from such play that art evolves?'

Nolan's plans for going to Europe were consolidating, but he now had to convince a reluctant Cynthia to make the trip that would be regarded as a great adventure for him and an unwarranted imposition on her and Jinx. In addition, he needed more money to travel overseas, and the only possible source was fully to establish his reputation in Sydney by having a third successful selling exhibition. He needed to know more about the real Australia behind the coastal fringes as a background to what he hoped to paint next and Cynthia agreed that they should invest their time and some of the proceeds from the shows in an extensive journey to the outback.

The Nolans and young Jinx, with her well-worn teddy bear tied by string to a small pack, set out on their adventure on a chilly afternoon in June 1949. As the plane ascended, the cultivated areas below, made green by early winter rains, gave way to a greyish chequerboard of vast paddocks intersected by yellow dusty roads. There were half-empty dams waiting to be filled, reflecting the sun in a silvery brilliance and Nolan thought there was something of Paul Klee down there in an almost abstract landscape of apparently random patterns drawn upon the earth's surface by unseen artisans. He kept his head pressed to one of the aircraft's small windows to watch the scenery drifting by from a viewpoint that remained exciting because he was still a relative newcomer to flying.

Cynthia had decided to keep a journal and her observations indicated that she found Adelaide a rather prim place with the people dressed in a way she remembered from Melbourne before the war. They rose early to catch the train to Port Augusta at the head of Spencer Gulf that would connect with the famous Ghan on its long journey to Alice Springs in the centre of the continent. Nolan's visual interests now became earthbound and he spent most of the daylight hours scanning the flat landscape through his field glasses as they rattled northward. Scattered trees on the horizon, interrupted by the occasional windmill or wheat silo, gave way to a featureless plain as he searched for the southern extremities of the dry bed of Lake Eyre which he had thought of cycling across as a youth. Cynthia noted in her diary that the luminous brilliance of noon was replaced towards evening by a pinkish hue that deep-etched a range of purple hills on the horizon. There were three days of slow progress, sleeping on hard wooden bunks as the train jolted on its way with frequent stops to deliver mail and supplies to lonely railheads along the track. The speed of the Ghan, named after the camel drivers from Afghanistan who once provided the main means of communication in these parts, followed the pace of outback life.

Cynthia was surprised at the straggling suburban character of Alice Springs, considering its small population of barely 2,000, but there was, at least, plenty of foliage to soften the starkness, with oleanders and eucalypts masking the ugly facades of mean little fibro structures with peeling paint and rusty tin roofs. These were early days for tourism in the Northern Territory with sparse facilities for the traveller, although the Nolans were fortunate to secure a room with a bathroom in the new wing of the Centre Hotel. Nolan carried an introduction to Eddie Connellan, a former barnstorming pilot who had established an aerial mail service for the remote settlements of the territory with weekly deliveries to many of them. Connellan was happy to take the Nolans on one of his runs which left Alice Springs at dawn and returned in the late afternoon of what, he warned, would be a day full of noisy and often turbulent travel. Cynthia could not face the thought of so many hours in the air and protested that she had a sore throat and needed some rest after their arduous train journey, but Nolan convinced her that flying was, in fact, the best cure for her condition.

Next day, the surprisingly chilly dawn saw the sky brightening across the eastern horizon while the amber runway lights guided the twin-engined Beechcraft into the air. Over the next few days the Nolan family would ride much of the company's network, often with Connellan himself at the controls of the Beechcraft or the larger De Havilland Rapide, with Cynthia soon losing her weariness in the exhilaration of seeing so much colourful and rugged beauty. They became almost addicted to flying with the skillful and good-humoured pilots who seemed to know every feature of the vast terrain. There was so much to see and Nolan was already storing away images which he hoped to turn into paintings when he got home. They flew low through rock gorges with still pools reflecting the sun from their inky blue surfaces and the next moment they would be soaring up into the sky to look across at the spectacle of the massive outcrops of Mount Connor, Mount Olga and then the great monolith of Ayers Rock with the Musgrave Ranges as a backdrop.

Their journey continued with Cynthia suffering from a high temperature combined with a throat infection which she attempted to keep at bay by taking dozens of aspirins. Nolan remained in high spirits at what he was seeing and confident that he could depict this unique landscape in a series of paintings. One flight took them across dry river beds and clumps of occasional scrub. It looked like a barren wilderness, which was only revealed as brown earth with a light covering of salt bush for grazing when they descended to land at lonely cattle stations. They also put down at remote mining sites where wolfram was being wrested from the earth and then set off again to Tennant Creek, a gold mining and cattle community with a population of little more than 600. The Nolans remained there for just twenty-four hours, putting up with rough accommodation, tasteless food and a scarcity of water which they were told had to be trucked to the town from many miles away. A disturbingly strong wind blew across the area, bringing a penetrating chill which seemed to emphasise the remoteness of the little community. It had the effect of clearing the atmosphere, however, providing a crystal-clear light that made every feature for miles around stand out in bold relief with saturated colours.

After this breath-regaining stopover there was more distance to be conquered the next day with a flight up to the Gulf of Carpentaria for a brief touchdown at

Borroloola, the site of an abandoned mining venture, where a token police station, store and hotel survived to service a vast tract of the gulf country. But it was pointless to linger here because the hotel offered no accommodation, serving merely as a refreshment stop on the way to the town of Katherine to the north-west. The climate of these northern latitudes, with their heavy seasonal rainfall, was reflected in tropical greenery, although this was the middle of the dry season. The verandah of the hotel where they stayed was festooned with lush vines and there were mango and paw paw trees laden with fruit. They lingered in Katherine for a few days and then accepted an invitation to stay on a property a few miles out of town, which allowed a vivid insight into the way of life in the district. Cynthia found plenty of material for her burgeoning journal in meeting a colourful cross-section of the people centred on Katherine: peanut farmers, mine owners, crocodile shooters, station bosses, drovers and labourers.

It was an easy, relatively dust-free journey up the sealed road to Darwin, the capital of the Northern Territory, with the Nolans looking forward to a few of the conveniences that only a sizeable centre of population could provide. After six weeks in the outback it was a bitter disappointment to arrive in the small city of Darwin to find there were no rooms available except at the expensive Hotel Darwin. They experienced a shock to be back in what was regarded as civilisation and having to put up with petty formalities such as not being allowed to stroll in the hotel's gardens wearing shorts and the men having to wear coats and ties in all the public rooms. To make matters worse, there was a curious segregation of the sexes with the male and female guests accommodated separately for sleeping.

The next morning they caught a commercial flight for the two-hour trip to Wyndham on the Indian Ocean. Nolan found the Kimberley Ranges an impressive sight, indented and mysterious with their ancient formations, standing tall and stark in the crisp morning light, but the destination proved to be less than engaging; a sleepy little community of untidy tin-roofed houses, a scattering of shabby stores, hospital and the inevitable, and prominent, police station. They managed to book rooms in an old two-storied hotel where, once again, the sexes were segregated for sleeping by the curiously rigid morality that permeated the outback. The hotel's cook had left two weeks earlier and a replacement had not yet been found, with the consequence that guests were required to lend a hand among the flies in the kitchen, although it was hardly worth the effort when the menu offered a repetitive diet of meat and potatoes served on greasy plates, followed by jelly and custard for dessert. At the end of the main street stood the rambling and smelly pile of the meatworks, the main reason for the town's existence, with its lonely jetty stretching far out into the tidal reaches of the shallow sound. The Nolans soon discovered that its cafeteria provided better eating than the hotel.

This Australian odyssey began to take on an aura of permanence as it stretched from weeks into months and by the time August came around they were staying on a cattle property in the East Kimberleys with both Nolan and Cynthia tirelessly noting their experiences and surroundings; she filling exercise books with words, while he used his camera to expose an impressive number of films. In fact, Cynthia observed that her husband's method of assessing a scene was rather like the 'quick blink' of a camera shutter. He would turn his back on something interesting and then wheel around for the briefest moment to take in the view.

With thoughts of home beginning to impinge on their consciences and funds rapidly declining, Cynthia knew it was time for Jinx to return to regular schooling and Nolan was ready to start work painting an exhibition based on the experiences of the journey. At first, it was intended to return through Alice Springs, but as they were within steamer distance of Shark Bay and the old pearling port of Broome, it seemed a good idea to take the motor vessel *Koolinda* from Wyndham, sharing the limited cabin space with the meat workers and their families going back to Perth at the end of the killing season. It was a crowded trip by way of Derby to Broome where, once again, accommodation was limited for travellers and lingering proved to be pointless.

After a couple of days in the capital of Western Australia the Nolans made a conventional and speedy trip across the continent by train to Adelaide and then by plane to a rain-sodden Sydney. Cynthia recorded her delight at returning to Wahroonga:

> As we ran through our garden, the rain came down in sheets, falling upon ripe oranges hanging from the trees whose wet-blackened leaves dripped over blue forget-me-nots run wild. We were home, thank God. And yet — I would always be grateful to Sidney for taking me on a trip that alone I would have never contemplated. Jinx would now grow up with this continent and the Aborigines an accepted background, while behind my eyes there would always be a land flat as a strap and flooded by the light of dreaming.

Few Australians had seen so much of their own land and the journey would soon pay dividends in Nolan's fine series of Central Australian landscapes, while Cynthia's copious notes might find a publisher to become her third book. The attraction of a freewheeling existence, travelling extensively to gather experiences and impressions for paintings, became central to Nolan's existence as an artist.

Meanwhile in Melbourne John Reed was closing down his publishing activities, which had never really recovered from the Ern Malley affair. With Nolan out of their galaxy, the cultural orbit had changed for John and Sunday and many of the other painters and poets who had contributed to a vital, angry decade moved overseas or away from the Heide circle. The Reeds also took off

112

for Europe accompanied by the Kelly series, which Nolan had given to Sunday, for two exhibitions, the first arranged for Paris by Peter Bellew, who was now head of UNESCO's visual arts section. Few Parisians were aware of the show, which was held in the Organisation's building on the Avenue Kléber from the middle of December 1949, and it received little notice from the local critics, in common with the first public showing the previous year in Melbourne. An exception was Jean Cassou, an art writer and administrator who was so impressed with the Kelly paintings that he agreed to write the catalogue introduction. Cassou, who was also director of the city's Musée National d'Art Moderne, thought Nolan had captured the freshness of a world in formation in a narrative series that had become, through the artist's poetic vision, 'a tale of chivalry, a wonderful episode, a wonderful romance . . .' Perhaps the translation into English tended to transform the desperate bushranger into a medieval knight, although Cassou also noted, 'With Nolan, Australian painting itself appears as a new revelation, full of instinct, of a primitive truth, abandoned to the joys of life. And the country revealed by this painting is also new and of desert purity. We greet this enrichment of our experience.'

These comments came as a pleasant surprise to Nolan when he saw a headline in Sydney's *Daily Telegraph* of 15 December 1949 which read 'French art critics praise Australian' and quoted from Cassou's introduction as well as Peter Bellew's opinion that this was the highest praise that had ever been given in France to an Australian painter, overlooking the fact that Rupert Bunny had been extensively and favourably reviewed in Paris nearly fifty years before. This single news item, much more than the less-read art critiques, was a boost for Nolan's name and useful publicity for his next major exhibition three months away. He suddenly found himself in demand by the press, following up the Paris story with an interview two days later which appeared in the *Daily Telegraph* under the curious heading 'Aborigines "best artists"'. Nolan stated that he and his family 'existed' on the income from paintings and was 'thrilled with the criticism' only because he believed it would help to advertise Australian artists. He was quoted as saying, 'I feel sure that in the future the works of many other Australian artists will be hailed in Europe. But I am of the opinion that the Australian Aborigine is probably the best artist in the world.' Nolan explained that he and his wife had recently toured Central Australia and were amazed by Aboriginal art. 'The Aborigine has a wonderful, dreaming philosophy which all Australian artists should have.'

There was the suggestion of ancient forms seen through the eyes of the original inhabitants in Nolan's forty-seven Central Australian landscapes that filled the walls of the David Jones Gallery from the end of March 1950. Great patterns of red, mauve and ochre covered the Masonite boards with an imagery painted in Ripolin, broken in parts to allow the underpainting to show through, filling the pictures with light so that mountain ranges and monoliths seemed to glow from within. Gone were the previous quirky elements of his Queensland outback subjects; no inverted birds, abandoned mineshafts, forlorn agricultural machinery or outback characters looking as if they had strayed out of colonial photographs. This view of the interior, seen from an aeroplane, appeared as devoid of life as the surface of the moon. The effects on the eroded shapes had come not from man but from successions of wind storms and rain showers over aeons of time. Many of the pictures shared a common horizon line and Nolan knew he had composed a kind of fiction that looked like nowhere on earth. The contours were indeed reminiscent of the lunar landscape, making what appeared to the eye as a generally flat and featureless surface seem high, craggy and mountainous. This apparent change of style in Nolan's work was unsettling for a public conditioned to expect another series of narrative paintings as a successor to Eureka. But the modest proceeds from this exhibition, together with the substantial rewards from his two major shows of the previous year, provided enough money to consider taking off for Europe to try his luck, at long last, in the international arena.

CHAPTER SEVEN

First Blood

§

The three Nolans arrived in England during the early winter of 1950 to make Cambridge their base, staying with Cynthia's sister, Margaret, a doctor in general practice there. Apart from somewhere to live and a year-old promise from Kenneth Clark to help arrange an exhibition in London, they had no specific plans.

Everything around Nolan was a journey of discovery and revelation, making up for all those years when the direct stimulus of great art and any sense of historical continuity had been denied him. He and Cynthia would soon make a tour of Europe, leaving Jinx at school in Cambridge, and with this in mind they bought a Hillman Minx estate car. There was enough money from the Australian exhibitions, together with a modest allowance Cynthia received from her family and a small widow's pension, to stay away from Australia for about a year, perhaps longer if the promised London show was a success. But whatever happened, their sea passages home were already paid.

Nolan contacted Kenneth Clark and received an invitation to lunch at his Hampstead home in north London, driving there with a couple of Central Australia landscapes from the last exhibition to show him. They arrived late for the engagement and parked outside the substantial mansion named Upper Terrace House, which sat behind a high brick wall at the end of a drive. Nolan pressed the bell at the entrance and the black iron gates clicked open automatically and then closed behind them with a metallic clang after he and Cynthia entered and crunched their way along the gravel to the house. There was a distinguished looking elderly man standing in the porch waiting to greet them, immaculately dressed, whom Nolan took to be Clark's father. He rushed forward to shake his hand enthusiastically and comment, 'Sir, what a brilliant son you have, you must be very proud of him'. Without pausing, Nolan introduced Cynthia to the man who was now looking very confused by this curious behaviour. 'We had the good fortune to meet Kenneth at our home in Australia and I can't tell you

115

what a great pleasure it was for both of us.' Cynthia was well aware he was the butler and tugged at her husband's arm in an attempt to pull him away. At that moment Clark appeared in the doorway and saved any further embarrassment with his warm greeting. The man Nolan had taken to be Clark's father gathered up their coats and hats with an air of disdain and steered them into the dining room for lunch where Clark's wife, Jane, and the other guests were waiting.

After introductions, Nolan found himself sitting next to a middle-aged Frenchwoman who was apparently an official from the Louvre and spoke no English. Clark managed to keep the conversation flowing with pleasantries during the soup, which was followed by quail, a dish new to Nolan. He thought they looked like undergrown pigeons and when he tried one of them it proved to be undercooked as well. He toyed with the quail, eating only the vegetables, and hoped he was not noticed. The lady from the Louvre attempted to strike up a conversation, speaking so quickly that Nolan understood little. He smiled and nodded politely for a short while but then had to shrug his shoulders in defeat when she paused for his response, not sure if the subject had been about the doubtful delights of quail, the qualities of Poussin or the art of Vermeer. As soon as the meal was over, everyone left the table and then, in the Australian manner, Nolan sat down on a couch expecting there would be a chat accompanied perhaps by a convivial cup of tea. Clark glanced at his watch apprehensively and observed, 'It's 3 o'clock now'. 'Oh yes', Nolan replied, 'doesn't time fly? But we're in absolutely no hurry to go.' 'Well', Clark replied, 'I have an appointment'. Coats and hats were handed over by the butler and Clark accompanied them down the drive to the car, where he found time to linger for a few moments and look at the paintings in the back.

There had been no opportunity to raise the question of a London show during lunch, although Nolan continued to live by Clark's promise made in Sydney. Nolan thought he should try to get the show organised before going away and decided to take the matter into his own hands by showing a selection of paintings to the Leicester Galleries' Mr Brown. He proved to be polite but distantly formal with a world-weary air suggesting he had seen everything worthwhile in modern art. He appeared to be unimpressed by Kenneth Clark's recommendation, although he did consent to look at Nolan's work, taking his time to examine the striking landscapes that seemed to him primitive in their imagery and rather crude in execution. Finally he told Nolan that the gallery was soon to hold an exhibition of Drysdale landscapes, 'those same red prairies'. It was obvious that a Nolan exhibition at the Leicester was out of the question. Clark's suggestion that was so full of promise had proved to be as arid as the subject matter of Nolan's paintings, although he could only blame the unfortunate timing that had allowed Drysdale to score a show at the Leicester first.

Cynthia suggested that one of her Sydney friends now living in London might be able to help. Harry Tatlock Miller, who had moved to London in 1947, was running another of London's leading galleries, the Redfern, and Nolan agreed that nothing would be lost by visiting him, particularly as he had given very favourable press reviews to his exhibitions in Sydney. The sample paintings were taken around to the Redfern where Tatlock Miller was surprised and delighted to see the works and readily accepted them as the basis of an exhibition. The largest, a desert landscape, was hung on one of the gallery's walls for himself and a colleague to assess and while this was happening, one of the gallery's leading artists wandered in looking like a character from a Somerset Maugham novel. He appeared particularly striking because it was the depths of winter, yet he was sporting a light coloured suit, white hat and carrying a cane. It was Victor Pasmore, an artist Nolan had admired ever since he had seen his work at the *Herald* exhibition in Melbourne eleven years before. During this stage of his long and distinguished career, Pasmore was including abstract Chinese scroll effects in his paintings and was considered to be one of the leading modern painters in Britain. Pasmore leaned on his cane and gazed at the work in silence for what seemed an eternity and then turned to Nolan with the judgement, 'It's very fine brushwork'. He regarded this as a devastating remark from a painter of Pasmore's stature, thinking 'All his abstract art is ahead and mine is behind', but consoled himself with the knowledge that Central Australia is a very remarkable place, although Pasmore could never comprehend that unless he went to see it.

Nolan's show was held, just after Drysdale's had opened, during January 1951 and received kind notices from the London critics, although they were guarded in their comments because it was their first exposure to a new imagery coming out of a country whose previous art had looked familiar and staid. These outback, interior and Eureka Stockade paintings contained an element of challenge and the art writers chose to play safe for fear of making too many *faux pas*. The two Australian exhibitions led to a confusing episode when the Tate Gallery's Sir John Rothenstein had two of Drysdale's pictures and two of Nolan's up for consideration by the trustees. It was only after they had been despatched that Nolan remembered one of them was already sold to the Adelaide collector Kym Bonython. Sure enough, it was the painting recommended for purchase. After some hasty renegotiation with Adelaide, the Tate got its Nolan and both he and Drysdale entered the collection at the same time.

The Nolans set off for Portugal, taking a cargo ship from Southampton to Lisbon with the Hillman lashed to the deck. It was not long after leaving the Portuguese capital that their dream of carefree travel became tarnished when they realised it was not at all like moving around the countryside in Australia. Across the border, Spain was only just opening up to visitors after a long period of isolation from the time of the civil war in the mid 1930s and right through the Second World War. There were no other tourists around and it was bitterly cold away from the Mediterranean coast, with Nolan experiencing snow for the first time in his life. They soon discovered it was impractical to sleep in the car under these harsh conditions and had to rely on the availability of rooms in small hotels and inns in the towns and villages they passed through, few of which had electricity or adequate heating. Nolan had never been so cold in his life and Cynthia, who had experienced icy winters in central Europe and North America before, became increasingly tense about this foolish journey, although she was determined to persist with it because despite the cold her husband was revelling in his first experience of Europe.

After several visits to the Prado, where Nolan spent hours looking at the Goyas and Boschs, they were joined by Margaret and Jinx before heading south to where the weather was warmer and the sun managed to shine for a few hours each day. Nolan had rarely been happier since his St Kilda schooldays and filled dozens of notebooks with small sketches and descriptions of what interested him. They visited Torremolinos and Malaga because of the Picasso associations and were struck by the similarity between the countryside of Australia and Spain in these southern parts that were still virgin territory for tourism, remaining very much the same as they had for centuries. It was easy to get around on the empty roads and this lack of traffic probably allowed escape from injury when the overloaded Hillman skewed out of control on slippery surfaces or while negotiating unfamiliar hairpin bends, where it would sometimes finish up on the wrong side of the road as Nolan fought with the steering wheel to regain control while Cynthia clasped the dashboard, fearing the worst.

Their journey progressed through southern France and all over Italy with its blossoming fruit trees and great carpets of wildflowers. There were few other travellers as Europe was still recovering from the ravages of war. Cynthia lost count of the number of museums and galleries Nolan insisted on visiting while gorging himself on this huge cultural feast after such a long period of enforced fasting. Going through the Uffizi in Florence, following a winter of no heating, it was still necessary even in the spring sunshine to wear gloves to avoid numbed fingers and essential to keep moving to ensure circulation while peering at Botticellis and Michelangelos. The attendants, wearing threadbare clothes, failed to guard the masterpieces in their gloomy galleries as they huddled around small wood stoves in the corridors trying to keep warm and smoking endless cigarettes.

Nolan had made a promise to Cynthia before leaving Australia that they would remain in Europe for only a limited time. They must then return home to Sydney so that Jinx could settle down to a regular education without the disruptions of her mother being away or always on the move. After getting back to England from the Continent, however, Nolan found himself with a nagging feeling of uncertainty about the future because he had already exhibited in London with some success and was now beginning to meet influential people who could assist his career. There was also the cultural ambience that he enjoyed and which he knew he would miss in easy-going Australia. His misgivings were heightened on receiving press reports from home about the Redfern show and Drysdale's exhibition at the Leicester Galleries. These had caused an outbreak of cultural cringe, a peculiarly Australian affliction, which revealed itself in fears that the national reputation was at stake and the image of the country sullied by painted representations of arid, sandy wastes, occasional clumps of spinifex, rusted cartwheels sticking up from the desert and the grotesque skulls of cattle that had strayed too far from stock routes and perished. It was suggested, quite seriously, that this misleading impression should be countered by a renewed effort to promote the more appealing aspects of the unique wild-life, such as koalas and kangaroos, together with the human attractions of Australia's suntanned beach girls.

Nolan had second thoughts about his intentions as he travelled from Cambridge to London by train to confirm their return passages to Australia. On his way to the shipping office he walked through Leicester Square, wondering how he could remain in England, when he noticed that one of the cinemas was advertising an Australian film called *Wherever She Goes*, about the life of Eileen Joyce, who had risen from obscurity in Tasmania to become a famous concert pianist in Britain. On the spur of the moment Nolan went to the film, though he paid little attention to the screen, agonising about Jinx's education and wondering if there was any way he could convince Cynthia to stay in England. Suddenly the soundtrack jolted him back to reality with the familiar warble of Australian magpies, giving him a sense of nostalgia combined with a feeling of anticipation. Nolan dismissed any residual thoughts of remaining in England and when 'The End' flashed onto the screen he hurried out of the cinema, strode along past the National Gallery to the P & O office at the lower end of Trafalgar Square and confirmed the three passages for Sydney on the *Orion*.

A few weeks later they were on their way, Nolan happy at the prospect of being a professional, full-time painter. In the hold was a large crate of new work derived from the travels in Spain and Italy, and enough small studies for an exhibition planned at the Macquarie Galleries in Sydney during October. The first Australian port of call was Fremantle where the Nolans were entertained by the curator of the Art Gallery of Western Australia, James Cook and his wife Ruth. Professor Allan Edwards from the local university joined the party because he had an interesting proposal for a series of paintings similar to the Kellys, which he had seen as reproductions. He suggested Nolan might like to consider Joseph Furphy's picaresque novel *Such is Life* as a subject because

Furphy's son, Samuel, lived in the west and had endowed the Tom Collins Bequest at the University of Western Australia. Furphy's celebrated book was first published in 1903 and was described by the author as a 'vast and ageless volume of human insignificance', being 'certain extracts from the diary of Tom Collins'. It rejected all conventional techniques of story-telling, was intricately structured and had no plot. But it quickly became an Australian classic, reflecting many of the aspects and characters of country life, expressing a bush philosophy of the bullockies and swagmen and rural communities based on strong ethics, humour, religion and nationalism. Edwards suggested a series of paintings based on the novel for permanent exhibition as part of the bequest in the university's Winthrop Hall. Nolan was pleased that he had received such an ambitious proposal immediately on reaching Australia and promised to start work as soon as possible on a group of pictures that would form a continuous frieze inspired by *Such is Life*.

After a relaxing month at sea, adrift from the realities of the world, the Nolans arrived in Sydney on a dazzling late winter's morning in August 1951. When the ship entered the harbour Nolan was on deck early to experience this moment with Jinx and as the liner approached the dock and mooring ropes were hurled over the side, he noticed the workers below: burly wharfies wearing shorts and singlets, most of them with big beer bellies. They moved lethargically about their duties, cigarettes dangling from their mouths and with an apparent lack of interest in their task. Then came the sound of their voices drifting up from the wharf, flat, nasal and expressionless. The sun was rising higher in the sky, holding the promise of a perfect day, but as Nolan watched the torpid scene below, he began to think that he had made a terrible mistake in returning to Australia.

The well-travelled Hillman came on the ship with them and a couple of days later when it had been cleared by the customs, Nolan drove up the Pacific Highway to a place he knew in the bush some forty miles from Wahroonga. It was a stark landscape covered with a great number of dead trees where previously he had experimented with stereoscopic photography, taking the same picture from different viewpoints. He drove into this area as far as the track would allow and then walked among the bare trunks to the top of a hill to sit and ponder. The next thing Nolan recalled was banging his head against a fallen branch in complete confusion, shouting at the top of his voice, 'No, no, no!' His brain seemed strangely detached from the action and from the jolting pain of successive impacts, as if he were standing outside himself watching what was happening. After a few moments he came to his senses and stumbled back to the car. Nolan glanced in the driving mirror as he returned along the track, noticing blood on his cheek dripping down from the gashed forehead. He tried to reason with himself as he drove along and came to the conclusion that there was

Carcass, 1953

unfinished business for him in Europe and that he must go back. Nolan said nothing about these thoughts to anyone, explaining away his cut head as the result of tripping over an unseen branch while in search of a new angle on the landscape. He knew that he must work systematically for a return to Europe and that everything he undertook during the next year or so would be with that goal in mind. In the meantime, his name was kept before the London public with a show titled 'The European Scene' at the Redfern Gallery.

Nolan's reputation was spreading in Australia and he was commissioned by the Brisbane daily newspaper, the *Courier-Mail*, to take a trip during August 1952 through the north to document the effects of a chronic drought that had ravaged much of the grazing land and brought the cattle industry to a standstill. He and Cynthia flew to Darwin as the starting point of their travels. They covered a wide area by diesel truck and light aircraft, often sleeping out under the stars. For much of the time the scene was of bare earth with no remaining pasture and twisted, leathery carcasses littering the dusty stock routes. It had been estimated that more than a million head of cattle were lost in Queensland alone and another four million remained at risk. The sights were both impressive and depressing; a grim confirmation of the power of nature to rule the destiny of this ancient land. Nolan's commission was for a series of drawings

Photograph taken by Nolan during North Queensland drought, 1953

to illustrate several newspaper articles and, under normal circumstances, it was a subject that would be difficult to transform convincingly into a larger scale. But as he saw more and more of the dried up bodies of the animals, he realised there was a strong visual link with the contorted forms of the dog and humans trapped in the flow of lava following the great eruption of Vesuvius in AD 79. The plaster casts that had fascinated him in the museum at Pompeii were an unforgettable sight and they now provided a grisly sculptural prototype for a series of pictures of desiccated cattle which Nolan painted in the new studio he was installing at the bottom of the garden in Wahroonga. Work proceeded as if he was intending to live in Sydney permanently. Nolan knew that with Jinx's schooling becoming increasingly important, Cynthia would not agree to move overseas in the near future, but the idea stayed with him as strongly as the moment when he had made up his mind sitting in the Hillman with blood on his face.

Ram Caught in Tree, *1953*

His Australian travels continued when the film-maker, John Heyer, invited him on a trip to the remote Birdsville Track in Central Australia as the location survey for a planned documentary sponsored by the Shell Company about the people living along the loneliest mail run in the world. With journeys like this, Nolan was logging a vast amount of outback travel, filling his imagination with scenes and experiences that few others had known. The underlying purpose was to gather information for further local exhibitions or to take back to Europe. A career problem Nolan had to face at this time was a growing reputation for being too prolific. This began to upset a number of people, particularly Paul Haefliger, who until now had been the artist's principal champion, a man whose reviews in the *Sydney Morning Herald* were so influential that they could make or break a painter's career. The Nolans had become good friends with a group of Sydney artists, critics and designers including the Drysdales, Gordon and Mary Andrews, and Haefliger and his wife, who painted under her maiden name of

123

Jean Bellette. A few echoes of Heide days reverberated around Sydney as their discussions became over-heated, when the drink would flow and tempers flared in volatile exchanges of ideas. As time went on, however, it became obvious that Paul Haefliger was having second thoughts about Nolan.

Haefliger had hinted on a number of recent occasions that Nolan's work was becoming superficial and certainly too prolific. With the advent of the drought paintings, to be shown first in Melbourne during June 1953 and then at the David Jones Gallery in Sydney from the end of July, Nolan knew he faced the prospect of poor reviews because he suspected the subject-matter would work against him. With this in mind, he sought to protect himself to some extent by painting some small pictures of wildflowers, no larger than six inches by eight, to be beautifully framed and exhibited in a separate room of the Sydney gallery, as a contrast to the main exhibition. Nolan also devised a way of hanging the drought pictures to give an added element of drama by suspending them from a beam some fourteen feet above the gallery floor so they would hang out from the wall and suggest a sense of outback space. When asked by a journalist why they were displayed in this unconventional manner, Nolan explained with mock seriousness that if an irate viewer felt like putting a fist through any of his pictures, they would swing out of the way like an apple on a string at the apple-eating contests he had known as a child. He also asked the gallery director to ensure that when Haefliger arrived for his preview, the door of the smaller room containing the flower paintings should be locked, because he had the impression that an unfavourable notice would appear about the drought pictures if Haefliger were to see the more appealing but small-scale flower subjects.

The day after the press preview, Nolan eagerly bought the papers to read the reviews. The *Telegraph* responded favourably to the flower paintings and, more importantly, to the drought pictures. The review ended with a statement about the freshness of his approach, 'Here is Nolan at his best, and it is this quality, present in other works, which makes this an important, beautiful and original exhibition'. The *Sun* critic wrote:

> He sees miraculous harmonies in the most unlikely places — in the disintegration of an animal's carcass, in the collapsing architecture of their bones, or in the tumult of a desert storm. He sees as though he were perennially delivered from blindness and in the intoxication of seeing for the first time sees more deeply and more truly than the rest of us, whose eyes have been drugged into insensitivity by constant use.

Nolan felt reasonably happy with these comments, hoping that his fears about Haefliger were groundless. He had saved the *Sydney Morning Herald* until last and, sitting in the parked car, warmed by the winter sun, he hunted through the pages to discover a small review headed 'Sidney Nolan's Exhibition of

Nolan and Cynthia at the opening of Drought *exhibition, David Jones Gallery, Sydney, 1953*

Paintings'. Haefliger's opening statement read well enough, referring to his 'agility of mind, more daring than ever' and Nolan thought he had escaped. But reading on he came across:

> When the effect wears off, little remains except polite interest and the recognition of an accomplished craftsman. Here indeed lies the apparently insurmountable weakness of this painter's work. Immediate emotion and impact are not sustained, imagination is not allowed to wander or to discover, all that remains is work most decorative and without destiny.

Nolan feared for the sales of the drought paintings which had a top price of 100 guineas, but as there was no reference to the flower pictures in this review, he thought there was every prospect they would sell well. He read and re-read another part of Haefliger's critique with increasing annoyance. It stated, 'In all the years that Nolan has painted, his work has not improved, nor has it regressed; it has merely changed. With all his great talent this is indeed something to mourn.'

125

That evening there was a party at David Jones in the room containing the flower pictures and Nolan was happy to see all these works bearing red stickers, although their prices were low at only £10 apiece. Paul Haefliger and Jean Bellette came into the gallery; she pale and unsteady, obviously concerned that a close friendship was in jeopardy and he looking furious when he caught Nolan's eye, who was ready for a fight. Haefliger accosted the artist, accusing him of engineering things so that he would not see the flower pictures and would praise the other works in the main gallery. 'Well, it was hardly praise you managed to write', Nolan replied with a taunting note in his voice. Further angry accusations were exchanged before the critic turned his back on Nolan to rejoin his wife, who was now weeping at this turn of events, while Cynthia was looking on, furious at the confrontation. It was the last time the Nolans would see the Haefligers, although the critic had the final word, in effect, because none of the drought paintings in the main gallery was sold. It was time for the Nolans to make an exit from an increasingly claustrophobic atmosphere of pettiness and suspicion in the Sydney art world. Cynthia had to agree with her husband that if he was to develop as an artist and she as a writer, only England could give them that opportunity. Jinx would have to leave the experimental Artarmon Opportunity School and resume lessons in Cambridge.

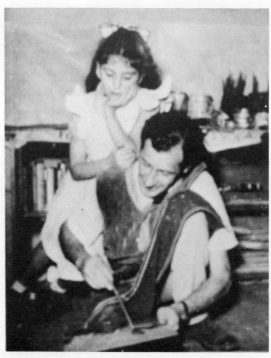

With Jinx, Sydney, 1953

126

The Joseph Furphy proposal for the University of Western Australia was not forgotten in the intervening two years and the Nolans had made a journey to the Riverina, where *Such is Life* is set, to gather information for the paintings, but none eventuated. Nolan wrote to Professor Edwards explaining that he was abandoning the idea because he was leaving Australia for an extended period, although he had in his possession several works from the Queensland outback series, mostly painted during 1948 as part of a lapsed project to publish a book about colonial days. He thought that the desert landscapes, deserted mines, ghost towns, and dilapidated hotels were in the spirit of Furphy's novel and that the Tom Collins Bequest might like a selection of these instead. The university agreed to buy a dozen pictures for a total of £1,000 and they arrived in Perth in late 1953, a few months after the death of Samuel Furphy. This largest single group of Nolans in a public collection was exhibited for a month at the Art Gallery of Western Australia and, as Allan Edwards observed, 'Admirers could be numbered on the fingers of one hand; mockers, scoffers, the puzzled, the indignant and the shocked were as usual both numerous and vocal'.

CHAPTER EIGHT

Expatriates

§

Back in England at the end of 1953 the Nolans continued their peripatetic life, planning extensive excursions through Europe while Jinx returned to school in Cambridge. Cynthia became more involved in her writing and, although she had completed a full account of their outback trip in the middle of 1949, publishers were yet to show interest in the manuscript. She persevered, however, making extensive notes while travelling in the car to many places on the Continent she had known before the war. Nolan regarded the journeys as essential for extending his knowledge of European art, and at the same time they provided Cynthia with material for what was accepted as her own career.

Their presence in Europe at this time led to an interesting appointment for Nolan, who had been selected, together with Russell Drysdale and William Dobell, to represent Australia at its first participation in the Venice Biennale during the summer of 1954. The trio now was considered the 'big three' in Australian art and, because Nolan was already in Europe and one of the few Australians having any connection with painting, it seemed appropriate to a penny-pinching administration back home to appoint him as the nation's commissioner in Venice, even though it was unusual for an exhibitor to take this role. The position meant co-ordinating the exhibit, ensuring that the works arrived on time and were hung appropriately. There was no problem with Nolan's own contribution of ten paintings which came direct from an Arts Council of Great Britain touring show titled 'Twelve Australian Artists' circulating to six cities during 1953–54, together with a series of drawings related to John Heyer's documentary film *Back of Beyond*, which was entered in the Venice Film Festival held concurrently at the Lido. The two dozen paintings by Dobell and Drysdale that were sent from Australia were delayed by shipping difficulties, however, and caused a rushed hanging in the temporary exhibition space that was equipped with inadequate partitions and lighting. Nolan's credentials were presented to the mayor of Venice in a little ceremony that gave him quasi-diplomatic status but, in reality, unlike the major contributors from the United States and Britain with their professional staffs, Australia's rather makeshift showing had to rely almost entirely on the efforts of one man.

Nolan became so frustrated by the experience that he wrote a stinging letter to Daryl Lindsay in Melbourne, who was responsible for Australia's official participation, pointing out that considerable mismanagement at home had been compounded when Italian help had to be recruited to assist in the last-minute preparations. An encouraging aspect of Australia's involvement in the Biennale was the Italian government's offer of a generous plot of land for the construction of a permanent pavilion on the site. The area would be donated without cost provided the exhibition building was designed in consultation with Italian architects and local labour was used in its construction. A total of £30,000 would give Australia a handsome stake in the world's most prestigious international art event. Nolan was enthusiastic about playing a key role as his country's representative in this exciting development and he passed on the details to Melbourne, assuming that approval for the scheme was merely a formality. He was dismayed to learn later that his efforts to secure the site were wasted because the Australian government turned down the proposal, with Prime Minister Menzies rumoured to have said the Italians were likely to trick one into accepting a bit of useless swampland. Nolan enjoyed the experience of sitting on the international art judging panels and supervising the Australian entries at the film festival where, by a happy coincidence, John Heyer's production won the Grand Prix.

As a result of his extensive travelling in Australia, Nolan thought little of facing a drive of 300 or 400 miles a day in Europe, although Cynthia soon became exhausted by this, having little but the concentration on her writing to ease the strain of many hours' sitting in a car. He continued to assess instantly a scene and store it in his memory, to paint it later as if it had existed for just that moment. When they had returned for the second time, Nolan had regarded England as a convenient springboard for the more exciting prospects in continental Europe, but when their finances became depleted after so much travel, it was obvious that London, where he could best earn a living, must become their base.

They took a small flat near Paddington Station and he began to immerse himself in the artistic life of the capital, visiting the museums and galleries, getting to know his fellow artists and meeting people who might help him to build his reputation. It was vitally important to nurture the interest of dealers so that London exhibitions could be planned and to continue sending shows back to Australia where the main market lay for the moment. By now Cynthia was accepting an expatriate life, saying, 'You can be more anonymous in London. Everyone has their own lives, they're very busy and you see them a few times each year. In Australia, you'd be part of the community, it would be much harder to keep your inventiveness going and to remain anonymous.' During this time of working, travelling and career development, the Nolans met the Australian author and journalist George Johnston and his wife, Charmian Clift, who was also a writer. The two men soon discovered they had similar backgrounds, with Melbourne boyhoods spent close to Port Phillip Bay; Nolan's schooling had been at St Kilda and Brighton, and Johnston's in the adjacent bayside suburb of Elsternwick. But now their lives were centred on Europe with George and Charmian recently returned from Greece, bringing with them a stack of photographs that Nolan found exciting. Although they were in black and white, Nolan could appreciate the clarity of light in the Greek Islands; and the dazzling whitewashed houses looked fascinating as subjects to paint. George Johnston had come to the conclusion that he smoked and drank too much in London, and had to spend too much time earning money as a journalist to pay the bills instead of getting on with writing novels. He suggested the Nolans might like to join them later in the year on Hydra where he, Charmian and their children were going to live far away from the pressures of England, to work in congenial surroundings at a fraction of the cost of London. The Nolans were intrigued by the idea, particularly when they thought about the prospect of another British winter.

In the meantime, Nolan had heard through the British Council of an Italian government scholarship that might be available to him if a suitable subject could be suggested. Earlier, he had made a pilgrimage to Padua to see the wonderful art works in the city's churches including Giotto's great mural *The Raising of Lazarus* in the Arena Chapel, Giotto's bronze relief for the high altar of S. Antonio on the subject of *The Healing of the Wrathful Son* and Andrea Mantegna's murals combining elements of architecture, painting and sculpture, in the Ovetari Chapel of the Church of the Eremitani. The two legendary Mantegna murals, representing the martyrdom of St James and the martyrdom of St Christopher, had been badly damaged during the bombardment of the city in March 1944, almost destroying the fifteenth-century artist's first masterpiece. While in Padua, Nolan had seen photographs of the chapel taken immediately after the intense fighting, showing huge holes in the murals through which the buildings outside could be seen. It was an intriguing sight which prompted him to propose a series of paintings on this theme based on multiple images with a cubist context. The idea appealed both to the British Council and the Italian authorities and he was awarded the scholarship with enough money to live on for the next few months. The plan for the latter part of 1955 was to spend some time in Greece and then move on to Italy in the new year to start work on the Mantegna project.

The Nolans were visiting Hydra long before it became one of the most popular places in the Mediterranean for foreigners to buy holiday houses at bargain prices. At the end of 1955 there were a few Scandinavians and Germans who made the effort to get there on the infrequent, lumbering ferries making a four-hour trip from Piraeus, but there were no hotels to accommodate them and few facilities for tourists. Hydra in the winter was essentially a working community of 2,000 people whose income derived from the sea, its picture-postcard port surrounded by a semicircle of sea captains' houses. Hydra had yet to become a painter's cliché or to be exposed by Hollywood, and most of the developments of the twentieth century had passed it by. During the late autumn and winter, rainstorms lashed the rocky hills behind the port, sluicing out the soil, which ran down to the harbour as rivulets of mud, staining the water red.

George Johnston proved to be an entertaining and voluble host, becoming noisier with each glass of raki, taken, he said, to ward off the chills of the rain and howling gales outside. There would be conversation long into the night at the Johnstons' house a few streets back from the waterfront when the two men discussed their boyhoods in Melbourne and planned books and paintings, while Cynthia and Charmian often talked guardedly about their current work. Sometimes at the taverna too much wine was consumed, too many cigarettes smoked and, after violent argument, George was left in a state of stupor until the blinding light of dawn brought him to his senses and he could stagger home. The Greek language remained a mystery to Nolan and one of the few phrases he managed to master was the New Year greeting *kali chronya*, which he used incessantly. The locals put up with it until the following Easter, when finally an old sponge diver pointed out that 1956 was well advanced and it sounded foolish to be wishing everyone 'Happy New Year'.

Nolan with part of lamb-roasting spit on the roof of Ghika's house, Hydra (left). Leaving the island, 1956 (right)

131

Soon after arriving on the island Cynthia had become friends with the wife of a leading Greek painter, Nikos Hadzikiriakos, who was known professionally as Ghika. She intended to spend the next few months in Athens and Paris with her husband and invited the Nolans to stay in their house, set in a terraced garden filled with almond trees, cactus and wildflowers and set above rocky headlands. The Johnstons' villa was too small for them to remain as guests for long, and now the offer of the Ghika residence meant they could remain on the island for some months. The Nolans' new home was a large 200-year-old whitewashed fortress of a house, out of sight of the port, surrounded by a substantial stone wall which gave shelter from the howling Aegean winds, although on some nights the kerosene lamps swung in the draughts, throwing mysterious shapes onto the walls as if Greek myths were being re-enacted in a shadow puppet play.

There was not much spare money for the Johnstons or the Nolans, but luxuries were unobtainable and living was cheap. They met at a small taverna on the quay where the food was basic and often in short supply when no provisions could reach the island from Piraeus. On those occasions they had to be satisfied with a limited menu of small fried fish, rubbery octopus, rice, and retsina from the barrel, followed by a visit to the *kafeneion* for small cups of thick Greek coffee accompanied by glasses of the harsh local brandy called *koniak*. The Johnstons' financial survival depended on publishers' advances and royalty cheques arriving in their Athens bank account and the Nolans found themselves in much the same situation, waiting for money to arrive from dealers in Australia when pictures were sold. It was a great help to have a rent-free house but there was never quite enough cash to pay for a return trip to England to see Jinx, who remained at school in Cambridge, and both Cynthia and Nolan were unhappy about this.

Greece was proving so seductive that Nolan found the Mantegna proposal difficult to develop. He dashed off preliminary sketches of work in progress to ensure that his allowance was maintained, but his thoughts were now centred on a time long before the Renaissance. He read a lot, learning about Greece, studying the Hellenic myths, Homer's *Iliad* and Robert Graves' book of Greek mythology. From his reading Nolan developed the idea of Troy as a subject for a series of paintings. He was interested in it, not simply as a battle that had taken place quite near, on the other side of the Aegean, but as a composite subject incorporating memories of life in Australia. There might be the tragedy of drought or images of the naked swimmers at the St Kilda baths who had looked to him like Greek gods; elements of two entirely different worlds, separated by time and distance, and yet curiously linked in mood and spirit.

He began to play with the idea in experimental ink and oil sketches, attempting to combine the weapons and accoutrements of the Trojan war, the human figures and the horses, with a landscape that might have been Central

Australia, the flat plains of the Wimmera, or a country of his imagination. Johnston would find him immersed in his task, the hand-woven rugs pushed aside and the floor littered with dozens of discarded sketches. He was having trouble working out the design and decided the work required metal and a forge rather than canvas and paint. Nolan had got to the heart of one aspect of his subject, that of Troy itself. He knew he could depict it from Homer's descriptions of sweat and dust, cruelty and death, coupled with the grandeur of the human spirit. His treatment would not be like the idealised Renaissance images of noble Greeks propounding democratic ideals; it would have blood and guts and relevance to the greatest Greek defeat of modern times, only thirty years before, when the ambitious forces of the Hellenes had been forced to retreat from Turkey in what became known as the Smyrna catastrophe; Greece's Gallipoli, a defeat remembered with ignominy instead of the glory acquired by Australians and New Zealanders.

Nolan learned that another Australian had recently been living on the neighbouring island of Spetse, just south of Hydra, while working on a book. Alan Moorehead's *Gallipoli* was not yet available but Johnston had a copy of the *New Yorker* magazine of early April 1955 which contained the author's long essay on the subject titled 'Return to a Legend', which commented on parallels between the Gallipoli campaign of the First World War and the ancient story of Troy. Its effect was dramatic and immediate, providing Nolan with the key to a combination of ideas for a series of paintings that would link a pivotal moment in Australia's brief history with the heroic events of the Trojan wars.

This conjunction of the two themes was not a new concept, however; several writers at the time of the campaign had used it, including the Englishman Compton Mackenzie and an Australian poet named Arthur H. Adams, whose verse *The Trojan War, 1915* had appeared in the *Anzac Book*, which was published in 1916 and quickly assumed the status of an Australian bible of nationhood in honour of the young men sacrificed in battle at an unknown cove in a distant land. Nolan recalled seeing the photographs taken on the Gallipoli battlefield that were included in the *Anzac Book* and he remembered snatches of Adams' verse:

> We care not what old Homer tells
>   Of Trojan war and Helen's fame.
> Upon the ancient Dardanelles
>   New peoples write — in blood — their name.
>
> Those Grecian heroes long have fled,
>   No more the Plain of Troy they haunt;
> Made sacred by our Southern dead,
>   Historic is the Hellespont.

Homeric wars are fought again
    By men who like old Greeks can die;
Australian backblock heroes slain,
    With Hector and Achilles lie.

No legend lured these men to roam;
    They journeyed forth to save from harm
Some Mother-Helen sad at home,
    Some obscure Helen on a farm.

And when one falls upon the hill —
    Then by dark Styx's gloomy strand,
In honour to plain Private Bill
    Great Agamemnon lifts his hand!

With such sentiments spinning around his brain, the next step was to visit Troy and the Dardanelles and make a pilgrimage to Anzac Cove.

Nolan was able to continue work on the Gallipoli theme and also to paint a few local scenes of Hydra, including the white churches, black-robed priests and the island's rocky coastline, whose sea changed colour from purple to pewter during storms. The paintings had to be small because access to Ghika's house was difficult, with anything heavy having to be carried up on a donkey, although Nolan did manage to get half a dozen larger canvases to the house and they became local landscapes. But when the time came to depart in the early summer of 1956, there was no way they could be transported safely across Europe and he decided to leave them stacked out of sight behind the huge stone fireplace in the living room. Nolan left Hydra frustrated that its light and landscape had proved to be so difficult to capture in his paintings. Cynthia would remember their stay, with its gardening, fishing with the sponge divers and visiting other islands, as the happiest time of her life.

When he returned to London after a sojourn in Rome to fulfil obligations to the Italian Government scholarship, Nolan received a manuscript from the Australian writer Patrick White of his novel *Voss* with an accompanying letter asking if Nolan would design the dust jacket, because as an art lover White felt Nolan had explored the interior of the Australian continent in a physical sense, while he through his story of the explorer, Voss, investigated it mentally. Nolan read the manuscript and was impressed with the narrative and White's command of language. Nolan felt his jacket artwork was a strangely unsuitable design, but it was the beginning of a long association with the writer.

By the latter half of the 1950s Australian art was making an impact in London and the national tag was enough to generate considerable interest. One of its leading promoters was Bryan Robertson, whom Cynthia had originally met at Heffer's bookshop in Cambridge during the Nolans' first visit to England. Robertson was then only 17, although already he ran a small gallery and would soon move to London. He kept in touch with the Nolans and became a friend of Kenneth Clark, so that the unlikely trio came to regard themselves as a sort of art gang — the painter, the director and the *éminence grise*. Bryan Robertson's vigorous directorship of the Whitechapel Art Gallery in London's unfashionable East End made it an unexpectedly lively centre for the visual arts. He had proved himself a good administrator as well as an excellent entrepreneur, taking a big exhibition by the American, Mark Rothko, which was on a European tour, and showing it in London with a promotional flourish that gave the impression it had been assembled there. To exhibit at the Whitechapel soon became a prestigious event for any painter and Nolan jumped at the opportunity when Robertson offered to stage a retrospective to celebrate the artist's fortieth birthday.

He suggested Robertson should write to John Reed asking him to send over a selection of early works from Heide so that this London show could be fully representative of his career. Unfortunately, this initiated a series of tiresome communications with many excuses for delays in despatching pictures from Melbourne, most of them blaming the lack of suitable shipping space. Nolan knew this was nonsense because he was sending considerable numbers of paintings and drawings back for Australian exhibitions and there was never a problem with their delivery. John Reed had been given plenty of time to make a selection and get it to London on time, but as the date for the opening loomed closer it became obvious this was going to be a retrospective with few backward glances, lacking pictures from many of the most important periods of Nolan's early years as an artist. He began to panic when the Reeds' reluctance to loan works hardened into refusal and he feared that the show, which was due to open in the middle of June 1957, would have to be cancelled or greatly modified.

After discussion with Bryan Robertson a solution was found which demonstrated how prolific Nolan could be. Nearly half the works in the show, which included 153 paintings and studies and was no longer called a retrospective, were painted during 1956 and 1957, including new versions of the Mrs Fraser theme. Nolan felt less than proud, even embarrassed, about his face-saving actions, regarding them as a rather misleading way of compiling a comprehensive survey from 1947 to 1957, but Robertson was quick to point out that this kind of thing happened more often than the public realised.

A spell of unusually hot June weather did little to deter the crowds from making their way to the Whitechapel, with the daily attendance often reaching 500, and most of them found the pictures curiously poetic, highly imaginative and exciting, and were intrigued by the creation of an Australian mythology. What mattered most to Nolan was that the leading Sunday newspapers took him seriously, with John Russell writing in the *Sunday Times*, 'He is one of the most civilised of living artists. When he paints landscape the texture of the paint

135

Nolan in his London studio, 1957

is consistently and originally beautiful, the placing of the intervals in space has an absolute assurance and the transitions of tone are never forced or abrupt.' Russell summed up his impressions by stating, 'I can think of few painters of his age (40) anywhere in the world of whom we may legitimately expect so much'. Neville Wallis writing in the rival *Observer* made no attempt to define Nolan's style, simply stating, 'The bizarre poetry of the earlier painting and the visionary nature of his latest are matters more for wonder than for probing'.

The atmosphere at the Whitechapel had none of the stuffiness or formality of a major exhibition in one of the fashionable London galleries. Robertson's gallery, supported by the local community and with grants from the Arts Council, attracted a more cosmopolitan clientele; a mixed audience of workers from the East End, crocodiles of schoolchildren accompanied by their teachers standing fascinated in front of Ned Kelly, and West End art lovers, looking a little apprehensive at straying into unfamiliar and decidedly unfashionable territory, attracted by the newspaper notices and a discussion of the show on the BBC radio programme *The Critics*. Nolan's exhibition, together with the success of Ray Lawler's play *The Summer of the Seventeenth Doll* and the publication of Patrick White's *Voss*, became talking points in cultural circles and no dinner party conversation seemed complete without at least one Australian event being discussed in detail. This heady atmosphere was summed up by Kenneth Clark's comment after he saw Lawler's play, 'You were right, Sidney, you Australians are certainly pedalling along quite well'.

136

Near Bourke, *1948*

Goulburn Valley, *1950*

Angel Over Ely, *1950*

Antarctica, *1964*

Selection of works sent by Nolan to his family in Australia.

Icare *design, 1941*

Il Trovatore *design, 1983*

Nolan supervising the painting of
Il Trovatore *backcloths, 1983*

Rite of Spring *design, 1962*

Nolan's position in England was consolidating on the strength of his notices and he could expect a successful and lucrative career in London with successive exhibitions. But, ever the wanderer, he now had plans to spend the winter in Paris to study printing techniques, an aspect of art he wished to know more about. The Nolans had moved from Paddington into a spacious house beside the Thames at Putney with a large studio above and fine garden below. They now let the house, packed their bags once more and prepared to spend the next couple of months in the French capital, living in a studio arranged for them by the well-known British graphic artist, S.W. Hayter, who founded the famous Atelier 17 in 1927 for teaching and research into printmaking. He had attracted a long line of painters, including Picasso, Miró, Dali, Ernst, Pollock, Rothko and De Kooning, and had an outstanding reputation as an innovator and teacher.

Although Hayter continued to introduce his students to various printing techniques, he now held rather rigid views about the type of images that were suitable for the medium, preferring bold incisions on the metal plate combined with cross-hatching that would register clearly. Nolan soon discovered that he was learning very little because Hayter considered his designs were inappropriate. This did not worry Nolan for his wish to live in Paris was greater than the need to study with Hayter, who seemed somewhat hidebound in his methods, and had an inordinate number of American women students attending the school and working on a limited range of subjects based almost entirely on lace and leaves. Hayter was a patient and pleasant man, however, and he attempted to teach his Australian student how to use a burin for achieving the best impressions on copper engraving plates, preferring this traditional method of incising an image to Nolan's experiments with a flow pen.

Nolan had used these broad-tipped marking pens for a number of years, having done hundreds of drawings with them in Greece, developing the skills to produce very fine lines or bold, fat strokes that had been particularly effective in the outback drawings shown at Venice. Nolan now discovered that if he used one of these pens to work directly onto the surface of a copper plate, its ink would inhibit the biting of the acid, leading to some interesting effects. He adopted this technique to make elaborate designs on six etching plates without any traditional engraving from a burin. They were left overnight in an acid bath and when Hayter arrived the next morning he found the studio full of fumes. It was quite obvious who had broken the rules.

The Nolans enjoyed their time in Paris as a prelude to crossing the Atlantic to live in New York on the first leg of a two-year Harkness Fellowship. Through the novelist and scientist C.P. Snow, Nolan had met the representative of the Harkness fund. There was no specific category for painters and Nolan had been interviewed informally about his intentions when in the United States. He described a night flight he had taken previously along the eastern seaboard, noting from the lights below that every valley seemed to hold at least one small community. He was also interested in the contours of river systems seen on another flight from Florida to New York. Nolan talked about America as an extraordinary conglomeration of communities and how he would like to make a comparative study with the Australian continent. No mention was made of any specific paintings to come from these observations, but the Harkness representative was so impressed with his detailed knowledge of eastern United States that he asked jokingly, 'You've never flown over Russia in that way, have you?' A fellowship was granted, giving Nolan virtual *carte blanche*, although there was the helpful suggestion that he might like to go to Yale and observe its art school. Nolan was able to avoid that because he was determined that New York was the only place for him and Cynthia to live.

They arrived in New York harbour aboard the *Liberté* on a misty morning in the early summer of 1958 and proceeded to clear their twenty-seven pieces of baggage through customs. His folios contained a new book jacket design for another Patrick White novel, *The Aunt's Story*, first published in 1948. Unknown to Nolan, another Australian painter long resident in London, Roy de Maistre, was under the impression that one of his paintings was to be used for the cover. After reading the book, Nolan had found it difficult to come to grips with the illustration because the novel was structured as a three-part narrative, but he had made a likeness of what he assumed was the correct woman's face. He would hand it over to the author when they met for the first time during this trip to the United States, as White would be living in Florida, which the Nolans planned to visit.

After checking into a hotel, the search began for a studio apartment that would become the core of Nolan's painting activities, while Cynthia made enquiries about a suitable school for Jinx. Trying to find an acceptable space with enough light and storage in crowded Manhattan proved to be a tiresome introduction to the United States as the hot days grew ever more airless, with work demands taking precedence over domestic considerations such as suitable sleeping areas and adequate bathroom facilities. The excitement of being in New York soon began to pall when Nolan failed to find any accommodation at a reasonable price. He had stated in his Harkness application that the prime purpose for visiting the United States was to see as much of the nation as possible and he realised he should follow this literally by giving up the frustrating search for a studio and seek solace among the art at the Museum of Modern Art, the Metropolitan and the Whitney. The family could then tour, getting away from New York to see America first. Cynthia agreed with this course of action and Nolan went out to buy a Chevrolet station wagon, gaudily painted in crimson and white with whitewall tyres. Most of their possessions remained in the numerous unopened cases, which were put into store, and on 22

July 1958 the trio set out in high spirits on a journey of discovery that would be documented in words, sketches and photographs. Nolan planned to keep a diary of impressions and a photographic record to assist him with subsequent paintings, while Cynthia would take copious notes with the intention of compiling a travel book that might appeal to a publisher more than her account of the Australian outback completed more than eight years before. It was now eleven years since a book of hers had been published.

Nolan wrote about their first day on the road: 'This expensive ribbon, a million dollars a league, gives access to the American dream. For one cent a mile toll one grasps this Ariadne's thread and drives painless, gearless, into the labyrinth of Lolita Land.' He was amused by the instructions given on the road signs: 'Maximum speed, minimum speed, caution soft shoulders, do not speed, frost heaves, remove sun glasses before entering tunnel . . .' The journey into America became a visual adventure and not since Central Australia had he been so moved by forms such as those to be seen on the edges of cities and towns along the highway. They included the dumps of discarded automobiles, 'Burnt, gutted, hoisted one above the other as if they were old jam tins, they dwarf the trees'. Nolan imagined them being dug up by latter day archaeologists. There was no fixed itinerary, just a vague south-westerly direction with overnight rests at roadside motels, which were a revelation of high standards and reasonable prices to travellers more familiar with the conditions of post-war Europe and outback Australia. The Nolans covered miles in their gas-guzzling automobile, negotiating Virginia, Tennessee, Alabama and Arkansas in a blur and then, after only five days away from New York, found themselves driving along the Will Rogers ('World's Greatest Humorist') Turnpike in Oklahoma to visit 'The World's Greatest Buffalo Ranch'. Nolan noted, 'Outside the buffalo steak cafe and Indian gift shop stands a curious collection of galloping and bucking stuffed animals. A giant moose, poised on hoof tips, seems ready to take off, using its antlers as wings.' Pretty girls in floral dresses posed for photographs, giggling on a giant artificial bison. These uniquely American vignettes punctuated their easy progress of long days on the highway filled with the sights and sounds of a confident, rapidly-developing nation. Jinx often found the travel hot and uncomfortable, fidgeting her way across much of the United States. Cynthia also began to feel the strain of sitting for long periods on the unsupporting seats and she had to ease her aching back by stretching out across the middle seat while Jinx rode in the front on the wide bench with her stepfather.

There were visits to rodeos and country fairs, art museums, historical landmarks and in New Mexico, two weeks into their journey, a detour up into the mountains to a shrine at Taos, where they were greeted by lightning flashing across the purple sky as columns of rain fell on the sage brush, whose moistened scent reminded Nolan of the countless cowboy novels he had read as a boy. There was a memorial to D.H. Lawrence and Nolan jotted down his response to it:

> A phoenix, painted on tin, is nailed like a totem to the wall of a log cabin next to a small, sunny chapel-building. Inside, the ashes of D.H. Lawrence are sealed in concrete. His hat, typewriter and faded blue shirt are kept in a wooden box with flowers painted on the lid by Frieda, his wife. A rose window, which is instead a sunflower, is above the gaily painted sunflowers of the tomb. Outside in the thin clear air at 7,000 feet, lies the beautiful afternoon. Birds, beasts and flowers, men and women.

The long distances they travelled often led to strained relations for the Nolans, with tensions developing and evaporating as quickly as the summer storms around Taos. Nolan's boundless energy kept them all moving at a furious pace so that Jinx's adolescent irritations would sometimes erupt and she taunted him with questions about his abilities as an artist. At other times tempers became frayed when Nolan took what seemed an excessive time to get the right combination of light and angle for a perfect photograph, while his passengers waited with mounting impatience. Cynthia observed these moments from a horizontal position on the wagon's seat, knowing that her husband's implacable confidence in himself would not buckle under any threats or comments, which he would counter with puns until the tensions dispersed. She had watched him on many occasions ignoring distractions, working with a single-minded purpose when his adrenalin flowed and energies redoubled, embarking on a flurry of painting that might take weeks of sustained effort. Cynthia realised that this self-centred certainty and apparent oblivion to those around him could be disastrous but his humility counteracted his less attractive characteristics.

Just over three weeks into the journey, they reached the Grand Canyon and Nolan viewed it in its multicoloured splendour through half-closed eyes like a camera shutter stopped-down against the glare. He was beginning to feel the landscape and thought that after the myth-making pictures he was already contemplating — Gallipoli and a series based on Leda and the Swan — he must attempt to depict this experience, perhaps in the spirit of Mark Tobey, Sam Francis and Jackson Pollock, whose works he admired.

Cynthia thought that Los Angeles was infinitely more crowded and looked less prosperous than she remembered it twenty years before, although the hospitality offered them was never less than generous and often overwhelming. They carried an introduction to the screen actor Vincent Price, who invited them to the studio where he was making a film called *The Tingler*. Following a melodramatic scene involving him as a mad surgeon, the urbane actor resumed his real identity between takes and chatted to them about Kenneth Clark's book

American sketches, 1958 'They blow as if to bring down the walls of Jericho' (left), 'This expensive ribbon' (right)

on Gothic architecture and discussed the influence of Ruskin on British painting. This seemed an unlikely conversation to be taking place on the set of a B-grade horror movie, but Price had studied at the Courtauld Institute in London and his passion was collecting modern art. That evening he entertained the Nolans at his mansion in the Hollywood Hills, which contained an impressive number of paintings including a good representation of contemporary Americans, a memorable Modigliani and two small Nolans. Price suggested that Nolan have an exhibition at the Los Angeles University Museum and promised to approach the authorities but, like many conversational gambits, the proposal came to nothing. While in California they were also invited to stay at Santa Barbara with the poet Stephen Spender, who was enthusiastic about a book of poetry by the American Robert Lowell titled *Life Studies*. Nolan reacted instinctively and enthusiastically to the work by drawing a series of illustrations, hoping that he could meet Lowell back in New York.

By the end of August the Nolans decided it was time to start heading back on a long looping journey across the south before returning to the task of finding a New York studio. The route took them back to New Mexico to watch the residents of Lincoln County re-enact the drama of their favourite son, Billy the Kid, and Nolan felt a strong link between this colourful pageant and the drama of Ned Kelly. There were certain similarities between the two outlaws, such as Irish origins, although Billy left no poetic statements after his shabby demise.

141

Cynthia suggested that Kelly was perhaps one of the few truly heroic figures of modern times, but Nolan felt he was just a misplaced revolutionary with a gift of the gab and reasoned that his long commitment to Kelly was because 'misplaced revolutionaries always attract conservatives'.

The artist's scribbled notes described New Orleans as 'a kind of sweet hot hell' and he thought its architecture reminiscent of Sydney, particularly the terraced houses with their decorative cast-iron balconies. He went in search of the legendary jazz performances and found some, although they turned out to be highly commercialised. 'They still play here', he wrote, 'famous names in rather crumby restaurants. They blow as if to bring down the walls of Jericho. They produce a piercing kind of poetry, quite religious, acutely nostalgic; as if they were thinking of a migration of angels. Pigmented ones.'

Next came Florida, with an introduction to its delights at one of the water shows made famous by Hollywood, an extravaganza of Roman proportions that could have been conceived only in the United States. 'Six goddesses of desire rise from the foam of the tropical sea', Nolan observed, 'form themselves into weaving geometrical pyramids, and finally are landed by speedboat on the grass at our feet. The air is balmy, orchids are everywhere. Cinerama has made these gardens famous, Esther Williams has consecrated them.' The Nolans explored the natural world of the Everglades, another of the superb areas of the United States preserved as a national park. During a boat trip, with the assistance of field glasses Nolan entered an Alice in Wonderland world of egrets, ibis, heron, cranes and roseate spoonbills, a continuous pageant of bird life that seemed to display itself in tribute to the naturalist, John James Audubon.

While in Florida, the Nolans visited Patrick White who was staying near Fort Lauderdale with his companion Manoly Lascaris, whose sister lived there on an orange grove. White was in a tetchy mood because he had nothing in common with the locals and detested a climate that supported every type of insect, most of them anxious to attack him, although he found some small consolation in the profusion of delicious fleshy avocados which were there for the picking.

White was impressed with the open-heartedness of Nolan and his obvious energies and enthusiasms, which were complemented by Cynthia's cool intellectual qualities. A bond of friendship grew from this first meeting with Cynthia as they discovered they had similar outlooks and seemed to speak a common language that Nolan assumed had something to do with their pastoral backgrounds. They spent two days driving through the flat Florida countryside, Nolan charming White and Manoly with his anecdotes of their trip and pouring praise on *Voss* to the discomfort of its author. They were sitting in a small tea-room when Nolan brought out his cover design for *The Aunt's Story*. There was silence for a few moments as the author inspected it and then erupted, 'Damn it! That's not the woman.' Nolan had illustrated the wrong character,

142

but there were more covers to follow and White became a keen collector of the artist's work.

The Nolans returned to New York and checked into a modest hotel to conserve funds while looking for an apartment. After the long car trip Cynthia's back was giving her almost continuous pain and she had to spend several days stretched out on a bed. Nolan painted small imaginary flowers on sheets of paper for amusement and to keep up her spirits. Eventually he found a place they could call home, a studio apartment owned by the abstract expressionist Harold Rosenberg on 10th Street in the Greenwich Village area. It was essentially one large room with high white walls and extensive windows on two sides letting in good light for painting, together with an impressive view of the Empire State Building.

They could now both embark on a concentrated period of work during the harsh months of winter, with Cynthia methodically assembling her notes made on the trip and Nolan working up the Gallipoli theme in hundreds of sketches which occasionally resulted in a completed painting. He was aware that in tackling this subject, an event that happened two years before he was born, he was stepping on a sensitive area of the Australian psyche that could easily give offence to the survivors of the campaign. He regarded the tragedy of Gallipoli as the first great drama in the nation's brief history, when young men from all walks of life and every part of the continent were taken to the other side of the world to face an enemy they knew little about in a pointless strategy engineered by unknown leaders. Nolan felt that those who returned from the rocky cliffs and sandy wastes of the Dardanelles must have harboured a feeling that there was a new world, perhaps even a whole new civilisation, to be built in Australia. Now, in his studio, he reasoned that the best way of approaching the subject was to regard it as part of the imagination in the way that the modern reader approached Homer's *Iliad*. The Australian and New Zealand troops, their horses, guns and equipment would become larger than life if the campaign took on mythical qualities like the exploits of Achilles and Hector. Nolan felt that if he pushed Gallipoli far enough back into history, treating the participants almost as dream figures, he could achieve the right balance.

Nolan knew that he had to pitch his narrative so it could be seen as a myth that related to the entire history of Australia, a symbol of what a young nation had achieved and what it was capable of becoming. Standing watching the snow falling outside, he recalled the dazzling days of sunshine on St Kilda beach and the regular meetings at the baths when his father and the men from the Tramways stood naked around the pool, bronzed and healthy. They were from the generation that had gone off into the unknown to become Anzacs and, with their efforts and sacrifice, forge a symbol of nationhood, like the brave young Greeks at Troy. The key to painting Gallipoli lay in Nolan's own memories.

During this long winter in New York many hours were spent in the city's art museums and walking through Central Park and visiting its zoo. There were also frequent visits to theatres and concerts and dinners with friends, including one of the most entertaining people the Nolans had met, the celebrated cartoonist Saul Steinberg, whose work was well known from the *New Yorker* magazine and whose dinner parties with his wife Hedda were always witty occasions. At one of them he told Cynthia, 'Every word that Sidney says is camouflage. Everything he says goes off on a trail away from what he really believes, thinks, intends to do, has done in the past. He is like the bird dragging a wing, leading the hunter away from its young and nest.' It was a perceptive character analysis.

With spring beckoning them outside into a new world of greenery and wildflowers, Nolan broke with months of sustained work, taking Cynthia and Jinx to Washington to see the impressive sight of its avenues of flowering cherry trees. They decided to extend their trip north to Chicago, where Cynthia had worked many years before at St Joseph's Hospital, and Nolan was able to see the fine collection of Renoir, Degas, Monet, Picasso and Braque at the city's Art Institute. Never ones to journey modestly, and true to the terms of the Harkness Fellowship, they set out for Nebraska, followed by a circuit through the south again before returning to the summertime delights of New York.

By the time of their return to New York Cynthia had developed an almost continuous cough and a doctor recommended exploratory X-rays. They revealed an anomaly which suggested tubercular infection. Nolan and Jinx were quickly screened to see if it had been passed to them but were found to be clear. Cynthia, however, with an apparent problem in both lungs, would need to spend time in hospital having treatment, although her doctor thought an operation would probably be unnecessary. She was admitted to the so-called permissive ward of a large New York teaching hospital, loathing the incarceration and its enforced inactivity, spending most of the time in a room on her own. Cynthia could assume an air of aloofness better than most and she soon gained the reputation of being a strange, unco-operative limey, which had the effect she wanted of maintaining a barrier of solitude. Nolan's regular visits to the ward became a nightmare for him in an atmosphere he thought reminiscent of an asylum. He brought gifts of small paintings, books and flowers that were regarded by the other bored patients, who missed nothing, as wildly eccentric.

These lonely and aimless weeks led to artistic inertia with absolutely no will to work, although Nolan had accepted the commitment for a major show in London in a few months, his first in Britain for three years. Without Cynthia's support and encouragement he was lost and unproductive. As their second successive Christmas in the United States approached, the intense cold and the sight of skaters on the Rockefeller Centre rink seemed to him like the approach

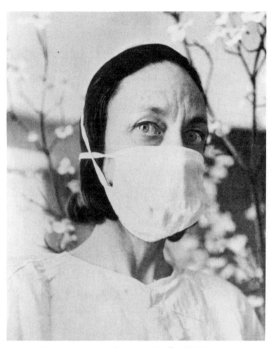

Nolan's photograph of Cynthia in TB ward, New York, 1960

of an ice age. He watched the automobiles arrive in Manhattan from upstate New York with deer strung across their hoods; the proud trophies of brave shooters.

Nolan left Jinx in New York studying speed writing while he returned briefly to England to check on financial affairs, make sure the house in Putney was in good condition and finalise arrangements for the London show at the Mathiessen Gallery, which was due to open in mid-June 1960, with a catalogue introduction by Stephen Spender. In fact, many of the people he met on his rounds assumed from their absence that the Nolans had returned to Australia to live. Cynthia's condition did not worsen and after several months, during which she was able to observe with the clinical accuracy of her nursing background every detail of the hospital system and its patients, she was allowed to leave. A final medical report gave her condition as 'open negative', indicating that the infection had been arrested and she could safely leave to recuperate at home. This was now an apartment kindly loaned them by Brian Urquhart, a British official working for the United Nations Secretariat, who was away from New York on business. Nolan was able to get down to work again, painting with his former energy and striving to meet the London deadline with works on a new subject he regarded as a 'dry run' for the all-important Gallipoli series that was yet to be fully resolved.

145

During Cynthia's absence he had re-read Robert Graves and become attracted
to the myth of Leda and the Swan, which was made more vivid through an
unpublished poem by the Australian Alwyn Lee. Its concluding lines read:

> Until black Jupiter with
> snake-like head
> Has taken lubra Leda to her bed,
> And everything, including tears,
> are shed.

As Nolan painted away every night, inspired by Graves and Lee, the muted
tones of England seemed to be emerging rather than the dazzling light of the
Mediterranean. His reputation in London as an Australian artist remained high,
in spite of the long absence, but he needed to prove himself without the national
tag. That probably meant embracing a local ambience: the dark greens, a poetic
mood, English behaviour, and what he described as 'a sometimes swooning
atmosphere'. Leda was transformed from her Greek origins, acquiring perhaps
some Aboriginal overtones, and the setting became much closer to the pigeon-
grey Thames at the bottom of the artist's London garden than the translucent
Aegean.

Nolan was repaying a debt that had worried him for the ten years he had
made England his base. During that time he had absorbed much of the landscape
but never attempted to paint it. Now it would be revealed in his half-English
Leda, which had none of the high-pitched light and peculiar poignancy of the
works Nolan had shown in London before. There were no figures placed in
identifiably Australian landscapes with plenty of sky and a strong sense of
loneliness. This was mainly a collection of dark paintings with the principal
figures of the drama often bloodily intertwined, not his recent recognisable style
and yet receiving a good response from the public at the show's opening and
recording excellent sales.

The professionals reacted differently. Herbert Read told everyone that he
disliked the works intensely and Kenneth Clark remained tight-lipped about
them; Nolan assumed it was his gentlemanly way of registering disapproval by
outward politeness and inner chill. The critics seemed to be thrown off-balance
by the absence of bright blue skies and the impossibility of finding anything
Australian from a painter who had become inextricably linked with his native
country. Nolan was not too worried at this reception, knowing that the delicate
balance between public response and critical reaction was easily upset and, being
a showman, he tended to side with the public. Influential critics, many of whom
had been Nolan admirers, were so incensed that one of them, David Sylvester,
vowed he would not even acknowledge the existence of the exhibition by writing
about it. 'How could you do such a thing, Sidney? How could you do it?' was

Leda and the Swan *lithograph, 1960*

his remark at the opening, although his critique did appear in the *New Statesman* a week later. Nolan's fellow Australian artists, Albert Tucker and Arthur Boyd, both had exhibitions in London at this time and, although Boyd was enthusiastic and encouraging about Leda and the Swan, Tucker was uncertain about Nolan's new direction. The playful remark, 'I suppose it's all right, Ned, but how much would you sell the stencils for?', referring to the repetitive imagery, was not received very kindly by Nolan.

With Leda and the Swan a good seller, Nolan was riding high again after a lengthy absence from what he called 'the English art game'. He was approached by the editor of *Queen* magazine to contribute a series of articles because in fashionable circles Nolan and Francis Bacon were seen as likely to be the dominant painters in Britain during the 1960s. The influential Lilian Somerville of the Arts Council had become one of Nolan's champions, suggesting he integrate more into the English scene with the possibility of a show at the Venice Biennale as a British exhibitor. All that was needed was to drop the Australianisms, which he had done with Leda, and change his passport. As Nolan's friendship with Clark blossomed, Somerville warned Nolan that the association could mean 'the kiss of death' to his career. She detested what she called the 'scented handkerchief' approach, supporting such critics as Laurence Alloway and David Sylvester in resenting Clark's apparent aloofness and his view that this was not a good century for art. Nolan was able to survive quite comfortably in this game of wits by sitting on the fence and letting critics talk

147

among themselves, although he wondered why Clark continued to be so supportive. The only possible explanation could be that Nolan was the exception to Clark's rule about modern art. He remembered that no matter how outrageous he became in making deliberately contentious statements, Clark would never dismiss them. He was always helpful, saying, 'Let Sidney have his say, after all, he's an Australian'.

The long association between Nolan and Kenneth Clark had now developed into a firm friendship, close enough for the two men to discuss the tribulations of their marriages. This bond far exceeded what appeared to many observers as an inexplicable mutual admiration society and the closeness of their relationship was unknown outside their own intimate circle of friends. Nolan was flattered by Clark's concern and constantly intrigued by the patrician demeanour of the man whose way of coping with emotional problems was to dismiss them with a remark such as, 'Well, Sidney, we men sometimes take strange women to be our wives!'

The Nolans were regular weekend guests at the Clarks' country estate, Saltwood, in Kent, with its house based on a large medieval building with twin towers which had been remodelled during the Victorian era. It was the custom for the two men to breakfast together in a small upstairs study where the Sunday papers would be waiting for them. The unchanging ritual was to take boiled eggs from the lidded dish, pour a cup of coffee from a Georgian silver pot, butter some toast and select a newspaper to read while breakfasting in silence. After several of these experiences Nolan found it an annoying restraint on his natural desire to discuss the news of the day and especially the reviews of the latest gallery shows in London. One weekend he finally plucked up the courage to question this routine, saying to Clark, 'We always have this silence at breakfast time which seems very strange to me. After all, the *Sunday Times* is only the *Sunday Times*, eggs are only eggs, and we know each other very well by now.' Clark seemed shocked by this statement, as if it were a heresy, and immediately rose from the table, stepped over to the window, and stared at the sunshine playing on the leaves of the trees just outside.

Nolan became embarrassed by this reaction and stammered an explanation of what he was trying to say, 'Well, there are things about our friendship that remain a bit puzzling, certainly to me'. Clark slowly turned round, presenting an immaculate silhouette in his silk dressing gown. 'Oh dear!', he exclaimed, 'I couldn't possibly discuss this with you, Sidney'. He returned to the table, picked up his newspaper and added, 'I understand what you mean, but we'll just have to continue as we are'.

It was incidents like this that gave Nolan the impression that Clark continued to regard him as a kind of phantom from the antipodes. To Nolan breakfasts in silence were a pointless exercise, even for a guest politely observing the rules of somebody else's house, and on subsequent occasions Nolan went out of his way to bait his host with random remarks. 'I frankly don't quite see the importance of Cubism', he would state as a mock naive comment. 'After all, do you have to look at it in the same way as you assess the Masaccio frescos? Do you feel the same emotions, or, if not, what is the basis of regarding them? And where does that leave Cubism?' Clark listened patiently and apparently seriously, but rarely was drawn into discussion saying simply, 'It's all right for you to think that, Sidney, but it is not the way it really is'. It seemed that Clark continued to place Nolan in a special category reserved for Australians, who were expected to break all rules and conventions. Nolan wished for a less convoluted relationship, but having failed by the most direct methods to clarify their association, accepted the situation and used it to understand better the complex personality of his friend.

The *Observer* had planned a feature article to coincide with the opening of the Leda and the Swan exhibition and contacted Nolan several weeks before about a story. Kenneth Clark had just completed the foreword to a Thames and Hudson monograph about him and Nolan suggested that the newspaper approach the publishers and read the foreword rather than interviewing him. A couple of weeks later the Nolans were staying again at Saltwood and the men engaged in their ritual of silent breakfast with the newspapers. Clark leafed through the *Observer* on this Sunday in June, stopped to read the article about Nolan and exclaimed 'Oh my God!' on seeing his own words prominently displayed on the page because he was under exclusive contract to write for the rival *Sunday Times*. He put down the paper without revealing the reason for his surprise and nothing more was heard about it until afternoon tea when Jane said to the Nolans, 'Do you know what's happened? Thames and Hudson have given K's manuscript to the *Observer* and they've printed it almost in its entirety'. 'I don't believe it', Nolan responded, trying to sound as if it was the first he had heard of the article.

Clark was in the corner of the library propped on a pile of cushions writing a long letter to the editor of the *Sunday Times* and when Nolan tentatively approached him he explained, 'I'll only be a few moments, Sidney, and then perhaps you'd like to take a walk with me down to the post box'. Nolan asked, 'Is it an urgent letter, then?' 'Yes, extremely urgent', Clark replied with a worried look on his face, 'extremely urgent and a rather delicate matter'. Nolan never dared to admit that he was responsible for the mistake and Clark did not reveal the contents of his letter, but the generous exposure in the *Observer* assisted the exhibition to become a sell-out.

CHAPTER NINE

Carrying the Flag

§

The Leda and the Swan exhibition, together with its well-publicised purchasers, including the Queen, Agatha Christie, and Rod Steiger, generated intense media interest in Nolan. On the night of the exhibition's opening Robin Day had interviewed the painter on his television news programme, while *Monitor*, the BBC's highly-acclaimed arts magazine, showed a film directed by Peter Newington about Nolan's life as a painter. It was well-received by a large viewing audience, although the programme had experienced a rough passage before being ready for screening because its ending was awkwardly inconclusive. To overcome this, Huw Wheldon, who strode like a Welsh colossus through television's world of the arts, had suggested the artist participate in a live studio discussion to express his private thoughts about being a painter. Nolan, however, was convinced that the film should say everything that needed to be stated and refused to take any further part in the project. He was aware that a film documentary could be edited until it was right, whereas a live interview, particularly one discussing paintings, would probably sound pretentious, however seasoned the performer. This was a technique that could take years to master, if ever, and he was not prepared to make a fool of himself in this way.

Following Nolan's two forays into television, Wheldon saw that his art and personality worked well in the elusive electronic medium. The counterpoint between bold painted images translated into black and white and the apparently modest, self-effacing artist provided fascinating television and Wheldon wanted to develop Nolan's talents in this direction, coming up with the idea of him and Cynthia travelling to various countries with a cameraman to make a series of programmes under the title *The Painter's Eye*. It seemed an attractive proposition, combining many elements that interested Nolan: travel, photography, and gathering material in remote or unusual locations. The series could further his career and income by helping him to become known to a large audience in a medium that was turning people from many professions, but particularly science and the arts, into popular personalities. Nolan agreed to the proposal and set out with Cynthia and a BBC cameraman to visit Egypt as the first stop in a tour of the Middle East during the spring of 1961. They travelled on a small steamer down the Nile, filming all the way: Nolan getting on the boat and then getting off, running up the side of Abu Simbel, rolling down a sand dune, standing beside the monuments and generally showing off with a child-like enthusiasm. Once this burst of activity was exhausted, the cameraman remained puzzled about what was intended to be shown in the series, unsure of just what he was supposed to be looking for. Standing in a camel yard he asked, 'What are you wanting here?' 'Just set up your camera and let the camels walk through the shot', Nolan replied. But he soon realised that he could not direct the camera adequately because of a lack of experience in film techniques. He was clear enough in his own mind how the completed programme should look; it was the means to the end that eluded him. When planning a series of paintings Nolan knew the process of assessing all the elements and then working them into finished pictures; Huw Wheldon had hoped the same procedures would apply equally well in a television film, but it was obvious they did not. The cameraman became increasingly disillusioned because, without adequate direction, he felt he was failing to do justice to the subject and his reputation was likely to be damaged. After a couple of weeks he returned to the BBC taking the exposed footage with him, but leaving enough film stock and a small 16mm. camera for use at the next locations in Jordan and Iraq.

Nolan kept shooting as they roved around the Middle East until Cynthia became exhausted and insisted they go home. The film was processed and a screening arranged of all the material from the beginning of the trip in Egypt. Much of it, apart from the sequences shot professionally, proved to be disappointingly shaky; in fact, Nolan thought there was no hope of salvaging any acceptable sequences, and told Wheldon so. The optimistic Welshman thought otherwise, convinced that with judicious editing and the addition of scenes of the artist at work in England on drawings and paintings inspired by his travels, there would be worthwhile results. Nolan remained unconvinced and declined to proceed with the art sequences because he felt sure the documentary material did not represent his painter's vision of places and incidents in the Middle East. And without that, the credibility of the project was suspect. The film was committed to the BBC's vaults, unloved and untouched, leaving as one of the few tangible results of the journey an article titled *Nolan on the Nile* published in *Queen* magazine.

With the overseas reputation of Australian art higher than ever before, helped principally by individual shows from Nolan, Russell Drysdale, Albert Tucker and Arthur Boyd, a mixed exhibition under the title 'Recent Australian Paintings' was organised by Bryan Robertson for his Whitechapel Gallery in

151

June 1961. Apart from meetings with Boyd and Tucker, Nolan felt rather on his own as an Australian painter in London. He had been around England for the past decade and sensed he was somehow helping the cause of Australian art when he had an exhibition. His thoughts only became focused on the matter, however, when attending the Whitechapel opening, where he was represented by one of the Leda paintings and the first major Gallipoli picture to be seen in public, a figure on horseback called *The Myth Rider*. At the opening, Nolan was approached by a young man with close-cropped curly red hair who introduced himself as Brett Whiteley, a painter from Sydney who was also represented in the show. Nolan had been impressed by his pictures; fleshy seductive landscapes hanging prominently on the gallery walls.

As the evening progressed and the wine flowed, inhibitions loosened until some of the Australian artists began making pointed remarks about Nolan's successes and he found himself facing some unpleasant attacks on himself and those close to him. He was made to feel in no uncertain terms that he was fooling himself to imagine he had been carrying the flag for the past few years, with one drunken painter pointing out that all he had achieved during that time was to muddy the waters, blocking the public's acceptance of real Australian artists who had not compromised their integrity. Rather than merely carrying the flag for the nation's art, Nolan was now being accused of trying to steal it.

He listened to the tirades of his fellow artists, restraining himself from arguing with them until Whiteley said he despised Nolan's picture plane. This had nothing to do with misplaced chauvinism or opinions about the uniqueness of Australian art. Flatness of the picture plane was the theory behind the success of contemporary New York painters and extended back through the early days of the modern movement, certainly as far as Cézanne. All painters in the twentieth century were supposed to have a flat picture plane. 'The problem is, Sid', Whiteley continued, 'you just haven't got one. You've got a terrible idea of picture planes and many of us think you've not only betrayed our art, but also the picture plane.' This sort of talk could easily lead to blows and Nolan knew there would be no rational conversation under these circumstances. He suggested to Whiteley they meet for coffee, 'So that I can tell you what I know about picture planes'.

They met a few days later in amiable circumstances, talking generally about art, and then Nolan put aside the coffee cups, took out a sheet of paper from his pocket and proceeded to draw the outline of *Moonboy*. 'Brett, you've got a lot to learn', he said, pushing the paper in the younger artist's direction, 'particularly before you start to talk about picture planes. I don't know if you've ever seen my painting which looks something like this, but when you get back home, go and take a look, check the date, and then refer to the American works from that time whose picture planes you probably admire, like Elsworth Kelly.'

Gallipoli Horseman, *1959*

Soldiers Bathing, *1959*

Miner, *1972*

Mine, *1972*

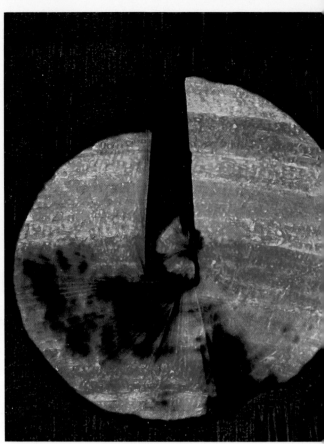

Selection from Paradise Garden, *1971*

The Whitechapel exhibition gained a great number of press notices, most of them favourable, with critics noting the emergence of a recognisably Australian style of painting. Most artists of the 111 works in the show were names new to Britain including Charles Blackman, Clifton Pugh, Robert Dickerson, Frank Hodgkinson and Robert Juniper. Terence Mullaly, writing in the *Daily Telegraph*, thought that they displayed a rare directness of approach coupled with a degree of integrity 'that makes most of the painting we see in London look wearily academic or, even worse, like the facile pursuit of the latest craze'. Mullaly considered the show's strength lay in the fact that the majority of the painters had succeeded in evolving styles which both exploited new techniques and rested upon ancient verities. The *Guardian* critic, Eric Newton, also followed this theme in noting that the Australians paid no lip service

> to grace and refinement that we in Europe have inherited from the Renaissance, and beyond that from Greece — and in order to feel at home with them we must shed our Renaissance prejudices and attempt to identify ourselves with the continent we vaguely connect with desert and drought and decay and human pioneers.

That connection could only have been made from the one-man exhibitions of Drysdale and Nolan, Tucker and Boyd. It was confirmation, if he needed it, that Nolan had been carrying the cause of Australian art in Britain and making his mark.

Nolan lost his Australian innocence as a result of the Whitechapel mixed show and the events surrounding it, retreating from his previous stance of believing it was an honourable thing to uphold the cause of Australian art. As he remarked to Arthur Boyd, 'The honeymoon's over; I no longer regard myself as the lone battler, beavering away in London.' Boyd was developing a highly successful career for himself on both sides of the world and agreed that they were both suffering the same fate for their expatriate successes. Nolan stated the position dramatically, 'I say with all honesty, Arthur, that I can no longer admit, with hand on my heart, that Australian civilisation deserves, *ipso facto*, to flourish, as I thought up to now!' He saw many of the visiting Australian painters, eager to cash in on the impact Australian art was having in London, making a beeline for Kenneth Clark's door on the assumption that it was a short-cut to success. Clark told him with growing dismay of these embarrassing attempts and he, too, retreated from his previously wholehearted admiration for many things Australian.

It was not only in Britain that Nolan came under fire from his fellow artists. He was sent a newspaper clipping about an exhibition at the National Art Gallery in Sydney where the acquisitions for 1960 had gone on display in early 1961. Its principal painting had been purchased from the Leda and the Swan series at the Mathiessen show for £500 and caught the eye of John Olsen, a promising local painter some eleven years Nolan's junior, turning his hand to art criticism for the *Sunday Mirror*. He described Kenneth Clark as the 'blue blood of English criticism', stating that he seldom left the safe arms of the old masters to 'flirt with such lovely creatures as contemporary artists', not knowing, presumably, that he was a close friend of Henry Moore and had long held Graham Sutherland in high regard. More importantly, Clark had certainly not given his blessing to this particular series of Nolan's. Olsen expressed the opinion that *Leda and the Swan* demonstrated the danger of artists losing their roots in the country which gave them inspiration, describing Nolan as a 'regional' painter. '*Leda and the Swan* is a picture contaminated with the over-ripened atmosphere of Bond Street', he wrote, pulling no punches. 'As a consequence the painting is superficial and confused.' He did have the grace to admit that Nolan at his best was 'the greatest lyric painter the country has ever produced' but warned that this quality would be lost unless he returned to the source of his inspiration.

Comments like these seemed to commit Nolan to remaining in England, where he was widely recognised as an Australian painter, while there was the growing impression in art circles at home that he had sold out and become British, although there was a grudging admiration for his international status. From the time he had arrived in Europe on his second visit, lived in Greece, travelled around Italy, had the Whitechapel retrospective, and then spent nearly two years in the United States, Nolan had rarely thought about living in Australia again, and Cynthia was adamant that she would never return except for visits. His fellow trail-blazer, Russell Drysdale, remained in Australia and the other art hero of the time with a small international reputation, William Dobell, did not go to Europe again after living in England throughout the 1930s. Nolan's presence in Australia after the mid 1950s was to be as a visiting expatriate.

By now, the Thames and Hudson monograph on Nolan was attracting considerable attention because it was the first time a major book about an Australian painter had been distributed internationally. It had three distinguished contributors, including an introductory essay by Kenneth Clark in which he made an interesting comparison between Nolan and the composer Benjamin Britten: 'Both are ready to assault with a sort of reckless innocence, subjects from which more prudent men would have drawn back. Both draw their strength from a locality, but transcend it, so that the local becomes universal.' The other contributions came from Bryan Robertson and the Australian writer Colin McInnes, who had also lived abroad for many years. The 119 plates, sixteen of them in colour, showed the development of Nolan's work and included a large number of drawings and paintings from his own collection that had not been exhibited before. Publication of the monograph was an exciting moment for the artist and he hoped to become better understood as a painter who happened to be an Australian by birth and background, but who wished to remain a free spirit to express something of what Kenneth Clark had noted in the book's introduction. 'Both', he wrote, continuing the link with Britten, 'are horrified by the smugness and grossness of biological aptitude, and their heroes are the odd men out — Peter Grimes and Billy Budd, Ned Kelly and Bracefell . . .'

Such words proved too much for some to swallow, and it was Nolan's fate to become a continuous moving target in the sights of several critics who saw success stunting his progress. The young Robert Hughes, described as 'artist and art critic of *Nation*', an Australian political and literary paper, called the monograph 'a blatant promotion job', so that the impression someone unacquainted with Nolan's work would get from the book was 'of a talented, agile and eclectic lightweight'. He admitted that Nolan was deceptively easy to 'knock' because that was a penalty of being the one Australian artist to have successfully captured the imagination of England. Hughes stated,

> He is the best painter this century has produced; and during the decade, from 1941 on, he did more to make articulate the image and metaphysical contours of Australia than anyone else. His present paintings are now reaping him the reputation his earlier ones earned, and this involves him in a perilous course along the tightrope of fashion; as soon as people ask 'What will Sid do next?', it is time to watch out.

Nolan's answer to such comments was to shrug his shoulders and go off to design the set for Harvey Breit's play *The Guide*, produced by Frank Hauser at the Oxford Playhouse, prepare an exhibition of American pictures inspired by his Harkness travels for the United States Information Service Gallery at the American Embassy in London, and send off a major show of thirty-four recent paintings to the Bonython Art Gallery in Adelaide. Most of his energies were now concentrated on the systematic production of a large output of paintings from the studio in Putney before making his next trip to Australia.

Nolan began each workday rather like an actor preparing for a difficult role, a tennis player limbering up for a final, or perhaps a matador going through his pre-fight ritual; each knowing he had the determination and skill to master the occasion, but also being aware that unknown variables could ruin the result. Paintings, too, tended to interact and become unpredictable like audiences and opponents. The first move in Nolan's performance was donning a pair of overalls to guard against paint splashes before entering the studio and closing the door against the outside world. He then put on a Mozart piano concerto or perhaps one of Beethoven's late quartets, selected from a huge variety of recordings tossed untidily in a great stack in the corner. The music, played at low volume, set a mood and assisted his concentration. Nolan found it could take up to an hour to reach the right state of mind. In the meantime he would be playing around with the painting materials, selecting brushes, flexing arms and wrists, fidgeting while half-listening to the music and waiting for the moment when his brain would trigger a signal for the start of action. None of this had much to do with recognisable shapes or the application of colour; it was rather waiting for the crystallisation of many thoughts that might have been sifted for just a few days, a couple of months or even years.

Nolan described the curious combination of thought and action:

> I must rehearse in my mind how the images will go down on the canvas or board sitting there on the painting table demanding to be transformed. At some indefinable point I cease to hear the music and my fiddling with the tools of trade gives way to the first patch of paint on the surface. It is now imperative to get something down fast, whether it feels right or wrong, acceptable or awkward. If it doesn't work to my satisfaction I hover over it, looking accusingly, muttering 'You bugger!', take it off the table and stand it against the wall, hovering in front, rather like a slow motion film of an Australian Rules football match with a player looking for an opening that will lead to a successful mark or deciding how to pass the ball for the best tactical advantage — how to continue with the painting.

Sometimes this could take half an hour with Nolan being able to pick up the threads after the interruption and complete the work.

On other occasions he found himself blocked, like being trapped in a bunch of riders during the competitive cycle races of his youth, trying to push through the pack but failing and falling to the ground, with a painful gravel rash on legs and arms as the only trophy. Nolan thought nothing of staying up all night in the studio to complete a work, drinking black coffee until the pot was drained and then chewing the grains for concentration. On many occasions he lay down on the floor, frustrated and disconsolate, admitting that his adversary remained on the painting table undefeated; having to accept the fact, as bitter as the coffee grains still in his mouth, that much of an artist's life is spent being beaten.

On another day the element of confrontation would be inexplicably absent and the artist, unlike an actor or sportsman, felt he had the power to decide whether to stop or continue. 'If the moment is right', Nolan explained, 'you start to work away quite consciously and the paint itself, which is just an intractable material, actually begins to spread itself into forms; you think of a tree and a tree evolves; you think of a horse's head and that appears'. But these were only fragments of a mosaic that needed resolution to give them credence. Nolan often seemed to lose himself at this point, drifting into a sort of weightless trance while the images continued to build to their conclusion. He said, 'If you are lucky enough to achieve this state, which might last for twenty minutes, something inexplicable happens and when you come out of it, the picture more or less is completed, or at least it can be finished quite consciously'.

Nolan sometimes discussed this with fellow painters and they agreed there seemed to be no way of putting a picture together except by the hand and the brain working together in harmony within this trance-like state. Unfortunately, there seemed to be no rational explanation for the processes. Neither artist nor critic could be aware of the steps leading to the creation of a work of art, leaving them free to discuss every other aspect of the business, except how a picture actually came to be painted.

His use of classical music as a background for painting in the studio was a reflection of his growing interest in music and the theatre. He was a regular visitor to orchestral concerts and recitals at the South Bank and attended opera and ballet at Covent Garden. It had been a long time since he had designed for the stage, apart from the one-set effort at Oxford recently, and he was thrilled to be contacted by Ninette de Valois for discussions about a new production planned for the Royal Ballet. When they met at the end of 1961, the formidable director asked Nolan if he was familiar with 'Lac' and he felt rather puzzled. '*Le Lac des Cygnes*', she explained in rapid French and he thought it sounded like 'Lake of Sin', assuming it to be a new work based perhaps on Aboriginal themes in Central Australia, which would explain why there was interest in his designing the decor. That production of *Swan Lake* did not eventuate, but Nolan was contacted a few weeks later by one of the leading British choreographers, Kenneth MacMillan, with the suggestion that he might like to consider designing his new version of *The Rite of Spring* because Jean Dubuffet, who had originally been approached, was unable to accept the commission and they needed to proceed without delay for the premiere of the work scheduled for May 1962.

Nolan was more than happy to play second fiddle to Dubuffet, although it was a much larger project than anything he had attempted before in the theatre, a complex ballet requiring the use of unfamiliar techniques. MacMillan understood this and suggested that Nolan should first attend the choreographic sessions to get the feel of the designs from them. Remembering his initial thoughts about *Icare* more than twenty years before, Nolan rekindled interest in the concept of incorporating the backcloth, dancing surface and wings into one comprehensive effect. He recalled how Colonel de Basil had abused him for suggesting a painted floor-cloth, or *tapis* as he called it, claiming it was impossible for the dancers' movements and, what was more important, would cost an extra £50, which was out of the question. Covent Garden was a long way from the Theatre Royal in Sydney and the budget was not quite as tight, so Nolan was able to develop these ideas into a workable stage design, although he was still missing a central motif, a visual device that could bring the whole production into focus. Once again, the shards of his imagination helped, as he began to piece together thoughts about *Moonboy*, the subject of his altercation with Brett Whiteley, and the centre of that wartime security scare when he had painted the bold outline on the roof at Heide. This image, originating beside the beach at St Kilda, might have seemed a strange device for the centrepiece of a ballet based on primitive themes from another continent, but *Moonboy* seemed curiously appropriate to help tell this story of 'scenes of pagan Russia in two parts', based on fertility rituals.

The Rite of Spring is a notoriously difficult ballet to stage successfully, famous for its first night presented by Serge Diaghilev's Ballets Russes in Paris in May 1913 when the earthy vigour of Nijinsky's choreography combined with the pounding dissonances of Stravinsky's music caused a riotous reaction in the Théâtre des Champs-Elysées. There were almost continuous boos and catcalls from one section of the audience contrasting with applause and cheers from another, so that the dancers found it impossible to hear the music and perform the complicated steps. *Moonboy* was reborn, bigger than ever, as a menacing totemic disc at the back of the stage during the second part of the ballet. Nolan's initial idea of cladding it in gold leaf was, like his *tapis* for *Icare*, too expensive and a substitute gold-coloured foil proved to be excessively reflective, failing to give the desired primitive effect. Cliff Bayliss, who had worked in Covent Garden's model room for many years, came to the rescue with a suggestion to burn off the foil's paper backing and thus dull the surface. Nolan had last seen him in early 1936 when cycling near Goulburn in southern New South Wales after he had won the prized travelling art scholarship from the National Gallery School in Melbourne. By a strange coincidence Bayliss' companion, John Sinclair, had later shared a flat with Nolan and it was his head and shoulders, silhouetted against the rising moon at St Kilda, that became the inspirational basis for *Moonboy*. The gold foil soon assumed a crinkly, metallic texture after it was treated, turning into a range of subdued rainbow hues, which Nolan and Bayliss regarded as a perfect effect for the stage. Attention was then concentrated on the costumes with MacMillan wanting his dancers to appear as naked as possible by wearing flesh-coloured leotards which seemed to leave little scope for any additional design. Nolan came up with the idea of stencilling hands onto the fabric to emphasise primitiveness in a universal sense, while realising that the audience might regard them as an Australian Aboriginal motif. His Australian nationality was being emphasised at the time by an exhibition, *Nolan '37–'47*, at the Institute of Contemporary Arts in London, including drawings, monotypes, collages and paintings from his first decade as an artist. He had also seen outlines of hands in photographs of African rock art and, whatever their origins, they became a simple and effective way of suggesting the celebrants touching each other in tribal rituals.

The first night audience at the Royal Opera House was not expected to riot like the Parisians in 1913. In fact, Diaghilev thought *The Rite of Spring* had become 'perfectly safe' to perform in the French capital by 1924. The London audiences of 1962, however, were stunned by the look of this new production and the originality of its choreography. For the first tableau, 'Adoration of the earth' Nolan had designed a backcloth that looked like a rugged cliff face with zig-zag geological formations echoing his original thoughts for Lifar's *Icare*; and in the second part 'The sacrifice', *Moonboy* rose mysteriously behind the frenzied dancing as Monica Mason in the role of the Chosen One was raised high over the male dancers in front of the great sacrificial symbol. It was a triumph in the theatre and the critical response next day was excellent, including high praise for the decor and costumes from Clive Barnes, whose review in the *Daily Express* was headed *Moon Boy*.

Nolan with Kelly and his Horse, *Institute of Contemporary Arts exhibition, London, 1962*

Cynthia, who seemed to have accepted the minor professional role, continued to work wherever they went, jotting down her impressions while travelling on aeroplanes, in motor cars and staying in countless hotel rooms. These notes would be expanded into longhand drafts and eventually transferred to a type-written manuscript. She and Nolan worked together on the American experiences, although Cynthia had almost given up hope of getting anything further published because of the apparent indifference to her work and the fact that Nolan's painting commitments increasingly sapped her energy. Her ambitions as a writer were stronger than her husband realised for many years. She felt her wide experience in Europe before the war had led to a way of thinking that she was never able to explain back in Australia, and she was bitterly disappointed that her novel *Lucky Alphonse*, based on those experiences,

159

had not been better received. Once *Outback*, the story of their Australian travels in 1949, was finally issued in 1962 there was a growing interest in Cynthia Nolan's work and for a period, with good reviews, she gained confidence as a writer. Painting continued to absorb most of the Nolans' joint efforts, and although he played his part in talking to publishers on her behalf and offered to do illustrations for the books, the way ahead for Cynthia's talent looked decidedly uncertain. In fact, her principal role was perceived by acquaintances as a shield against annoying interruptions to her husband's work. This was experienced by the actor and satirist Barry Humphries, who was in London to try his luck in the theatre and mixing in Australian expatriate circles. He was very interested in art and became a close friend of Arthur Boyd and Nolan. On one occasion when they met, Nolan suggested he come back to Putney for a meal and asked if Humphries would call Cynthia to tell her of their arrival. Cynthia answered the phone and Humphries identified himself. But before he could give the message, Cynthia said brusquely, 'I'm sorry, but Sidney is not available; he's at work in the studio and can't be disturbed. You will have to try and get him at some other time.' The call was terminated without comment as Humphries, still holding the receiver, turned around to make sure that the painter was standing behind him.

It had been a while since they had been on a major journey, but the autumn of 1962 would soon change that with a trip to Africa followed by another visit to Australia for an important exhibition in Perth coinciding with the Commonwealth Games there. The African journey came about through Lilian Somerville, Director of the Fine Arts Department of the British Council, after she had been approached by a wealthy Kenyan named Malin Sorsbie, who wanted to know if there was a prominent artist in England who would accept a commission to interpret some of the frontier aspects of Africa. The initial suggestion had been to paint a narrative series about a young man, Ewart Grogan, who had walked all the way across Africa from south to north as a wager to win a lady's hand; a story documented in his book *From the Cape to Cairo*. Lilian Somerville suggested that Sidney Nolan would be ideal because of his considerable status in the British art world and his love of travel and adventure. The conditions were excellent, with air fares and accommodation provided, and Sorsbie, who apparently took pride in his prowess as a big game hunter, undertaking to escort his guests to several of the famous game parks. Always keen for new experiences, and convincing Cynthia that Africa would provide plenty of colourful material for a book, Nolan accepted the offer and they flew to Nairobi where they were met by Sorsbie and his wife, Constantine.

A certain friction was generated at their initial meeting with Nolan regarding his host, eleven years older than himself, as a great bull of a man with a scarred face, although displaying a persuasive charm that he modestly claimed had made him a fortune selling aircraft engines from surplus stock, after being a pilot during the war, and later becoming a director of East African Airways. At their first meal together the conversation seemed to be dominated by firearms with descriptions of the arsenal kept in the house as security against intruders and, particularly, the Mau Mau terrorists. Cynthia took an immediate dislike to Sorsbie, which was reciprocated, so that prospects for a pleasant stay in Africa were soured from the start. She also took exception to Connie Sorsbie's vivid accounts of how she could look after herself if threatened because she was a crack pistol shot. A week was spent in the city getting fitted out with safari clothes and the plan was to go to Serengeti, with the women flying to the lodge while the men took the overland route in Sorsbie's four-wheel-drive vehicle with a roof aperture for viewing wild animals.

After an unpromising start to their relationship, Nolan began to enjoy himself on the three-day journey with some interesting conversations and plenty of game to note on sketch cards and record with his camera. At their destination they stayed with the game warden, away from the other tourists, leaving the way clear for Nolan to study at his leisure elephants and lions, buffalo and giraffes and especially the prolific bird life of the area. Cynthia wrote up her notes every day in this generally relaxed and stimulating atmosphere, although she continued to hint at her distaste of the Sorsbies, which led to strained moments when they were together for evening meals. They survived the Serengeti visit reasonably unscathed and it was followed by a week back in Nairobi before Sorsbie flew them in his own aircraft for a stay at Lake Rudolph in the far north of the country near the Ethiopian border.

It was a region where tribal fighting was endemic and strict precautions had to be taken to make sure their camp was well guarded from attack. The plane carried a cache of weapons together with a large medicine chest for any emergencies in these remote areas far from hospitals. After they had landed at the dusty airstrip and while supplies were being unloaded, Cynthia drifted across to talk to the wife of the camp's manager and noticed that many of the local people were suffering from glaucoma, probably tuberculosis and other diseases connected with food and vitamin deficiencies. She discussed the conditions and it became apparent to her that their diet was extremely limited, based almost entirely on the Nile perch that was caught in the lake. With knowledge of some of their problems from her training as a nurse, Cynthia asked Sorsbie if she could take antibiotics from the medicine chest to treat the blacks. He flatly refused, saying it was none of her business, and she accused him in return of ignoring a moral duty to assist these wretched people.

They all flew back to Nairobi, nerves in tatters. All Nolan had been able to produce were the small postcard sketches done on location, which he had handed over so Sorsbie had something tangible from their agreement. The plan, as

161

discussed, was to paint a large exhibition for Nairobi based on the theme of the Cape to Cairo walk and also the African animals. Nolan had flippantly suggested that some portraits of the Mau Mau might be saleable, but now there could be little chance of anything eventuating. He had decided that it was unwise to stay and told Cynthia to pack quickly. While the Sorsbies were resting, the Nolans stepped out into the dazzling Nairobi afternoon, brilliant with bougainvillea and heavy with heat, and stumbled along the leafy street of the fashionable suburb, soon sweating from the exertion of carrying their heavy bags. Nolan went up to the first approachable entrance along an avenue of heavily guarded mansions, knocked on the door and asked the black servant who answered if he could use a telephone. He wanted to call a taxi to take them to a hotel but, as luck would have it, this was the residence of Doria and Jack Block, a likeable couple they had met at one of the Sorsbies' social gatherings. Block invited them in and listened to their story, suggesting he make a reservation for them at Nairobi's best hotel, the Norfolk, which happened to be one of a chain of lodges and hotels throughout Kenya managed by his company.

After checking in, Nolan's first action was to arrange money to be telegraphed from his bank in London and notification arrived the next day, just as the hotel's reception informed him that an urgent message had been hand-delivered. It was from Sorsbie, who had found little difficulty in tracing the Nolans' whereabouts. 'Dear Mouse', it read, 'I hope you will be able to explain your strange exit. In the meantime, I have had a meeting with my colleagues and we decided in the circumstances to cancel your return tickets to London. This has been done and I now await your reply.' Nolan bought his own tickets with the telegraphed money and made arrangements for a trip to Dar Es Salaam to see an Australian friend working for the United Nations there.

Nolan was determined to paint an African series as soon as there was time, but it would have to wait until the new year because he was off to Australia to attend his exhibition at the Skinner Galleries in Perth and then travel on to Sydney for the release of a film about his work. Perth in late November 1962 was full of visitors for the Commonwealth Games and this carnival atmosphere seemed to spill over into the Nolan show of twenty-nine recent works whose opening was attended by Prince Philip, the Duke of Edinburgh, describing himself as 'a spare-time painter today' as Nolan guided him around and discussed techniques, including the use of a windscreen wiper blade to achieve an unusual streaked effect. Nolan explained how he had first used this in Greece, where he bought a dozen rubber-edged blades to be used for painting. The Duke bought a picture titled *Strange Fruit*, which formed one of the illustrations in a new book of poems called *The Outrider* by Randolph Stow. This purchase served to consolidate Nolan's London reputation and all the works in the exhibition sold quickly at high prices, including the top of £1,800 for *Escaped Convict* bought by the Art Gallery of New South Wales; a picture from the Burke and Wills series which went to James Fairfax of Sydney; *Burke and Wills at the Gulf* bought by John Reed's Museum of Modern Art in Melbourne; and a landscape for the Western Australian Art Gallery. The show grossed almost £20,000, establishing Perth, through his energetic dealer Rose Skinner, as an important market for Nolan's work.

His subsequent visit to Sydney was brief, just long enough, he told a journalist, 'To charge my batteries, and by the time I leave for England again early next week they'll be topped right up'. He was treated as a celebrity, putting on a good performance for the press as he sat in front of the window of his eleventh-floor suite of the Chevron Hotel at Potts Point. Nolan said everything they wanted to hear: 'I don't think Australians make very good expatriates, you know. Something that has been drummed into us since childhood keeps asserting itself. This business of the great egalitarian nation, the country where everyone is equal and as good as the next man.' He said the thing he noticed most about returning was 'the flashbulb quality of the Australian light'. He explained that his paintings in England had become

Press conference, Chevron Hotel, Sydney, 1962 (News Ltd)

noticeably darker and this had been emphasised by a visit to his home at Wahroonga where he experienced vivid hues, 'I could see the colour in the old bark of the lemon-scented gums peeling away and showing the bright new bark underneath'. He thought the brilliant sunsets, the bright blue jacarandas and deep red flame trees were like an hallucination and were revelation enough for him to return with his wife and daughter to settle permanently in eighteen months time, obviating the need for further battery charging. Nolan was also interviewed on the ABC television programme *Spotlight*, billed as 'one of the century's greatest artists'.

At this time the national airline, Qantas, was using Australian art as one of its marketing devices, including a commissioned series of short films about Australian painters from Dahl and Geoffrey Collings. The first had been *Russell Drysdale* released in early 1961, followed by *William Dobell* later in the year. Nolan was the third subject, but where the other productions were earnest and uncomplicated treatments, gaining strength from a straightforward approach, Geoff Collings, who was a friend of the Nolans from Wahroonga days, decided on something lighter for this latest film. He employed a local jazz group for the soundtrack, added some smart opticals, and used prominent sound effects to enhance the paintings. One hundred and twenty works flashed onto the screen during the twenty minutes running time, giving a correct impression that Nolan thought and painted quickly, but allowing few opportunities to learn how the artist developed his ideas. With its multiplicity of images and a banal commentary, the film fell between the aim of presenting a knowledgeable survey of Nolan's art and appealing, with its flashy gimmicks, to a general audience. The experience of *Monitor*, *The Painter's Eye* and now this production should have served as a warning to Nolan against future forays into film and television.

Nolan returned to England in time for Christmas, knowing it would be announced very soon that he had been appointed a Commander of the British Empire in the New Year's Honours list. The award came, not on a recommendation from Australia, but for his services to art in Britain. Nolan was worried that the award was not appropriate for someone with his background and doubted if painters should accept such honours because they might become swallowed up by the establishment and ruin their work. Nolan had approached Kenneth Clark for advice and he had no hesitation in recommending acceptance. 'Don't be a fool, Sidney', he said. 'It's nothing to do with background or guarding your integrity. Nobody really takes notice of where you come from; it bears no relation to painting. After all, Rubens accepted high honours and so did Titian; there's an honourable tradition of painters as ambassadors and representatives of their countries.' Nolan took the point, respecting Clark's knowledge of the workings of society and the means of consolidating a public for art, though he was still not entirely convinced, being strongly influenced by Cynthia's objection to his becoming a CBE. Clark had warned Nolan that if he declined the honour he'd never be offered anything like it again.

Nolan managed to concentrate on his African series during the early days of 1963 in bitterly cold weather that contrasted strongly with memories of the light and heat as he looked at his sketches and read the notes of the unhappy trip. His main impression on seeing animals in their free state had been that they looked like brand new works, freshly painted by an unknown artist. He recalled their distinctive markings, thinking that they must possess an aesthetic sense when looking at each other, and in painting them Nolan felt he was participating in this act of recognition. He began to depict some of the creatures with their natural camouflage so they became, in a sense, abstracts, although if you stared for long enough, as was necessary in the wild, the form would reveal itself. This was shown to good advantage in the picture of a leopard whose low, slinking profile melted into the background of an arid plain so that spots and boulders became interchangeable. Several paintings were sent to Sorsbie in Nairobi as compensation for the works that never eventuated in the form intended.

The show of thirty-four paintings at Marlborough Fine Art was Nolan's first selling exhibition in London for three years and his return was greeted with enthusiasm by the buying public and with considerable disdain by the critics in a further polarisation of his reputation. The type of patronage he was receiving could only confirm for detractors back home that he had completely uprooted himself, and that any pious comments about returning to the jacarandas and sunsets of Sydney should be treated with scepticism. The Queen bought two of the pictures an hour before a private viewing was due to open and then Princess Margaret arrived at the gallery and took a liking to one of the works, only to be informed that it was already sold — to her sister. The art public found Nolan's colourful 'African Journey', as the show was named, very appealing, perhaps because, as the critic of the *Times* observed, in the landscape and wild life of the great African plains, Nolan clearly had found something corresponding to what haunted him about Australia. Most of the work appeared to be deceptively simple, almost straight reportage, although the pictures of monkeys and gorillas were painted in such a way that some people detected a likeness to Francis Bacon's powerful portraits and figure studies. In fact, in a rare public comment, Bacon himself was complimentary about their colour. Young people seemed to find an affinity with the African series but the London critics generally regarded them as something of a fraud. There was even the suggestion from Eric Newton, who previously had been a supporter of Nolan's work, that the artist had become a modern-day Baron Munchhausen and fabricated the whole show without ever setting foot on the African continent.

Kenneth Clark admired the picture illustrated on the catalogue's cover, *Blue*

165

From the African series, 1963, Figure, Zebra, Lion, Elephant and Mountain

166

Monkey, painted, like all the works, in oil on hardboard. Nolan wanted him to accept it as a gift, but he declined, agreeing instead to exchange the painting for a bronze plaque by Jean Renoir. The gallery recorded good sales, particularly to agents acting for collectors in the United States, but Nolan lost the support of a number of critics who imagined he was travelling the world trying to find new roots now that his Australian themes were apparently exhausted. With this exhibition he became fully aware how fickle the British critics could be when confronted with what they perceived as an unwarranted change of style. The Leda and the Swan series had been difficult to comprehend after the outback, and now the African subjects began to look like an ersatz Australia or Nolan's version of Scheherazade. The main problem was that few of the critics knew anything about Africa and, always placing art in categories, assumed that animal painters should show in the specialist galleries of Dover Street, certainly not at Marlborough Fine Art.

Nolan was now financially secure for the first time in his life. Approaching the age of 47, he dismissed suggestions that success was affecting his work, admitting to an Australian newspaper man in London, 'I'll not say it isn't a good thing not to have to worry about money any more. It makes you more mobile for one thing. I can afford to get around a bit. I can pop back home any time I fancy because Australia's not so far away any more.' He still felt Australian, in spite of the obvious permanence of his life in Britain. 'I know there'll always be a kind of refracted Australianism in my work', he added, 'no matter how long I stay away'. By his own admission, he was doing 'quite well', although there was the constant consideration of looking after Cynthia, whose physical frailty had to be respected so she could avoid being 'put through the mill' in his obsessively mobile life. Consequently they travelled well, flying first class and staying at the best hotels, which made their expenses considerable. Living at Putney with the garden backing onto the Thames was a comfortable base where Cynthia spent many hours among her flower beds and climbing roses in a country-like atmosphere. In the spirit of a closely-knit Irish family Nolan felt he should share good fortune with his parents, paying for them as well as his sisters and their husbands to come on a visit, providing rental cars so they could tour, believing it was essential to enjoy life to the full while they were still active enough. His greatest joy was to greet his old father, who was now troubled with a heart complaint, although it had not stopped him from having a lively time on the sea voyage over, regaining something of his former gaiety by dancing with most of the women on the ship and then becoming quite sophisticated in getting around Europe for the first time in his life, loving what he saw.

The Nolans' friends in London were mainly from the art and literary worlds. He would listen to their conversations about work, aspirations and techniques, translating what they said into mental visuals and getting what he described as 'a sort of free ride' in the process. Nolan met Arthur Boyd for lunch every week when they were both in town. They were completely at ease with each other and able to enter their private world of communication in a kind of painters' shorthand. The two men would sometimes walk around the National Gallery viewing the pictures with a professional eye, noting that the big toe of Leonardo's *Madonna* was twice the length of her nose and detecting, like sniffer dogs, the faintest whiff of oil paint where the restorers had been at work. After so many years of close friendship, each understood almost instinctively the other's view of art, like members of a family whose idiosyncracies are so well known they need never be discussed.

The close relationship with Kenneth Clark and his wife was consolidated, and the Nolans dined regularly with the novelist and politician C.P. Snow and his wife, the writer Pamela Hansford Johnson. The Nolans enjoyed the Snows' company and met many of the people in their circle. Particularly memorable was an evening in Cambridge when the author gathered together many of those who had been the inspiration for the main characters in his *Strangers and Brothers* series, for which Nolan provided several jacket designs. Many of Cynthia and Nolan's friends came to Putney, including the historian Stephen Runciman, who invited them to stay at his house in Scotland, and several artists, one of the regulars being Lynn Chadwick.

Thoughts of travel were never far from Nolan's mind. John Russell was going to the Soviet Union with his Russian-born wife, Vera, to interview premier Nikita Khrushchev for a feature in the *Sunday Times* and he invited Nolan to join them and do some illustrations for the article. It would be a winter trip and, in preparation, the artist equipped himself with a fur coat and hat with ear flaps. The arrangements with the Russians became complicated, however, and the project failed to materialise. Soon afterwards, Alan Moorehead approached Nolan with the idea of going to the Antarctic where he was planning to gather material for articles in the *New Yorker* magazine. The journey had been arranged for a group of admirals who were making a tour of inspection of United States bases on the icy continent during its short summer. There were places available on the plane for Moorehead and Nolan, who were continuing their professional association; *Cooper's Creek*, Moorehead's account of the ill-fated Burke and Wills expedition to the interior of Australia, had just been published and was high on the best-seller lists, with a striking Nolan painting on the cover. After their visit to the ice, Moorehead would return the compliment by making the opening speech at his friend's exhibition of African paintings at the Adelaide Festival of Arts.

The two men arrived in a blazing hot Sydney in mid-January 1964 on their way to Christchurch, New Zealand, where the Antarctic flights originated. The long journey south in a specially-equipped Hercules aircraft was the last trip of the season, with nothing to see through thick clouds except an occasional uninviting glimpse of the grey, storm-tossed Southern Ocean far below. The penetrating throb of the four motors made normal conversation impossible and the passengers wore ear plugs to block out the worst of the noise, although one of them kept pressing Nolan to discuss watercolour techniques with a persistence that seemed ludicrous in the circumstances. As soon as he could, Nolan brushed aside these enquiries, an action he regretted later when he learned that the man was a specialist designer investigating conditions the American astronauts might encounter when they first ventured into space. The base at the South Pole was an isolated environment and his task was to study its effects on humans brought together in close proximity for long periods. Nolan wished he had been more tolerant in talking about painting because he would have liked to learn more about space flight in return.

As the Hercules finally arrived over the ice shelf on the edge of the frozen continent, Nolan and Moorehead watched from the jump seat at the rear of the flight deck. It was an extraordinary visual experience combined with the emotional impact of reaching Antarctica so easily while the explorers of previous times had been forced to battle an ocean before coming to grips with the ice. Nolan told Moorehead he thought it looked like Buddha. 'Looking at that completely lethal environment, Alan, I have the feeling that if I was destined to die in it, I wouldn't mind at all. That's why it's like Buddha.' They landed at McMurdo Sound and Nolan was soon regarding this landscape of extremes, combining beauty and terror, rather like the contrasting elements in Titian's great painting *The Flaying Of Marsyas*, which was one of his favourites.

He carried with him a little box of watercolours and two hundred blank postcards to set about recording his impressions of men and wildlife in this seductively bleak environment, which seemed to be haunted by the spirits of Shackleton and Scott, Byrd and Mawson, the explorers he had read about as a boy. Nolan realised it would be a challenge to incorporate all these elements into a landscape of extremes, but whatever the difficulties, he was determined Antarctica would provide the background for his next series of paintings. After an extensive tour of eight days, much of it by helicopter around the base area at McMurdo and then to the South Pole, Moorehead and Nolan returned to the heat of Australia to find that the artist was in the news again.

Soon after leaving England Nolan had been the victim of an attack by the art critic of the *Times* who accused him of gross over-exposure. The hard-hitting article stated,

> If you are Leonardo himself and you produce hypothetical Leonardo greeting cards and design a ballet and travel down the Nile for a magazine and thus produce sketches and appear in person in a Leonardo film on television — then suddenly the public will become weary and your image, overdisseminated and overworked,

will seem lacking in surprise or, more seriously, in any real meaning.

Nolan was told about these comments in a Sydney bookstore where he was helping to promote George Johnston's newly-published autobiographical novel *My Brother Jack* with his cover design. Behind him on a large display stand was an extensive array of *Cooper's Creek*, its dustjacket also designed by Nolan. A nearby record shop was selling a new album of folk songs by Lionel Long with a cover that was also unmistakably Nolan's. There did seem to be a lot of Nolan around, although in fairness it could be pointed out that the record cover was a painting from 1946 and the Moorehead book displayed one of the Burke and Wills pictures dated 1948.

When asked for a comment Nolan replied, 'What does it matter if there are two hundred different books on the shelves with my covers on them? If people like it that way, then it's a matter of supply and demand.' He denied, however, that he painted with the public in mind. 'It's more like having a child. You like people to admire the infant, but that's not the reason you had it.' Nolan added, 'What the public or the critics think about my work doesn't matter. They are just spectators; and spectators, particularly at football matches or the cricket, are often one-eyed and wrong.'

In 1960 the first of the biennial Adelaide Arts Festivals was held featuring a fine Turner exhibition, Dave Brubeck's jazz group, symphony orchestras from Sydney, Melbourne and Adelaide, pianist Phillipe Entremont in recital and the Elizabethan Opera Company performing Richard Strauss, Verdi, and Puccini works. To everyone's surprise, except its originators, the festival survived and flourished so that the next occasion in 1962 was more closely able to emulate its Edinburgh prototype, with the London Philharmonic Orchestra on tour, Dave Brubeck making a return visit, recitals by Hepzibah and Yehudi Menuhin and a dance company from India. The main art event was a large survey of national painting under the title 'Australian Art — Colonial to Contemporary', which contained six Nolans among hundreds of pictures, and was destined for the Tate Gallery in London followed by tours to Ottawa and Vancouver.

By 1964 the Adelaide Festival was big business and had established itself within the short space of four years as the undisputed focus for the arts in Australia. This time there were 165 scheduled performances of music, drama and dance, together with nearly thirty exhibitions. Sir William Walton arrived for a new production of his opera *Troilus and Cressida*, making himself unpopular with the management by stating that he did not believe in festivals at all. There were the Black Theatre of Prague, a selection of paintings from the Queen's collection, Eddy Condon's jazz group, an Arthur Boyd retrospective and the world premiere of Robert Helpmann's ballet *The Display*, to be danced by the Australian Ballet with sets and costumes by Sidney Nolan.

Nolan arrived in the city at the beginning of March in the company of Russell Drysdale, who was also having a show in a commercial gallery, and Hal Missingham, the director of the Art Gallery of New South Wales. Their transport across 900 miles of the south-eastern corner of Australia had been Drysdale's father's 1947 Rolls Royce and they claimed a national long-distance 'pub crawl' record, having called at twenty-seven hotels *en route*, although Nolan was on the wagon and downed nothing more potent than lemonade.

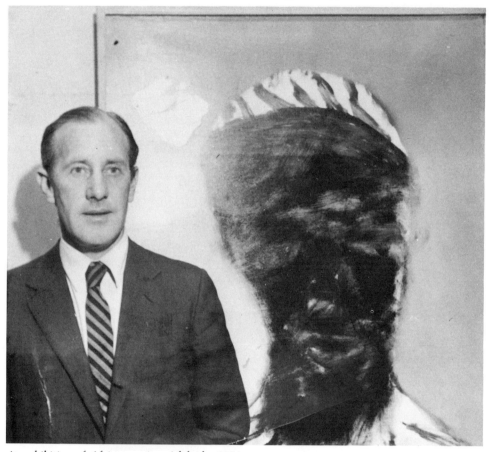

At exhibition of African series, Adelaide, 1964

Alan Moorehead opened Nolan's exhibition in front of a huge crowd of people crammed into the gallery, including the painters Len French and Arthur Boyd, composer Peter Sculthorpe and the writers George Johnston, Xavier Herbert and Patrick White, who had the first performance of his new play *Night on Bald Mountain* as a festival fringe event. The first night of *The Display* was a few days later. Some found weaknesses in the story but the dancing of Kathleen

Gorham, Garth Welch and Bryan Lawrence was superb and several critics thought Nolan's contribution, painted in London the previous year, was the most impressive part of the entire production. His sets and costumes, combined with Malcolm Williamson's sympathetic score, generated an atmosphere of mystery through the inventive use of gauzes and lighting that transformed the stage into an eerie rain forest where the sun barely penetrated the dense greenery. There were twenty curtain calls and a fifteen-minute ovation on the first night and the work took its place in the regular repertoire of the Australian Ballet.

Nolan discussing one of the gauzes for The Display, London, 1964

Nolan was delighted with the success of the ballet and returned to England to start work on the Antarctic paintings. As with his African series, he knew that the British art critics would have a preconceived notion of how the continent ought to look, and whatever he produced was unlikely to match that. His art transcended barriers of time and place, although this was a difficult notion to communicate and Nolan began to wonder if he would be forced back on the defensive again. The great numbers of paintings he began to produce in the studio at Putney used the background of Antarctica to incorporate his thoughts about the lonely land and its short history of human presence. Woven into the harsh landscapes were memories of Shackleton's expedition with the vivid image of his ship breaking up in the pack ice, based on a photograph he had seen years before taken by the expedition's Australian photographer, Frank Hurley. Elements of *The Ancient Mariner* crept into some paintings and others incorporated memories of explorers he had read about as a boy. The series was approached historically and became infused with that curious sense of suspended time that had become an element of much of his work. Nolan knew it was hardly the fashionable thing to be doing and that his public, in Britain at least, would probably find the results disturbing when they were exhibited.

While he was producing these Antarctic pictures in a sustained effort, Nolan received some of the greatest attention for his paintings when the original Kelly series of 1946–47, freshly restored and cleaned, was shown in London for the first time. The twenty-five works in the show were insured for £75,000 and went on display to the delight of huge crowds and overwhelming attention by the critics during June 1964 at the Qantas Gallery in Piccadilly. It was not the first time that the bushranger had been seen in London; in fact, ever since the Whitechapel retrospective seven years earlier, which contained a dozen new works on the subject, Kelly and Nolan had become inseparable in the minds of the British. But this series, almost twenty years old, came as a revelation.

Robert Melville, writing in the *New Statesman*, thought that the helmeted image of Kelly, if used as a poster, might well have the same effect on Australians as Picasso's 'Peace' dove on the French. 'One half might want to destroy it', he wrote, 'and the other half hang it up at home. For there is a fierce division of opinion about Kelly in Australia.' Melville explained that many Australians saw Nolan's act of painting the petty criminal as a disservice to his country for he thus gave Kelly currency as a folk hero. Others thought of Kelly as a great leader of men, even a saint. Melville continued: 'The odd intrusion of a suit of mail into a late nineteenth century story of banditry is possibly the secret of its hold on the Australian people. It's certainly due to Nolan's imaginative use of Kelly's armour that the rest of the world puts him in an altogether nobler class than Buffalo Bill.' Nobler perhaps, but the Kellys were helping to promote an airline in a spirit that was not dissimilar to the Wild West shows that toured the world late last century. Following London, the Kelly series would appear at the Edinburgh Festival, then have a return season in Paris, after an absence of fourteen years, before travelling to Sydney. In fact, Robert Melville suggested that the airline's treatment of the iconic figure indicated Qantas must have it in mind 'to advertise air tours to the Kelly country'.

Antarctic Landscape, *1964*

Some of the critics read the series as a parable while others, like Richard Walter in the *Daily Mail*, thought 'The simple incidents in his story are told with an intensity and a purity that seize you by the throat'. They were not at all 'the suave, civilised Nolan we know from his paintings today'. Several writers expressed the opinion that these early works possessed a vitality and originality absent from much of Nolan's later output and others found it necessary to explain the sophistication behind an apparently simple treatment of the subject. Robert Wraight stated in the *Tatler*,

> As I understand him, Nolan has tried not simply to illustrate the story of Ned Kelly but also to show the folkloristic nature of the myth that still surrounds him. The naive style parallels not only Nolan's own childhood image of Ned, but also the hero-worship with which adults of his own class surrounded him in his own day and continued to surround him long after his execution at the age of 25.

An expansive article in the *Times* by Edward Lucie-Smith gave the most penetrating insight into the original concept of the Kelly series. Lucie-Smith thought that the Australian hunger for national identity had swamped Nolan's original intentions and that the English public tended to search for significant statements in the pictures where none was intended. 'But what is most memorable about them', he wrote, getting closer than anyone else to the truth, 'is their insolence — the way in which an artist like Nolan treats the leaden certainty of historical fact as being something as flexible and as malleable as mythological material once seemed to a painter like Boucher'.

One of the continuing pleasures of living in England for the Nolans was visiting the annual music festival at Aldeburgh on the Suffolk coast, under the direction of Benjamin Britten. Nolan's first experience of his music was at a Melbourne concert by the Boyd Neel Orchestra in 1947 when one of the works on the programme was the song cycle *Les Illuminations*, based on the poetry of Rimbaud. He was able to relate the music to his own paintings inspired by several of the same verses, including his favourite, 'Royalty'. Nolan had been enthralled by the music, played with a verve and brilliance that was the hallmark of Boyd Neel's concerts, thinking to himself, 'This is the composer Australia needs; he seems to sum up everything to do with the desert, the bush and the continent itself'. Nolan had been introduced to Benjamin Britten at Aldeburgh in 1951 by Kenneth Clark with a fulsome description of the artist's talents that made the composer look askance at this apparent genius, four years his junior.

After this encounter Nolan took an increasing interest in opera, although it was several years before he could bring himself to attend regularly because he obstinately regarded it as a bastard form of theatre, boringly artificial. The tone of Nolan and Britten's friendship was established when they were brought together at an Aldeburgh lunch several years later. They went for a walk along the banks of the River Ald but at Britten's request they did not talk. They strolled along with only the sound of the wind in the reeds, the lapping of the water against the bank and the distant cries of herons out on the marshes. It was an experience that sealed a friendship and prepared the way for many future conversations. The Aldeburgh Festival attracted a group of distinguished artists who supported the aims of Benjamin Britten and Peter Pears, and there was at least one exhibition each year. In 1964 Nolan contributed a group of paintings based on Shakespeare's sonnets and began a closer association with Aldeburgh and its artistic directors.

It had been a relatively quiet year on the Nolans' travel barometer, but 1965 was already promising to be an extremely busy time. They would both return to Australia where he had accepted a fellowship in the creative arts at the Australian National University in Canberra. In fact, fellowships would repatriate both Nolan and the painter John Perceval, who had been living in London with his wife Mary. But before they met up again, Nolan needed to plan the showing of his Antarctic works, which would form part of separate exhibitions in New York, London and Canberra, with New York seeing them first at the Marlborough-Gerson Gallery as part of a mixed show of forty-three paintings. Alan Moorehead contributed an eloquent introduction to the catalogue of this exhibition which should have dispelled any thoughts of the paintings being mere geographical oddities or part of a continuing production of Nolan travelogues from various parts of the world:

> Anyone wishing to paint or describe these scenes turns naturally to the explorers. They were the first on the scene, they had the fresh eye, they suffered the first shock of contact. Knowing nothing of what lay before them, being without maps or records of any kind, they had the advantage of unprejudiced minds; every anthill and crevasse was a wonder, and was seen as it actually was, without comparisons. The problem of the artist who now follows in the explorers' tracks is to get back to their state of innocence.

CHAPTER TEN

The Reluctant Academic

§

When Nolan reached Canberra in early 1965 and learned what was expected of him as the recipient of a creative arts fellowship, he thought it sounded rather nebulous. As there was no art school or even a department of fine arts at the Australian National University, the duties of a painter in residence seemed to require little more than a token presence on the campus and making social rounds so he could be seen as an academic mascot. The prospect of using the university as a creative base had seemed interesting when the pro-chancellor, Dr H.C. Coombs, first suggested the position, but in reality there was little stimulation for a visiting painter and the location of Canberra, far from the vitality of Sydney and Melbourne, itself imposed an isolation. Cynthia soon wondered if she could survive for six months living in their flat at University House, in close proximity to the Percevals and surrounded by the surburban proprieties of the national capital built expressly as a centre for politics and associated bureaucracies.

With memories of the generous and undemanding Harkness Fellowship still fresh in his mind, Nolan thought that a painting journey from Australia on behalf of the university with an exhibition in Canberra at the end might be the solution to this personal and professional dilemma. He was keenly interested in going to Indonesia, and could extend the trip to Pakistan, Nepal, Afghanistan and then on to China. This group of nations to the immediate north and west were becoming an arc of interest for Australia in political, economic and cultural terms, so Nolan reasoned that an exhibition derived from his observations in these areas would be an appropriate project for a fellow of the Australian National University. He presented the idea to Dr Coombs, who responded with little enthusiasm, suggesting it would mean a long absence from Canberra and rather defeat the purpose of the fellowship, which was to stimulate an awareness of art by having a distinguished painter in the community. Nolan had a reputation for globe-trotting and the results in terms of his art were impressive, but being out of sight would mean out of mind, and Coombs, a leading banker,

177

could see little value for the university's money in allowing their star attraction to stray. After further discussions, when it became obvious that the Nolans were not going to be content tied to Canberra, Coombs agreed to put no obstacles in their way as long as the vice-chancellor, Sir Leonard Huxley, approved the scheme. The only stipulation was for the artist to mount an exhibition at the university on his return, to be seen as the fruit of his fellowship.

Before any painting trip could be organised there were other commitments to be fulfilled. The first was to attend the premiere of the latest film made by the Collings for Qantas. Titled *Toehold in History*, it had been produced for the fiftieth anniversary of the Gallipoli landing at Anzac Cove and incorporated some 180 paintings and drawings that had been Nolan's private obsession over the past decade: the hidden face of the traveller. Appropriately the script had been written by George Johnston, who had been part of the paintings' inception during those halcyon days on Hydra ten years before. Since then, between painting his major exhibitions, Nolan had produced hundreds of Gallipoli pictures in a range of sizes and treatments, although the public knew very little about them, except for an occasional picture slipped into a group or mixed show in London or New York. When he had amassed a great number of images covering all aspects of the landing at Anzac Cove, it was obvious there would be a problem in exhibiting them and Nolan became intrigued by Geoff Collings' suggestion of a film treatment that could give a kaleidoscopic interpretation of this epic event. *Toehold in History*, with a running time of 21 minutes, was accepted for general cinema release in Australia and New Zealand as a supporting short.

Its premiere was given in Canberra with the Governor-General Lord De L'Isle in attendance, a week before the film was released to theatrical circuits on 18 March. The main impression given by this cinematic cavalcade of subtle imagery was the immediacy of someone who had been on the spot at Gallipoli, not concerned with the grand designs of military strategy or the grandeur of battle, but with the human face of the engagement. The emphasis was on the personal and emotional aspects of men enmeshed in bloody conflict and haunted by the ever-present spectre of death. Nolan's journal of an event that happened before he was born combined with Johnston's words and the ingenuities of the editing to make a striking screen documentary.

Toehold in History may have had dignity, but it was also considered rather too serious for cinema audiences more accustomed to lightweight travelogues before the main feature. Amalgamated Theatres in New Zealand withdrew the Gallipoli film from exhibition because they said it was 'a bit on the arty side for general audiences' and the film faced additional problems across the Tasman. The president of the Auckland Returned Servicemen's Association said he regarded the film as a sincere tribute to the campaign. 'Nolan's paintings and drawings typified the Australian character — long, lean and raw', he said. 'But I would say they were not typical of New Zealanders.' During this time the Nolans were staying on Green Island off the Queensland coast, where he was informed of the death of his father at the age of 72.

The name of Sidney Nolan was synonymous with Australian art and his photograph appeared frequently in the newspapers, so it came as a surprise to read the critic of the *Sydney Morning Herald*, Wallace Thornton, stating that a Nolan exhibition had become a rare event in Australia. It was a fact, however, that, apart from shows of Italian and Greek drawings in the mid 1950s, his exhibition at David Jones during May 1965 was his first in Sydney for thirteen years. Its centrepiece was a series of ten pictures combining like a Japanese screen to form a single work titled *Riverbend*, five feet high and totalling some forty feet in length. It was a representation of the river at Toolamba in the Goulburn Valley, with its flooding billabongs; an area dear to his father's younger days. Most of the individual panels contained references to Ned Kelly, but they were small figures in a rich evocation of the Australian landscape,

A panel from Riverbend

179

painted in England and filtered by distance. The inclusion of six large portrait heads provided a colourful and witty contrast to the sombre, unrestrained panels. Thornton wrote about them, 'This reviewer remembers seeing together with the artist, the crowds of ladies, young and old, all similarly wearing flower-festooned hats as they paraded at the garden party at the last Adelaide Festival of Arts and no doubt these heads are a direct result of this impact-making image that struck forcibly the home-returning Nolan.'

In mid-June Nolan arranged for fourteen of his Antarctic paintings to be exhibited in the R.G. Menzies Library at the Australian National University. The show was opened by Sir Leonard Huxley but the Nolans were not present, being about to fly to Indonesia on the first stage of their Asian journey. Through an introduction from the Australian ambassador in Jakarta, Keith Shann, Nolan was able to meet President Sukarno at a time when the political situation in the country was at a critical stage. They had a brief audience with the president and the conversation remained on the level of good-natured banter. Shann had taken along a copy of Robert Melville's recently-published *Ned Kelly* combining text and notes, together with a spirited foreword by Alan Moorehead, as a background to the twenty-seven paintings illustrated in colour. This high-quality publication from Thames and Hudson was introducing the original Kelly series to a wider audience after it had achieved almost the same mythical stature as Kelly himself, because many knew about the paintings but relatively few had actually seen them. The book was presented to Sukarno, who proceeded to leaf through the pictures as the ambassador explained that Mr Nolan would welcome the opportunity of painting the president's portrait. Sukarno did not respond until he had examined every one of the reproductions with increasing amusement. He then looked up at Shann and said, 'Well, Mr Ambassador, he can't do that because I'd be a dead man'. He turned to Nolan, fixing him with an intense stare, adding, 'And so would Mr Nolan!'

The Nolans continued on their travels, looking at temples and ruins and archaeological sites, and Nolan realised a childhood ambition to visit the centres of the world's great religions. The Nolans were determined to see China, although the political climate was then very much against tourism. The only possible entry was through Pakistan, which had friendly relations with the Chinese. But Nolan was confident of achieving his aim, having pulled strings on both sides of the world, with a letter from the Foreign Office in London requesting an entry visa, and the initial backing of Sir James Plimsoll of the Department of External Affairs in Canberra, who was an enthusiastic collector of his paintings. The Australian connection had proved fruitless, however, because there were no formal diplomatic contacts between Peking and Canberra. Just before leaving Sydney, Nolan had received a typewritten note from the Chinese government explaining that because of a shortage of trained interpreters he would not be welcome at this time. He saw this as a neat diplomatic way of barring the entry of Australians, which made him even more determined to succeed.

Pakistan International Airlines was one of the few carriers operating a service to China, and soon after their arrival in Karachi Nolan was in the airline's office, flourishing a sheaf of traveller's cheques and demanding two tickets. The surprised girl at the booking counter explained to this eccentric foreigner that money alone was not enough to get seats on the plane; there was the more important question of a visa. She called the manager who ignored the question of tickets after hearing that Nolan was a painter who wished to study Chinese landscape, and introduced himself as a poet, in fact the best in Pakistan he claimed, with a disarming lack of modesty. He said that most of his finest work had been written in jail, where he had spent long periods during the partition troubles with India. 'But the most wonderful thing I've done with my life', he explained, 'was to take my four-year-old son to China'. Nolan was advised it was likely to be far too hot to visit the northern cities at this time of year and it would be better to delay the trip, if only for a few weeks. He took it as an excellent excuse to see Afghanistan, another country in this region which had long fascinated him.

He and Cynthia went to the Khyber Pass and then on to the city of Kabul, where they had an unexpected meeting with the film and theatre director, Peter Brook, who was doing some research there. The bare landscapes in this part of Asia soon palled, however, and they returned to Karachi during the rainy season to subject themselves to a heavy round of diplomatic, business and social gatherings that proved almost as exhausting as travelling the rough countryside. Nolan soon became restless at this increasingly aimless existence and Cynthia suggested that China in high summer could hardly be less comfortable than Karachi during the rainy season, and that he had better organise the visas. The Chinese consular official asked why he and his wife wished to visit his country and Nolan replied flippantly it was because the Pakistan Airlines man had said it was the best thing he had ever done in his life. The only other question was if any previous applications for a visa had been made. Nolan thought it best to ignore the documents he was carrying in his pocket from Britain and Australia and confirmed this was the only application they had submitted. Expenses in Karachi were mounting rapidly and it was fortunate that ten days later their visas were approved.

The route was via Dacca then across northern Burma and into southern China with a stop at Canton before going on to Shanghai where there would be a change of aircraft for the Nolans' final destination, Peking. But a delayed departure from Dacca because of a torrential rainstorm made their arrival in Shanghai too late to catch the Peking connection and necessitated an overnight stay in a local hotel. It was well after midnight when they checked in, with the roar of jet engines still ringing in their ears from the unexpectedly long flight and, although both exhausted, they stood for half an hour leaning out of an open window, taking in the muddy smells of the Orient and peering into the misty darkness, penetrated at intervals by the orange glow of streetlamps. An occasional cyclist passed silently below like a pedalling wraith, while the only sound came from ghost-like farm carts laden with fruit and vegetables making an early journey to the city markets.

Nolan felt that out there in the darkness must be the answer he had been seeking ever since, as a youth of nineteen in Melbourne, he first heard about the Long March. Perhaps now he would find that catalyst to combine elements of the east and west in his thoughts and paintings. In the morning there would be definable shapes instead of mystery and China would become a reality. For the first time in many weeks since the death of his father, the tight band of tension around his forehead seemed to loosen and Nolan fell asleep on his first night in China free from all cares and anxieties. There was a rude awakening just a few hours later, however, when it was time to be up early to catch the plane for Peking. Outside, the oriental fantasies of a few hours before had dissolved into an unattractive grey urban landscape of the Bund, obviously once elegant but now drab and rundown, the only splashes of colour coming from the red flags hanging limply in the heavy atmosphere.

The Nolans had arrived by 10 a.m. at a sunless and airless airport outside the Chinese capital which, to their surprise, seemed as bustling as any they had experienced in a dozen European cities. Their presence was completely ignored as if they were invisible as foreigners, becoming neither interlopers nor guests in this most foreign of locations at the worst time of year for personal comfort. Eventually an interpreter was found who arranged transport into the city and accommodation. The Friendship Hotel was a crowded place, segregated from the life of the city, housing a surprising diversity of visitors from all over the world: English women tourists, Eastern bloc delegates, old Communist sympathisers from France, Japanese businessmen, a Canadian journalist and a group of noisy Ghanaians, who annoyed everyone with their boisterous behaviour at breakfast.

Nolan carried a letter of introduction from Dr Coombs to the Governor of the Bank of China in Peking and that resulted in a stiffly formal lunch with an assistant. For want of conversation, and knowing almost nothing about international finance, Nolan talked about China being the only major country in the world on the gold standard and that seemed to please the official. Another Chinese at the meal was a person Nolan had been asked to contact by C.P. Fitzgerald, a China expert from the Australian National University. This man had been educated at Oxford and spoke fluent English which made for much easier conversation. He had translated Mao Tse Tung's *Little Red Book* for

182

distribution throughout Africa and was friendly and urbane, but Nolan was hesitant to suggest they meet again because he had been advised to take care in his relations with Chinese officials, both for his own and their sakes. After these official contacts had been made, the Nolans were keen to see the sights. They spent hours in the endless maze of buildings and pathways that made up the Imperial Palace — the former Forbidden City — revelling in the glories of its architecture with the elaborate pavilions bearing evocative names like Palace of Earthly Tranquillity and Hall of Supreme and Protecting Harmony. There were hundreds of old bronzes to inspect and Nolan was particularly interested in the hanging scrolls of Chu-Ta, the seventeenth-century monk and painter, whose influence seemed to be echoed in some contemporary American art.

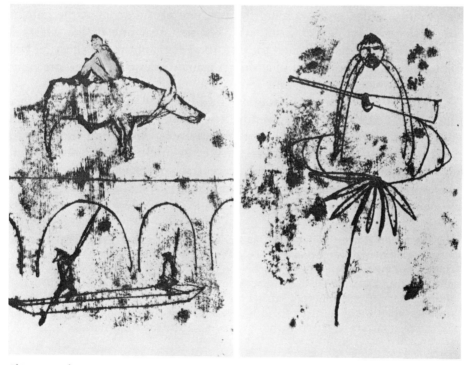

Chinese studies, 1965

There was only a small section of the country open to foreigners outside the three principal cities and after a trip to the Great Wall and the Ming tombs, Nolan began to feel as restricted as the pandas in the Peking Zoo. Many of the historic places he wanted to see, such as the site of Peking Man and the Marco Polo bridge, were in forbidden zones and he soon came to the sad conclusion that there seemed to be no place for painting in the new China. He was impressed with the way the Chinese had stimulated poetry and achieved a kind of collective harmony, but this was part of a long transitional phase that could be fascinating material for a writer, but was hopeless for a painter. The landscapes, temples and bronzes were all part of an ancient culture, having nothing to do with this great society in the throes of social upheaval. There was little room for art in this atmosphere; it had been drowned by both the past and the present. Nolan did not want to be just a sightseer any more. He discussed his disenchantment with Cynthia who, although tired by the rigours of the Peking summer, was enjoying her stay.

The Nolans' rounds of the capital became confined to a small, familiar circle of western diplomats and high Chinese officials and their wives. There were no performances of the classic opera to visit and everything else presented on stage was overflowing with propaganda prompted by the cultural revolution. One day Nolan heard muffled music coming through one of the doors in the hotel and stood in the corridor listening intently, realising that one of the guests was using a shortwave radio. Through the distorting static of the transmission Nolan recognised the slow movement of a Mozart piano concerto and knew precisely at this moment what he was missing.

Nolan found any discussions about art in China quite frustrating. The officials he met explained that western painting was meaningless because the Chinese themselves must strive to serve the common cause by employing art to illustrate the party line and rouse the workers to greater productivity. Nolan began to loathe the huge posters dominating the central streets of the city with their bland figures of rosy-faced soldiers, smiling workers and plump children. He felt they said nothing about the people.

> There's no art form. You can be sure there's no Chinese Shelley composing verses, or oriental Michelangelo sculpting, or local della Francesca painting. There's not even a Nolan here, more's the pity! These propaganda posters define attitudes that have travelled overland from Europe by way of Russia. They say nothing that's Chinese, nothing that's *theirs*. You never see the Chinese in those attitudes, they couldn't sit or stand like that if they tried. The figures, the faces and expressions are Western clichés expressing attitudes from Europe.

It was obvious they must move on and the Nolans returned to the more lively, cosmopolitan atmosphere of Shanghai that was curiously refreshing after the disappointments of Peking, which seemed in retrospect like a collection of dusty villages surrounding the Imperial Palace. After a few days in Shanghai with excursions into the surrounding countryside to visit collectives producing food and simple goods, the Nolans took a train to Suchow, the ancient city of canals and bridges famous for its gardens, pools and pagodas. It was a final reminder of the old China before they returned to Shanghai to make arrangements for the flight back to Karachi. As they strolled along the wide

Flying from England to Australia, 1977

*With Mary Perceval at a Melbourne
football match, 1977*

Burke and Wills exhibition, Sydney, 1985

Spray painting, 1986

Notes for Oedipus, *1976*
Nightmare, *1982*

Hand with Flowers, *1977*

boulevard beside the river, Nolan mused that the people rather than the landscape had been more interesting on this trip. A revolution, he reasoned, had to have more action than art, and that was why he held a feeling of unease and dissatisfaction from the day they had arrived. Cynthia pointed out that it was now possible to be a peasant or a proletarian and an intellectual at the same time. 'You yourself are an example of this breed', she suggested. They passed the great sheets of news and photographs pasted up on the walls that served as street newspapers for the masses, together with dozens of handwritten posters, and Nolan was suddenly aware they had not heard any news of the outside world for weeks, thinking what a joy it would be to read a western newspaper again and leaf through magazines.

Cynthia noted down her husband's thoughts on leaving China. He knew they would be difficult to explain to anyone else, although she was going to do her best because the notebooks she had filled for the past few weeks were the basis of her next book. 'A trip to China changes you', Nolan said. 'Something happens, a very quiet thing that's got to do with the future. It's a peculiar feeling to have been where we've been and come back again — like a dream in which you drown and fly at the same time.'

The direct result of the visit to China for Nolan was a group of small works in mixed media, mostly twelve by ten inches, shown at the Australian National University the following year. In his speech at the opening Dr Coombs referred obliquely to the Nolans' travels, pointing out that the pictures were the product of the artist's fellowship, the fruits of a short tenure. He said the university looked forward to a larger edition in due course. Nolan was aware that these works were little more than a string of impressions without a strong statement because of the difficulty of summing-up his feelings about the trip. He had told Coombs that the university was investing in a long-term project, and this journey was the start of a continuing painterly fascination with China that would show no signs of abating.

The Nolans planned to spend a few months in New York, taking up residence at the Chelsea Hotel, famous, even notorious, for its guests from the arts world. They rented one of its penthouses and Nolan negotiated to use a large space situated immediately behind the reception desk as a studio, where he could come and go unnoticed into a private world. Nolan could work almost anywhere he happened to be as long as he had access to the basic materials of his trade. Several major works would be painted there, including the multi-panelled *Inferno* and another version of *Riverbend* for display at the Montreal Expo. He also produced some large pictures, five feet by four, on a Greek theme, with thoughts of Hydra and the Hellenic myths still vivid in his mind. In fact, what eventually became *Inferno* was intended to be the start of a series based on Robert Lowell's translation of the *Oresteia*. During this period, he and Lowell met frequently. Nolan admitted that his own skills as a poet were little more than rudimentary, but found himself increasingly drawn into the construction of some of Lowell's work, discussing rhymes and the pattern of words. It became a highly productive time for them both with Nolan stimulated to delve deeper into the myths, fascinated by subjects like the sacrifice of Iphigenia at Aulis.

Nolan's intense burst of energy at the Chelsea came to an abrupt end, with many of the works remaining in the studio hidden behind the lobby. He was never able to explain afterwards what mental state led him to leave them at the hotel. It was a recurrence of a situation he had faced before, and which undoubtedly would happen again, where he abandoned whatever he was doing and just walked away. It was expensive living in the penthouse for such a long period and he had traded a number of paintings with the owner in lieu of rent. For all Nolan knew, his abandoned works and the exchanged paintings might have stayed behind the reception desk forever, rather like the pictures secreted at the back of the chimney of Ghika's house on Hydra. All he could do was to keep an eye open for their possible reappearance with dealers.

His mind had now turned to other challenges with the opportunity of realising his dream of introducing a large-scale mural art for Australia. Ever since *Moonboy* had been revived so successfully for *The Rite of Spring*, he thought about grander schemes incorporating that image. Why stop at thirty feet, when the image might be expanded to decorate one of the tall buildings springing up in the centre of Australia's cities? Nolan's thoughts raced in this direction when Dr Coombs, as Governor of the Reserve Bank of Australia, suggested he provide a major art work for the bank's new building in Melbourne, rising just along the street from where Nolan had lived almost penniless in the late 1930s. He imagined *Moonboy* decorating the entire side of the structure in gold ceramic tiles to reflect the sun, so that air travellers approaching the city might see it glinting in the distance. At long last Nolan thought he had an opportunity of following in the footsteps of the muralists from Mexico whose revolutionary art emphasised the importance of the individual and led to a new assessment of their nation's ancient Indian culture. Diego Rivera, José Clemente Orozco and David Alfaro Siqueiros had long been his heroes and this was an opportunity to emulate them.

None of Nolan's lofty dreams eventuated, however, because of cost, although Coombs did agree to commission a somewhat smaller but equally ambitious work for the entrance of the new building. Nolan wanted to know the specifications, and the area's exposure to the public, because the plans were for the entrance to be open to the street. Coombs answered that it had to be tough enough to survive being hit by a beer bottle and not show the mark. 'A full bottle?' Nolan asked and the reply was, 'Yes, better be on the safe side!' It was accepted as the remark of a cautious banker and Nolan suggested the area of 800 square feet would look good covered by a series of closely-fitting copper panels with a total measurement of 66 feet long by 12 feet high, 'painted' in jewellery enamel which would be hard enough to stand the normal dangers of urban life and which should last indefinitely.

All that survived from the Mexican concept was the revolutionary subject matter: Eureka, the uprising on the Victorian goldfields that led to accelerated reforms for the miners in an action where, according to H. V. Evatt, 'Australian democracy was born'. The romantic aura surrounding Eureka had intensified over the years, ever since Nolan's successful show on the subject in 1949, whose financial success had allowed him to travel to Europe for the first time. Now he would re-create Eureka on a larger scale in a new medium, which was the sort of challenge he enjoyed. If only in statistical terms he faced a formidable and expensive task in transferring two hundredweight of transparent jewellery enamel onto one and a half tons of heavy gauge copper sheet and making it into sixty-six separate panels. Nolan's design was fired at a heat of 800 degrees centigrade under the supervision of two London enamellers, Patrick Furse and Robin Banks, using Miss Banks' London studio. The panels were then carefully cleaned and assembled in the right order and a transparent enamel laid over the entire surface under the artist's direction. The whole mural was then refired piece by piece at varying temperatures that gave rich background effects in a large-scale version of a process known since medieval times. Enormous care had to be exercised at all stages of the work to ensure that the separate components of the continuous design did not become distorted after firing. The completed mural was shipped to Melbourne, but the new building was not ready to display it and *Eureka Stockade* found a temporary home in one of the large models for the Victorian Arts Centre being used by the architect, Roy Grounds, for assessing details of the interiors. He had wanted Nolan to work with him on various schemes to decorate the planned opera house, which eventually became the State Theatre. Nolan's ideas for continuous murals down the stairs and in the foyers interested Grounds, although he was not at all impressed with the new Reserve Bank effort. 'It's got to be another of your jokes, Sid', was his comment on first seeing it.

It might have been expected, with Nolan approaching the age of fifty, that his first Australian retrospective would be organised in his home city by the National Gallery of Victoria, which through its collection and school had been vital elements in his development as an artist. Although he was generally regarded now as the most famous, if not necessarily the best, artist the nation had produced, his work had long been ignored by the Gallery's director, Daryl Lindsay, who had been reported to him as saying, on seeing the Kelly series for the first time, that Nolan would only get into the collection over his dead body. It was a reaction that sprang partly from a bitter disagreement with John Reed over parochial art politics. Lindsay had retired in 1955 but Melbourne was still riven by these quarrels, leaving the Art Gallery of New South Wales to be first to offer Nolan a major retrospective to mark his fiftieth birthday year in 1967. The director, Hal Missingham, promised to organise the most comprehensive exhibition of his work ever, with attention to every detail. Missingham was a staunch supporter of the artist, having placed his own position on the line in the late 1940s by pressing for the purchase of Nolan's work in the face of trenchant opposition from the gallery's board of trustees.

Nolan had access to much of his output over a painting career that now went back more than thirty years. There was material available from his own collection, and from private collectors in various parts of the world and other public galleries. The main problem might be to borrow the key works of his youth and the original Kelly paintings from the Reeds. But that was a problem of diplomatic representation for Missingham and his staff to handle. For himself, at an extremely busy time of his life, Nolan was looking forward to seeing examples of his work from the different stages of his career in the largest show he had been offered. It would give him an opportunity to assess how the paintings he'd produced overseas related to his Australian work and, more importantly, to his current work. He began thinking about his start in art many years before when anything at all seemed possible, even a sudden switch to writing, and how circumstances beyond his manipulation had edged him into his present situation, which still held many personal uncertainties in spite of the outward trappings of success. Gradually he came to the view that the Sydney retrospective would be a pivotal point in his life. He would assess his work as objectively as he could and if it did not meet with his satisfaction, there was still time in his life for something else. Nolan had no idea exactly what he would do if the show gave him a negative impression; all he knew was he would not continue in his present ways for fear of realising at some future date that his career had been a waste of time. It was a matter of intense personal pride and he knew that art was too serious a matter to play around with if it was not going to satisfy him any longer. Nolan was anxious to have the show because he had determined that fifty was to be the testing point in his life.

In the meantime, smaller exhibitions continued to be arranged and mounted in various parts of the world, including a selection from Nolan's parents' collection shown at Shepparton in the Goulburn Valley of Victoria arranged by his sister, and the first showing of a comprehensive selection of Gallipoli studies, organised by Hal Missingham, and displayed at the Qantas Gallery in Sydney during April 1966 at the time of the annual observance of Anzac Day. There were 145 works in the exhibition and the Nolans returned to Australia for the opening, which received extensive press notices with many photographs of the Gallipoli images, so that this series became as familiar to a wide audience as

Anzac, *1964*

anything he had painted before, although the art writers were not unanimous in their praise. Wallace Thornton in the *Sydney Morning Herald* thought the pictures provided only slight, tentative skirmishes and, while admitting that much of the old allure was there, stated:

> The confident forms, the skilful arabesques, bring the touch of poetry and magic, so familiar in his best work, close at hand. But this is not enough for this theme, and on the evidence of the one larger work here — a painting labelled *Head* — the feathered hat, slippery forms and equally slippery colours hardly arouse one's confidence about the success of other larger works on this subject.

189

James Gleeson, however, writing in the weekend *Sun-Herald* took the opposite view, speculating that Nolan's claim to immortality would rest more securely on his Gallipoli paintings than any other of his works because they contained the highest concentration of all the most creative aspects of his art.

> Their brevity gives them a deceptively slight appearance at first glance but one has only to glance a second time to discover profound psychological truths in each brief note. These sketches — for they seem nothing more substantial than sketches — are as profoundly moving and as unutterably sad as the last movements of Benjamin Britten's *War Requiem* when the words 'let us sleep now' are sung over and over again and gradually merge into the texture of *In Paradisum*.

On this trip home, Nolan had further discussions about the all-important retrospective, which had now been scheduled for a Sydney opening in September 1967, and he considered including a few pictures for the show from his mother's collection in Melbourne. In fact, Dora Nolan had become the curator of the works that her son had given to her and to his sisters, Mrs Marjorie Sweet of Shepparton and Mrs Lorna Goslin of St Kilda. It was now a valuable private collection ranging over twenty years of the artist's work, regarded with fierce pride by the 70-year-old Dora who had often been urged to sell the paintings by friends and realise a considerable sum of money, but she always refused. The paintings were sometimes exhibited locally in aid of charity and Nolan was happy that *Northern Territory Stockman*, *Landscape Central Australia*, *Greek Sponge Fishing Boats*, a Leda and the Swan sketch, and *The Aswan Dam*, many with Christmas or birthday messages on the back, played their part in raising money for a cancer appeal or the hospital auxiliary where Mrs Nolan had been a member for twenty years. It continued to worry him, however, that his late father had never understood his desire to be a painter. Mr Nolan was constantly puzzled by his son's profession, although he never opposed it. Even when Nolan was sending him pictures he could be expected to appreciate, such as landscapes of the Australian bush or a hare caught in a trap, images that had been part of his youth in the Goulburn Valley, his father remained unmoved. Nolan tried to explain his concern to Cynthia:

> I put it down, not to a lack of intrinsic art education, which Dad certainly never had, but to the social and cultural deprivation that occurred if you happened to be educated at a State school in the bush in Victoria: you left as soon as you were fourteen, worked hard in a mine and then went on the land before becoming a tram driver, with your recreation based on swimming and bike riding and the horses. I can't blame him for any of that, but I'm absolutely determined to spread my appreciation of the enjoyment of art for everyone to understand.

After several years of journeys that had made him the most travelled painter

Dora Nolan with some of her collection, 1965

in the history of art, Nolan regarded his status rather in the same way as the content of many of his pictures: having a timeless, indefinite quality without allegiance to school or style. He no longer worried about being regarded by some Australian detractors as the pouter pigeon of his profession, or about those critics in Britain who saw him as nothing more than a show-pony of art, full of flash and short on substance. Nolan had heard too many conflicting opinions to take such things seriously, particularly as he was secure in the companionship of a circle of close friends, while Cynthia fended off those people and situations he wanted to avoid. His real dedication was to the transmission of emotions. Nolan cared about that so much that he revealed he would sometimes 'belt the paint across the canvas much faster than it should be belted; I don't care as long as I can get emotional communication'. Having done that for the best part of twenty years, he could admit to Cynthia and Kenneth Clark, 'I don't really mind where I stand — or don't stand — it has no interest for me personally', finding fame fickle, life inexplicable and nature relentless. He related the continuing challenge of exploring uncharted regions of the soul to the transmission of emotions, 'That is what my life has been spent doing and that's what I'm going to keep on doing, one way or another, and not be too concerned about the outcome'. These thoughts had nothing to do with trends and fashions which lasted for just a few months or years. They referred more directly to what he sensed in an audience's response to great music performed in a concert hall, where it seemed that everyone present acquired the same breathing rate. He had read that Berenson believed this type of kinesthetic reaction could come from a painting: the viewer's response determined by the nature of the work. But, ultimately pragmatic, he did not want to ask too many questions about these theories, believing instead that it was important to 'get working with the paint, the turps, the brushes and the fingers, going at it flat out until finished, and then getting a good night's rest'.

Nolan had always considered it essential for a painter to attend a show's opening, not so much for commercial reasons, but to assess how his brain had been operating while the exhibition was being painted. He admitted to a sinking feeling in the pit of his stomach on these occasions. Ruthless self-criticism was essential to retain integrity because the public and the press sometimes could be illuminating, but on other occasions simply irritating. Nolan often found himself playing devil's advocate, telling people they were incorrect in their assessment of his work, although this did not always assist sales. Then there was the type of opening where everyone was excessively polite, which quickly led to boredom for the artist, his eyes taking on a glazed expression and his lips fixed with the smiling responses of an automaton. Nolan slipped into this trance-like state, drugged by continuous conversation, often physically trapped in a corner with his mind many miles away.

The Nolans arrived back in Australia a full month before the big exhibition was due to open. And big it was going to be, with 143 paintings given a nominal value by the Art Gallery of New South Wales of half a million dollars. Over the preceding weeks the storage vaults at the gallery had been crammed with huge crates bearing numbers and stickers from galleries all over the world including the Redfern, Marlborough, Tate, Museum of Modern Art in New York, National Gallery of Victoria and the collection of Sir Kenneth Clark. Charmian Clift went along to meet Nolan and Hal Missingham in the midst of this planned chaos and it reminded her of an occasion in Piraeus eight years before when she watched a bronze Apollo, 2,000 years old, being raised from a trench in a hot and dusty back street. It was not Apollo that came out of the case Nolan was inspecting, but Sergeant Kennedy dead at Stringybark Creek. The artist looked surprised at the picture he had last seen twenty-one years ago, thinking that the hill in the background had grown pinker in the interim. He ran his fingers over Kennedy's spilt blood and joked 'Still fresh!' A clump of what Charmian thought must be snowdrops was growing from the gore. She commented on this and Nolan smiled, 'Yes, yes, Adonis and the flowers springing up eternally'. Missingham pulled out a large Wimmera picture completed only twelve months previously and now in the gallery's collection, stood it against one of the original Wimmera subjects and stepped back to make a comparison. Charmian Clift observed that little had changed in the landscape during the intervening quarter of a century, but a great deal had obviously happened to Nolan during the past thirty years of his creative endeavour.

Hal Missingham suggested they hang the show together but Nolan preferred to leave it to the director because he felt he was unable to face the task objectively enough. He had favourite paintings which were closer to him because of their associations, such as an intense struggle to achieve an acceptable composition or a desperate attempt to finish a work that had seemed to defy completion. Moreover, he had other commitments because September was shaping up to be Nolan month in Sydney. Apart from the retrospective, there was a show of theatre and ballet designs at Qantas, David Jones would exhibit a selection of the Burke and Wills and Antarctica paintings together with some new landscapes, and over at the Macquarie Galleries there would be the Shakespeare sonnets and other small pictures.

Hanging one of the Kelly paintings at 1967 retrospective, Art Gallery of New South Wales

193

In addition, the ABC had approached Nolan with the idea of making an hour-long television documentary centred on his homecoming for the retrospective. The script would be written by George Johnston, who was now living in Sydney, and the film would be directed by Storry Walton, a staff producer, who had been responsible for the highly successful television serialisation of Johnston's *My Brother Jack*. It was an impressive array of talent that would lead to the most comprehensive film coverage yet of Nolan's life and work, shot in colour at a time when the local television system was barely ten years old, with colour transmission still years away. The first sequence was filmed at Sydney Airport to catch Nolan coming off a plane from Melbourne. He was bundled into a waiting car to join Hal Missingham on the back seat and driven into town with the cameraman and sound recordist adopting contortionist positions beside the driver to catch their conversation. This type of sequence is difficult enough for experienced actors to cope with: trying to appear natural with a camera lens poking into the face, a microphone between the legs and a blinding portable light blurring the vision and raising the temperature inside the vehicle, whose windows had to remain closed against the exterior noise. Nolan and Missingham were a couple of old hams, however, with extrovert natures to make the best of an uncomfortable situation.

Later that day Nolan would go along to the Art Gallery to see the exhibition up on the walls, but in the meantime he joined Storry Walton and the film crew for an informal lunch with Allan Ashbolt, the assistant head of the ABC's Talks Department, who was administratively in charge of the production. After some rather strained pleasantries, Ashbolt shocked them all by announcing that the film would have to be cancelled through lack of funds. He regretted the last-minute decision and apologised for having to inform them so late. Understandably, this caused a moment of stunned silence until Nolan suggested that the film be reduced from sixty to thirty minutes. He expanded on this impeccable Irish logic: 'And if you can make a good film of thirty minutes under favourable conditions, for half the original budget, why not make the original length under less favourable circumstances?' He offered to pay his own fares around Australia and said he was prepared to accept no material benefits from the production, such as travelling allowance, as long as it went ahead. Ashbolt explained that the medium did not work in this way. It was not simply a matter of tailoring the film to existing cash because there was a point below which it was impossible to embark on a production. Nolan was persistent, however, suggesting that economies could be made by using less stock, reducing the amount of travel and working for fewer days. He was supported by the production team, while Ashbolt became increasingly irritated at being forced to reconsider his position, particularly since Nolan had declined to support him by agreeing to speak at a rally to protest against Australian and American involvement in the Vietnam conflict. Nolan made it clear that, whatever his personal thoughts about politics, he would not express them in public. Ashbolt promised to discuss their proposal with the administration, but Nolan realised that it would take too long in a bureaucracy and they would be certain to miss the opening of the retrospective. 'You don't have to do that, Allan', he said. 'You've admitted to having half the money, so we'll take that as read and all we need from you is a yes or no.' This resulted in Ashbolt agreeing to let the production proceed on a reduced budget and with an attenuated script.

At the gallery Hal Missingham showed Nolan around the three courts that housed the large retrospective. All the pictures were up, the labels in place and ABC electricians had installed battens for hanging enough lights to film at the opening. That evening Nolan paced the highly-polished floors on his own, making a solitary odyssey into his past and soon forgetting the question of whether or not he should persist as a painter by judging the individual works. He became absorbed in what seemed to be another's mental processes, twisting and turning in the action of creating images and emotions. Nolan was in the sort of trance-like state that sometimes gripped him when painting a picture, drifting past the big works, *Riverbend* and *Inferno,* as security staff stayed discreetly in the background. He realised as he came to the end of the exhibition, which had been hung in chronological order, that he had not really been looking at pictures at all; he was inspecting, as if from an outsider's viewpoint, the visual expression of an individual's thoughts, which he accepted from the signatures as his own. He walked out of the gallery thinking to himself, 'Well, if that's what painting's all about, it's just the kind of thing for me to be in.' At the entrance he paused to take out a small sheet of white paper and a red flow pen, drawing two red eyes which he cut out and then placed over a photograph of himself to give the impression of staring through a slit in Ned Kelly's armour. Hal Missingham asked him why he had done this and Nolan, in a mood of elation, replied, 'I think red eyes go with Sydney'.

The opening was one of the social events of the year and many people were disappointed because Hal Missingham had insisted that numbers be limited to 500, half invited by the gallery trustees and the others by the Art Gallery Society, with tickets at $5 apiece numbered and checked against a list of guests' names by security guards. The Lord Mayor of Sydney, Alderman John Armstrong, declared the exhibition open by saying, 'We are looking at the work of one man and we are moved with wonder at what we see'. Nolan faced the guests to make the shortest speech of the evening, 'I just hope you are as happy as I am'. His mother, who had travelled from Melbourne for the occasion, whispered to Cynthia, 'It's lovely. I feel very happy for Sid, he's worked hard for this.' The artist, wearing a blue suit, blue shirt and floral tie, joked to the Lord Mayor as they walked around the exhibition together, 'Now I feel ready to have another bash after seeing all this'. Armstrong, who was a collector of contemporary Australian art, asked which was his favourite picture and received the reply, 'The last one out of the oven's always the one you like best', referring to the final listing in the catalogue, *Camel and Figure*, painted in 1966. Next day the show would be open to the public at 20 cents a head, although the numbers, titles and dates attached to each of the works soon disappeared in an attempt to increase sales of the $1 catalogue. A gallery spokesman explained, 'You don't sell catalogues if you have titles and although we're not hard-hearted, we do hope to get something back on the cost of staging the exhibition'.

The critical reaction to the show was overwhelmingly good, as if many of the unkind thoughts and chauvinistic sentiments of previous years had been swept aside and Nolan's work could be assessed with a fresh vision. Wallace Thornton wrote about the artist's sense of apparent spontaneity and the infusion of lyrical poetry. 'There is an Irish lilt and *élan*', he stated in the *Sydney Morning Herald*, 'a style that encompasses simple visual story-telling, vast landscapes, dark history or pointed satire. One can trace through the descriptions, sagas and horrors the vital spirit of man himself.' James Gleeson enthused in the *Sun-Herald*,

> It is a tremendous perspective, yet when we have reached the final court and turned in mental retrospection, the whole body of work seems to take on the character of one vast symphony. It is unified, not only by the personal characteristics that impart a unique quality to everything he does, but by a constant recurrence and a continuous development of certain themes and motifs.

Elwyn Lynn in the *Bulletin* magazine referred to the impact of Nolan's colour, which had sometimes seemed eccentric in isolation, but became logical when viewed in this context. He related Nolan to 'pure painters like Watteau and Fragonard, when the medium was not the message'. Nolan's own final comment on the show was a lighthearted but prophetic remark that he was now looking forward to seeing a survey of half a century of his work in the retrospective that Melbourne might wish to mount to celebrate his seventieth birthday.

It continued to be a time for comment and celebration with many of Nolan's friends from former years rallying to pay their tributes. Elwyn Lynn's excellent book exploring themes and directions in his work, titled *Sidney Nolan: Myth and Imagery*, was published, together with a special edition of the magazine *Art and Australia* containing an appreciation by John Russell and a tribute by Maie Casey, together with essays on the student years by John Sinclair, the St Kilda period by Max Harris, John Reed's assessment of the Kelly paintings, Barrie Reid's Queensland reminiscences, George Johnston's recollection of the origins of the Gallipoli pictures, and articles on the Burke and Wills series by Geoffrey Dutton, Leda and the Swan by Charles Osborne, and Nolan's animals by Hal

Missingham. Published in September 1967, the magazine was a lavish symposium, illustrated with many paintings showing the multi-faceted aspects of the artist's achievements.

The artist himself was able to distance himself from the adulation and attention by being on location for the ABC film, becoming part of a team travelling to Mount Olga in the Centre, watching a bicycle race at Dimboola and taking part in a civic reception at the St Kilda Town Hall complete with brass band. In the Wimmera Nolan delivered a rather bitter monologue standing on a rocky ledge on Mount Arapiles, looking down to the salt lakes below. He was in an inexplicably sombre mood that day and reflected for the film that life was like standing with one's feet in vinegar. The wind was blowing a gale and affecting the microphone, but there was no chance of doing it again because of the strict financial restraints.

Cynthia's account of their long sojourn in the United States, *Open Negative*, appeared in Australia at the same time as the retrospective and was widely reviewed in the local press, most prominently by a friend, John Douglas Pringle in the *Sydney Morning Herald*. He began his critique of the book with the statement, 'Half of this book, which is the fifth Cynthia Nolan has published, is by far the best she has ever written. Unfortunately it is the second half — and some readers may never get to it.' The first part was devoted to an account of the extensive travels across the continent where Pringle thought she had found it impossible to portray her husband as a real person, remarking, 'He always sounds as if he is being interviewed by *Vogue*'. Although Pringle was highly complimentary about her account of incarceration in the New York T.B. ward, Cynthia was furious, deeply offended that anyone would think she did not understand her husband. She vowed never to talk to Pringle again and in spite of Nolan's offer to patch up their friendship she would not hear of it. But Nolan knew the review was correct in stating that Cynthia's portrayal of him was nowhere near as convincing as that of herself.

A small paragraph in the *Sydney Morning Herald* of 12 October reported under the heading 'Nolans leave for London',

> The artist Sydney (*sic*) Nolan and his wife left Kingsford Smith Airport last night by Qantas for London via Mexico. Mr Nolan had been in Australia for two months for his Retrospective Exhibition at the Sydney Art Gallery of N.S.W. and a tour of Central Australia. He gathered impressions which he will paint at his London studio during the English winter.

The past month had been the most eventful of Nolan's entire life, but it was a pleasing prospect to be returning to the real life of the artist, away from the showbusiness periphery.

197

CHAPTER ELEVEN

Paradise Garden

§

After the heady experiences surrounding the retrospective, Nolan's return to England saw him enter a long period of disenchantment with the commercial gallery scene. He felt he had lost touch with the art market and withdrew from it while he had the time and money to engage in several projects he was keen to develop. In Australia, however, the press was making him into a bigger personality than ever when Sydney dealer Barry Stern offered *Burke and Wills Leaving Melbourne* for sale at the unprecedented amount for an Australian painting of $35,000. It was not only the price that caught the attention of the general public; few readers of the *Sydney Morning Herald* of Saturday 27 April could have failed to miss the full-page advertisement and picture announcing the opportunity to acquire 'the greatest painting produced in Australia this century'. The results were immediate, with double the number of visitors to Stern's small gallery in the suburb of Paddington, and within the first couple of hours he had already sold twenty paintings from stock while people flocked to worship at the shrine of Nolan's expensive painting that had suddenly acquired the status of an icon. The dealer voiced suitably patriotic statements to defend what many regarded as a crass commercial stunt. 'I consider owning this painting', he said, 'is like owning Admiralty House so I would hate to see it going overseas'. He hoped a wealthy Australian corporation would buy it for presentation to the National Gallery in Canberra. Stern added a warning, 'But if it's not sold here I am free to do with it what I like because I have given first offer to the Australian public'. The dealer had owned Nolan's picture for the past five months, but since acquisition it had been travelling in the retrospective show.

The mass-circulation Sunday newspaper, the *Sun-Herald*, ran a prominent story capped by a photograph bearing the caption 'Sydney (*sic*) Nolan with his famous painting "Bourke (*sic*) and Wills Leaving Melbourne"'. It showed the unsmiling gallery owner standing in front of his goods for sale. The newspaper got it right the following week by printing an explanation which correctly identified Mr Stern and brushed up the spelling errors. That weekend a deal was

198

clinched with an anonymous buyer who, according to the gallery owner, had come forward as soon as the original advertisement appeared and was on the point of purchase on four occasions, but each time had hesitated 'because of the publicity'. Stern stated he was delighted the picture would now stay in Australia and claimed that if a buyer had not come forward, he had planned to present the picture to the nation — either for the National Gallery in Canberra or for the Sydney Opera House. The sale had the effect of releasing a flood of comment from art administrators, rival dealers and critics, particularly when the question of local prices was brought into focus with negotiations for the sale of *The Cricketers* by Russell Drysdale at a figure rumoured to be in the vicinity of $45,000.

Patrick McCaughey, the art critic of the *Age* newspaper, wrote, 'The prices of these Australian paintings are absolutely ridiculous in international terms. Melbourne can judge this for itself.' At the National Gallery of Victoria, the Felton Bequest acquisitions for 1968 were on display and included a Claude Lorrain landscape from 1637 and a full-size cast of Rodin's *Balzac*. McCaughey stated, 'It is not to decry the talents of either Nolan or Drysdale to say that the Claude and Rodin are incomparably greater in importance and value than either *The Cricketers* or the Burke and Wills painting. Claude and Rodin give us a glimpse into what major art really looks like and they make us realise why we continue to place value in the visual imagination.' The Claude Lorrain landscape had cost $37,650 and the Rodin in the vicinity of $30,000, which prompted McCaughey to fume, 'Granted the lunacies of the art market, it scales the heights of absurdity and borders on the frontiers of irresponsibility to suggest that Drysdale's *Cricketers* is of greater value than either of these works. It is a profligate provincialism that lets us believe this.'

Burke and Wills Leaving Melbourne originally had been acquired by the Adelaide dealer and collector Kym Bonython in exchange for a Central Australia landscape he loaned Nolan for his first British show at the Redfern Gallery in January 1951. The original transaction had been about £100 and Barry Stern bought it from Bonython some seventeen years later 'for considerably less than $35,000', according to the Adelaide collector. As a newspaper columnist commented, for a price that worked out at $1,750 a square foot, the picture must be the dearest bit of Masonite in Australia.

The extensive publicity surrounding Australian art prices flushed out another Nolan owned by an Italian businessman living in Japan, Signor F. Piacenti, who could hardly wait to send his Burke and Wills picture to Sydney for sale. The art manager of a leading firm of auctioneers confirmed at the end of May 1968 that this virtually unknown work showing the two explorers sitting on camels in a desolate landscape was for sale and an offer of $24,000 would secure it. There were no takers, however, and the picture was entered in the next auction along

Burke and Wills Leaving Melbourne, *1948*

with two Dobells, a Drysdale, four Arthur Boyds and a similar number of Norman Lindsay works. There were about 200 prospective buyers gathered for the occasion on 29 May when the auctioneer, Dick Wright, introduced the untitled Nolan and referred to recent publicity for another work in the same series by the artist. He then called for bids but the buyers gazed at the 35½ by 47 inch oil painting and remained silent. The painting was finally sold for $3,200 to a Mr O'Connor who said he had bought the Nolan for a private collector whose name could not be disclosed. Asked to comment on the price reported to have been paid for the other Nolan, he said, 'In my candid opinion that was inflated'. Concurrently with these art antics in Sydney, Nolan's latest exhibition, and his sixth in London, was selling briskly with small Australian landscapes at £500 each and paintings of coral going for £250. Barry Stern, questioned about the price disparity between the two Burke and Wills paintings, commented, 'The Nolan I sold brought ten times the amount of the untitled painting because it's thirty times better'.

Central Australia, *1983*

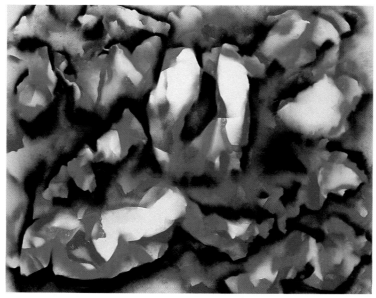

Abstract, *1986*

Self-portrait, *1986*

In between visits to the United States and Australia, Nolan began work on a huge project that would engage his thoughts and energies for nearly two years. It was to be a mural-like construction made up of hundreds of small panels depicting real and imaginary flowers that would combine to make a personal statement based on concepts he had been developing from his continuing fascination with the Mexican muralists. During his visit home in 1967 heavy rains in the desert areas had caused seeds that had been dormant for many years to germinate. This gave him the idea for a small series of wildflower paintings under the title of *Paradise Garden*. The project grew ever larger. Nolan carefully worked out the scale of what he had in mind and was not deterred at the prospect of dimensions extending to 150 feet in length and 20 feet in height, formed by 1,320 separate paintings each measuring 12 by 10 inches. These would be framed in sets of six to form columns of twenty-four complementary images. He realised it would be a long and expensive undertaking and unlikely ever to be a commercial proposition, but he felt committed to express himself in this way, where the small, individual components would combine to make a total statement. He got down to work in the studio at Putney using inorganic textile dyes to provide brilliant colour on heavy quality paper. A profusion of plant forms comprising leaves and stalks, buds and stamens, petals and anthers, gradually came together to form a decorative landscape where Nolan seemed to be manipulating nature and its colours into his own garden of earthly delights and despairs.

In September 1968 he flew to Canberra for a degree ceremony at the Australian National University where he was to receive an honorary doctorate of laws from the newly-installed chancellor, Dr H.C. Coombs, who was obviously satisfied with the institution's investment in its former arts fellow. The citation observed that Nolan was one of the few painters who had succeeded in 'imparting something of the real flavour of this strange continent'. He had abstracted its essence in paintings of the red desert, the drought-stricken countryside and dilapidated outback townships. He was 'an Australian who has been preoccupied with the landscape of this country and the place in it of man and beast'. Nolan said his honour was the first real step towards the recognition of the arts, using the term, he emphasised, not only in the form of painting. 'The new Melbourne Arts Centre and the Sydney Opera House are forms of art. They don't have to have anything inside to be recognised as works of art, although I have never seen so many people and children go through a place as I did last week in Melbourne.'

Kenneth Clark invited Nolan to accompany him on a visit to Amsterdam to attend one of the most important shows of the decade, the vast Rembrandt exhibition marking the 300th anniversary of the painter's death, which the art historian was to open. Nolan watched in admiration as Clark handled the

201

international audience, beginning in a disarming fashion by saying he was in the same position as a Dutchman going to England to talk to distinguished scholars about Shakespeare. The gambit worked so well that he held his audience from the start and proceeded to give a brilliant speech. Nolan later tagged along with a group of the world's leading Rembrandt experts on a tour of the exhibition and it soon became obvious that Clark knew more about the painter's work, especially the drawings, than most of them, although he remained diplomatically deferential to their opinions. The discussions ranged over the additions and alterations that the painter's work had suffered over the years and Nolan was fascinated to listen to discussions about the finer points of authenticity.

By contrast with former years, 1969 in Australia was a quiet one for Nolan with strenuous exhibiting efforts being maintained by his indefatigable mother. White-haired Dora had become an identity in her own right around the Brighton area where her son had once attended the technical school. Whenever a local cause needed help, she came to its aid with the family collection, which attracted large audiences who were prepared to pay handsomely to assist, for instance, the Brighton Historical Society's celebrations for the centenary of John Knox House. After the success of the show there, a reception was held in her honour which had to be limited to 70 people — although the organisers said that 500 wanted to attend the sherry party — before she left for England to stay with her son during the European summer. She was disappointed to miss the television screening of the documentary made almost two years before at the time of his retrospective, which was due to be shown at the beginning of June under its new title *This Dreaming, Spinning Thing*. She need not have worried because almost as soon as it was announced, the ABC deleted the film from its schedules in one of those mystifying behind-the-scenes sagas of disagreement, disenchantment and inevitable delay. Those who had seen the early versions in the cutting room were impressed with the photography and the eloquent way Nolan expressed himself, showing no signs of the larrikin nature that always seemed to play into the hands of his detractors. Whatever the reasons for delaying the film, its content was ageing rapidly so that when it was finally screened, all remnants of immediacy would be gone. It was hoped that the film would be taken from the racks and dusted off to coincide with Nolan's visit to Adelaide in October to accept one of three $10,000 Britannica Australia Awards for contributions to the arts, science and the humanities. But it was not shown until 6 January 1970 at 9.30 on a hot summer's evening when only a few art *aficionados* would have bothered to watch. The credits at the end were something of a roll call of departed colleagues. Storry Walton had left the ABC and was working in television in London, Allan Ashbolt's responsibilities were now exclusively with radio, and cameraman 'Stringy' Lowe, whose brilliant images caught everyone's attention, had turned freelance. Charmian Clift had

202

committed suicide six months before and George Johnston had only six months to live. It was a limp conclusion to a project that had started with such vigour. Nolan's luck in the world of art seemed unbounded but his record in film and television remained rather dismal.

The 1970 Adelaide Festival was one of the most exciting, with Sir Robert Helpmann at its helm. One of his biggest coups was signing the English Opera Group to perform, under the supervision of the composer himself, Benjamin Britten's church parables, *Curlew River*, *The Burning Fiery Furnace* and *The Prodigal Son*. Nolan and Cynthia were in Adelaide with Benjamin Britten and Peter Pears, who was performing in the operas, and they found the festival atmosphere rather like Aldeburgh with sunshine. Nolan's only commitment was the opening of his show of Wimmera paintings, which left plenty of time to spend with Britten.

One evening while walking back to their hotel after a performance of *Curlew River*, Britten started talking about his musical influences, revealing that, naturally enough, he had regarded Beethoven as one of the most phenomenal minds in the history of composition. In his late teens Britten had fallen completely under his spell but his feelings changed and he now thought of the music as the product of a deaf person with a disordered mind. Nolan found this attitude a shock coming from such an eminent composer and he said so, describing how he often played records of the late quartets when painting in the studio. Whatever the notes looked like on the score, Nolan said he was certain the music could not be the product of a deranged person. He was happier to hear Britten add that he thought he was now travelling on the same bus as Schubert, and Nolan thought to himself that walking under the trees along elegant North Terrace on a balmy night in the company of this man was not so far removed from a stroll on the Ringstrasse with Franz Schubert. Nolan found Britten a witty and straightforward person with an indefinable air of genius about him. He admired his grasp of English poetry, guided no doubt by W.H. Auden, which Britten set to music so beautifully. Britten pretended to have little visual sense, although he made some telling comments about art and responded instinctively to his friend's painting in a language devoid of jargon.

When the Nolans had been guests of Britten at Aldeburgh on several occasions in recent years, the two men had often discussed schemes they could develop together. There was an art gallery as part of the Maltings concert hall complex at Snape, the new focal point of the Aldeburgh Festival, and it was suggested that Nolan's paintings be displayed in one area, while another part of the exhibition space would be devoted to the composer's manuscripts. They agreed to embark on a systematic correspondence so that Nolan responded in paint to Britten's new compositions and the results would be shown together. It seemed an exciting prospect at the time, but they had not made a start on the work. While they were in Adelaide for the festival, Nolan took the opportunity of showing Britten some of the stark beauty of Central Australia, flying to Alice Springs where the composer was dismayed to see what had happened to the environment, but was enchanted by the grace and beauty of the young Aborigines.

There was a moment at Simpson's Gap, just out of the town, when he saw two youths silhouetted against the setting sun, framed by ghost gums in a golden glow. He turned to Nolan and remarked, 'Ah! the treasures there are on a boy's limbs', a line from the seventeenth-century metaphysical poet Henry Vaughan. They also went out to Mount Olga on their brief trip, walking along a remote track Nolan knew from a previous visit which led to an Aboriginal ceremonial site with a little rock pool that always contained water whatever the season. Britten stood surveying the idyllic scene, absorbing the spirit of the place, and finally breaking the silence with the comment 'Australia's soul has not yet spoken, Sidney. This great continent has not yet made a sound.' Nolan interpreted the remark to mean that he would do something about it.

Britten had, in fact, been commissioned by Covent Garden for a full-length ballet and this walk in the Australian bush gave him some ideas. On the return flight to Adelaide he told Nolan the story of a friend at Oxford who had hanged himself on his wedding morning. Britten said he regarded it as a tragic example of how people in Western society were often badly equipped to face the realities and pressures of life. He talked about his own upbringing, which had led to intense pain and soul-searching later. By contrast, Britten said how impressed he had been to learn about the initiation rites of the Aboriginal boys, which led to a total involvement in their traditions and to a harmony unknown to people of his generation. Britten wondered if there was a way of combining these two apparently disparate experiences to form the subject of a new ballet, which he would like Nolan to design. It was an exciting prospect to work in the theatre again and immediately Nolan began to imagine a snake as the unifying motif for both aspects of the story, a large symbolic creature based, perhaps, on Aboriginal art, to be made up of many smaller images rather in the way *Paradise Garden* was composed of more than a thousand small flower studies. One suggestion was for these designs to be flashed onto the stage during the action to fuse the contrasting Aboriginal and European elements of the story so that Oxford choristers and a tribal circumcision ceremony might merge at the climax when the young Englishman and his bride-to-be underwent the rites of fire, water and sexual initiation similar to that experienced by Tamino and Pamina towards the end of *The Magic Flute*. Britten was delighted with Nolan's enthusiastic response and they agreed to proceed with the work on returning to England.

After the festival the Nolans went to Melbourne where *Paradise Garden*, now assembled at the new National Gallery of Victoria, was part of the Captain Cook Bicentenary exhibition of Australian art to be opened by the Queen. The aim of the huge show was to give an historic overview of the nation's art and crafts, including costumes, silver, glass and furniture as well as painting and sculpture from both professionals and amateurs. Nolan was ushered into position beside his huge construction which took up an entire wall of one of the largest galleries. The tour of inspection began with the Queen, Prince Philip and Prince Charles discussing with Nolan his work, whose sheer size tended to relegate almost everything else in the show to a minor role. They talked about his infinite variations on a single theme, which seemed to vibrate with life, delicate and fragile as the Australian bush. It was impossible to see in the crowd the subtle composition sustained over the entire surface, with the central area of 768 little paintings in thirty-two columns, full of movement, colour and confidence. Closer examination of the individual forms and colour patterns revealed an impression of optimism and freshness at the beginning which changed at the end — a thousand images later — to reveal an air of studied caution, full of barriers against a hostile world. Whole flowers, nuts, bells, trumpets, leaves, stamens, pistils and anthers combined in this virtuoso piece to present a botanical front which masked a deeply-felt personal statement about Nolan himself and the nature of creativity.

Paradise Garden *installed at the National Gallery of Victoria, 1970 (News Ltd)*

Nolan thought *Paradise Garden* was his best large-scale achievement, but he was not sure about the Eureka mural now installed in the entrance of the Reserve Bank building. Nolan thought it was acceptable as a documentary statement on Eureka but it had not matched his desire for a major statement in the style of the Mexican muralists. Moreover the panels were difficult to light in their confined setting, and much of the colour was unable to be seen because of reflections from the copper.

During 1971 Nolan found the time and enthusiasm to pursue his writing by composing several 'notes for poems' to accompany a series of etchings on a Kelly theme. One of them read,

> Truth comes from the barrel of a gun said
> he, truth resides in the rope said the
> judge. Both were right and both are
> **dead, mixed in glory, shame and quicklime.**

Kelly *etching, 1971*

This pessimistic verse was attached to an etching titled *Carcass*:

> Screwed up by the sun, held together
> by maggots, dehorned and castrated anyway
> it stands like a rotting ship struck by lightning.

> The eye is a window to unmoving space, the
> brain inside defrauded. Any birthmarks
> are made by a whip.

> And yet nothing is forever, this universal
> victim will not be knocked, it was not
> mummified in the belief that God is a drover.

Many of Nolan's associations and preoccupations had been with writers and poets rather than painters and, with the completion of *Paradise Garden*, he decided to meet them on their own ground by publishing a collection of his verse. A de luxe volume was planned for 1971 in association with his collector friend and businessman Lord McAlpine, illustrated with plates from Nolan's luminous fantasy world of Australian wildflowers, together with added phallic imagery to counterpoint the obscure verse, most of it depressingly bitter and heavy with biographical content. It would be the first and only public exposure of the artist's sojourns with the Reeds. One of the poems, titled 'Cooked and Raw', included some revealing feelings about living at Heide in a *ménage à trois*:

> The basic story
> has been told before,
> loving in threes
> denies death's bruise,
> but war breaks out
> they break each other
> on the floor,
> and in a heavenly
> transcendental light
> they clear the dogs
> and do the flowers
> and eat each other
> cooked and raw.

'The Gardener's Wages' made reference to routine household duties and to Sunday Reed's domination:

> Dropping his spade
> he grew confused,
> the pollen on the stamens
> she explained
> grew in all of us,
> but once inside
> that bossy bower
> he found that
> flesh is paid for
> by the hour.

'Little Desert' is set in the Wimmera during the war after a visit from Sunday:

> Our eyes surfeit
> and cannot watch
> the evening destroyed,
> but the loyal wheat
> scents the little desert
> and the everlastings
> remain,
> longer than
> your dead bird arms
> waving falsely from the
> train.

'The Lawyer' provided a brief commentary on John Reed:

> He kissed his typist
> on his knee
> it broke his heart
> he took up art,
> it broke his heart again
> along with many other men.

For those without the key to these verses, the elegant bestiary of word and image published in *Paradise Garden* would remain an impenetrable thicket. Kenneth Clark pointed out that while the flowers were among the most attractive of Nolan's works, 'the poems they accompany are not so pleasant, and show perhaps what the Australian Rimbaud would have done if he had not discovered his extraordinary talent for painting'.

Benjamin Britten visited Nolan's studio in Putney to see the ballet designs which were now beginning to fill every inch of space in the way that *Paradise Garden* had grown and taken over. He inspected them for a while and then remarked, 'The strange thing, Sidney, is that they are so silent'. It was high praise from the composer and augured well for the realisation of their project. But soon afterwards Britten became chronically ill and the collaboration began to founder. With little hope of it continuing in its original form, there was a suggestion that Peter Maxwell Davies take over the score with Kenneth MacMillan creating the choreography. MacMillan thought the theme was too similar to *The Rite of Spring*, however, and he said he did not want to do another Aboriginal ballet.

Nolan ran into him in Hatchards bookshop in Piccadilly later and MacMillan indicated he would be interested to reconsider the proposal. But the moment had passed; Maxwell Davies had other commitments and Nolan was discussing a *Ring* cycle with Sir Georg Solti. There was always much talk in the uncertain world of opera and ballet, with high hopes but few proposals ever getting into production. The subject of Ned Kelly as an opera had been discussed for many years and the celebrated Italian composer Gian Carlo Menotti showed interest, but eventually declined a commission with the comment, 'You find me a horse that can sing, then I'll write you an opera'. When Peter Brook had suggested Nolan design a *Don Giovanni* for him, he thought his creative life might very well veer to the theatre. Before he committed himself to this, Nolan felt he should consult Kenneth Clark, who had a passion for music, particularly the works of Bach and Handel. His comments about the *Ring* were full of riddles and reminded Nolan of their first curious conversation in Sydney during 1949. 'In most circumstances I'd advise you not to do it, Sidney', he said. 'It would take such a lot of time out of your life. Painters are generally contemplative creatures and really shouldn't be exposed to the theatre. But in your case, being a man of action, it's probably all right.' Upon reflection, Nolan realised that Clark regarded him as some kind of showbusiness phenomenon as, of course, Clark himself had now become with his epic television series *Civilisation*.

None of the proposed stage designs materialised, however. Instead, Nolan accompanied Clark to Nuremberg for the great Dürer exhibition to celebrate the artist's birth there in 1471. Clark had been invited to make the opening address and when asked why he had declined what seemed to be a singular honour, he had replied, 'Because, Sidney, it is not wise to be associated with exhibitions when you know too much about the artist's weaknesses'. They walked around the vast show together, looking at the famous paintings brought from all parts of the world, then Clark led Nolan to a glass display stand containing Piero della Francesca's treatise on perspective, written in old age when his eyesight was fading, its cramped, spidery writing contrasting with the infinitely beautiful drawings. Clark waited a few moments for its effect to register, and then said, '*That*, Sidney, is the treasure in this room, and I will now leave you to examine it more carefully'. He merged with the large crowd, leaving little doubt in Nolan's mind as to why he had declined to open the exhibition. The della

Francesca book was a great human document which stood out from the surrounding art and Nolan felt that Clark's decision displayed art erudition of the highest order. Nolan decided that as soon as he returned to London he must go to the National Gallery and look with fresh eyes at the magnificent Piero della Francesca *Nativity*, because he imagined that seeing the work of a man in middle age, going blind, was rather like meeting the deaf Beethoven. To Kenneth Clark it was an unutterable tragedy that the *Nativity* was not to be followed by many more paintings, although della Francesca had lived long enough to produce this beautiful book on perspective. Nolan knew that Clark, like Plato, believed in an ideal state, and he saw in this peripheral exhibit in Nuremberg one of the finest examples of the adoration of ideal forms. This concentrated transmission of knowledge was one of the heady delights of their friendship.

An unexpected side of Clark's personality was revealed to Nolan during this visit to Germany with his impromptu performance in a crowded beer hall of a number of songs made famous by Sir Harry Lauder. This attracted a large wedding party from an adjacent table who brought their steins of lager and plates of Nuremberg sausage across to join in the fun. Clark later explained to a surprised Nolan that the great Scottish music hall comedian, most of whose songs he knew by heart, had been a close friend of his father.

While the Nolans and Patrick White were on opposite sides of the globe, they exchanged letters regularly, although those from England were invariably written by Cynthia because Nolan never seemed to have time. Initially, White regarded this as part of an inherent Irish charm. As the relationship had grown closer, he found he could have immensely enjoyable discussions with Cynthia, but it was a different matter with her husband. Secretly, the writer wondered how he managed to hold his own within a circle of eminent people such as C.P. Snow, Benjamin Britten and Kenneth Clark. He would then dismiss these suspicions, assuming that the painter must be aware of his own limitations. Whenever White and his companion Manoly Lascaris were in London Nolan saw to it that they were well looked after, often meeting them at the airport, driving them to their hotel and arranging visits into the country. Theatre tickets were purchased and they spent many evenings together at concerts, the opera and plays, including a memorable visit to a season of Samuel Beckett at the Royal Court Theatre. Nolan and White had many discussions about the Heide circle of the 1930s, especially Nolan's relationship with the Reeds, and for a while the author toyed with the theme as the basis for a new novel. On these visits, White watched the Nolans with a novelist's keen observation, noting every gesture when he was with them, listening to inflections, coming to the conclusion that without Cynthia and her will of iron, Nolan would have succumbed quickly to the flatteries of the art world and that his work, as worthwhile painting, would have collapsed. At the same time, Patrick White was full of admiration for Nolan's attention and devotion to his wife, particularly when she was in poor health. He realised that their relationship was interdependent, each relying on the other for support and encouragement; he with his painting and she with her writing. In spite of the apparent harmony of their marriage, however, White saw Cynthia as the dominant figure, more maternal than wifely because in his view Nolan needed a mother figure to look after him rather than a marriage partner.

Nolan's close association with prominent arts personalities gave him an insight into their characters and foibles which were often attractive, although occasionally perplexing. As he listened to more of Benjamin Britten's music Nolan thought he must have been influenced as a young composer by Stravinsky and he was sure he detected a return to Russian influences in the more recent works. The Nolans happened to be staying at Britten's home in Suffolk when Stravinsky's death was announced. It was the custom for the newspapers to be placed on a cabinet just outside the breakfast room so they could be picked up and read during the meal. Nolan was immersed in reading Stravinsky's obituary when Britten entered the room, noticed what he was doing and pointed to the newspaper report, remarking, 'Well, at least there won't be any more plagiarism now!' There was nothing that could be said in reply, but it set Nolan thinking about Britten's extraordinary capacity for the one-line dismissal that must conceal a reservoir of doubts and uncertainties.

It was another film project that took Nolan back to Australia in early 1972 where he would act as producer as well as the central subject of an ambitious documentary to be directed by a 29-year-old American named Stuart Cooper. Nolan had first met him in a London coffee shop where he listened to the young man's stories of working in the movies and particularly of acting in *The Dirty Dozen*. At this time Nolan was discussing with Norman Swallow at the BBC the possibility of a documentary and he hoped that Swallow himself, with a distinguished record in the business, might direct it. But now Nolan was presented with three possibilities: the production could be under the complete control of BBC Television, they could go into co-production with the artist, or Nolan could finance the entire project himself and sell it to the BBC for transmission, retaining all other rights for himself. Stuart Cooper had recently made a documentary about the Spanish artist Juan Genoves titled *A Test of Violence*, which won a gold medal at the Moscow Film Festival and attracted several other international awards. Nolan was impressed with the treatment and decided to have complete control of his own film, inviting Cooper to direct. This was agreed and they started working together on a shooting script and devising an itinerary for what would be titled *Kelly Country*. Nolan had been around the continent on so many occasions that he called this trip 'the milk run'. Cooper told the press that his treatment was going to be a 'vast magical mystery tour' through Australia, merging from landscape to Nolan's paintings and back again. 'There will be none of the usual scenes of a painter strolling round in front of a canvas', he explained. 'Nolan will probably be seen very little in front of the camera. His paintings will speak for him.' Cooper had some definite ideas about the style of his film, 'I intend to lay off narration. The sound-track will be original music, I think, possibly some electronic stuff as well, to tie in with the lunar landscapes.' He hoped to re-enact Ned Kelly sequences, mixing them with Nolan's own 'canvases'.

A film crew of three, together with Nolan and Cynthia, began a 10,000 mile expedition around Australia, setting out on 1 March and spending a few days at each location, shooting much more film than would be necessary. Nolan had at the back of his mind the idea that there would be enough material for a second production if the crew used twice as much stock. It was the same kind of logic he had employed five years earlier with the ABC and, of course, it failed. 'We shot good and hard', he said, 'but had to abandon the idea of the other film'. One of the most impressive locations was at Mount Tom Price, in the Hamersley Ranges of Western Australia, where the discovery of vast reserves of iron ore contributed to the Australian minerals boom of the late 1960s. Nolan was interested in the conditions faced by the construction gangs and miners who worked in extremely demanding surroundings. They reminded him of the Antarctic personnel because both sets of workers inhabited a lethal landscape where man was an intruder, the only difference between the two being the danger of either freezing to death or dying of dehydration. In the Pilbara region of the Hamersley Ranges the men had been stretched almost to the limits of their endurance building a railway line from the open cut mines to the coast through a desert wilderness. Nolan was fascinated by many of the faces, ravaged and tormented, expressing a kind of unspoken violence that matched the environment, but which if taken out of that context would seem frightening. These sequences were valuable for the documentary, but there was also material here for a series of paintings which he would work on later.

After the long haul from Western Australia to Alice Springs, through the Western District of Victoria, then to Melbourne, the Kelly country of north-east Victoria, and Fraser Island off the Queensland coast, the group completed their schedule at the penal colony of Port Arthur in southern Tasmania. By now tempers were getting frayed because the poor weather was hindering the filming. The previous week they had caught the tail-end of a tropical cyclone on Fraser Island, resulting in Cynthia catching influenza and causing production delays because of the rain, which had followed them all the way to Tasmania. Nolan decided he wanted no publicity for his film until it was completed and, although the team travelled to each of the major cities, surprisingly little notice was taken of their presence, partly because all the travel and accommodation reservations were made in Cooper's name. Philip Cornford made the journey to the Four Seasons Motel at Port Arthur for the *Australian*, arriving there with mists swirling low over the rain-sodden ground, to be greeted by Stuart Cooper emerging from the Nolans' unit, shaking his head in dismay and muttering, 'It's tense. It's very tense in there. They're very upset. Cynthia has got out of bed and insists on coming along today to guard him.' He was sympathetic to Cornford's desire for a story but could not co-operate or allow any pictures. 'Sid's got this thing about publicity on the job', he explained. 'He doesn't want a word mentioned until it's ready to show. *I* can't see any harm but, for God's sake, we can't finish without him. What he says has to go.' The six-week shoot ended with expenses exceeding the budget and they returned to London for the editing and general post-production to complete the documentary in time for its scheduled screening on the BBC in November. In spite of Cooper's insistence that there would be no dialogue, it soon became obvious there were advantages in having a commentary, and who better to provide this than the doyen of narrators, Orson Welles? Nolan admired him immensely and, in spite of the cost, relished the thought of engaging the man who had created *Citizen Kane*.

A fee was negotiated with Welles' agent and, remembering he had read somewhere that the actor enjoyed painting, Nolan took along two small pictures to the recording session with the intention of presenting one of them as a gift. Welles turned up looking even larger in real life than on the screen and not as young as Nolan had imagined. He responded genially to Nolan's offer of one of his paintings and took both. The session went smoothly with Welles also narrating a shorter film intended to accompany an exhibition at the next Adelaide Festival, where a new series of paintings on the Ern Malley theme was to be exhibited along with *Paradise Garden*. McAuley and Stewart's mock verses received their most distinguished interpretation and Welles also recorded some of Nolan's own 'doggerel', as the artist called it, from the *Paradise Garden* collection.

Kelly Country was coming together well. Cooper incorporated some visual effects based on optical experiments being carried out by two colleagues at the BBC. It seemed exciting to give the appearance of paintings merging with real-life scenes by bending and stretching the images, Dali-like. Used in moderation the results could be fascinating, but if overdone the excesses soon turned into clichés. Nolan admitted that they went 'into the deep end' with the visuals and the music. It had been decided that the film needed nothing less than Wagner conducted by Herbert von Karajan. The rights to use these recordings from Deutscher Grammophon were almost prohibitively expensive, but they wanted them and paid accordingly. The music worked most effectively as accompaniment to a train journey across the flat wheatfields of the Wimmera, but it became a near disaster when Siegfried's Funeral Music was played in the scenes where the great Central Australian monolith, Ayers Rock, was superimposed with whirling and bending carcass paintings. The BBC screened *Kelly Country* and Norman Swallow's comment to Nolan was 'Better luck next time, Sidney. You should have let us make it!'

After a lengthy absence from the London exhibiting scene, Nolan returned at the end of 1972 as a multi-media personality. The second of his great decorative constructions, *Snake*, was given wide attention when the work — 150 feet long and 19 feet high — was installed in the huge Studio 1 at the BBC's Television Centre to become part of the arts programme *Open House*. The 1,620 small pictures made up of Aboriginal motifs took studio technicians eleven hours to get into place and light, making it an expensive set as background for an interview with its creator, who afterwards answered questions from the studio audience. The work provided some spectacular angles on the screen with the lighter elements of Nolan's variations on an Aboriginal theme forming themselves into a snake-like arabesque across its entire surface. The following night, *Kelly Country* was shown and two days later Nolan's first exhibition in London for four years opened at Marlborough Fine Art in Bond Street, while the Tate Gallery was displaying *Paradise Garden*, which the historian Stephen Runciman saw for the first time and thought the nearest thing to the decoration of a medieval eastern European palace he had ever seen. The London art world was not so kind about the Marlborough show which presented a mixed offering of New Guinea paintings, illustrations for Lowell's *Near the Ocean*, six large painted panels titled *Troy — Dragging of Hector*, and a group of miners' heads deriving from the film visit to Mount Tom Price. In these most recent works Nolan had attempted to depict the men as a human response to extreme conditions. But once again it was an aspect of life unfamiliar to the British and he was accused of distorting the faces in a bizarre and unacceptable way. Nolan insisted that what he saw was what he painted; those miners in Australia were responding to an environment as the wild animals reacted to theirs in Africa. In the catalogue introduction Robert Melville likened the men to the damned who passed through the bodies of medieval devils and emerged as a kind of excrement.

> Yet they are individualists to a man, and they have congregated in hell for the high pay, and Nolan's portraits of them give him the right to echo some lines from Robert Lowell's translation of Dante's *Inferno* Canto V 'I fix my eyes with such intensity on his crusty face that its disfigurement could not prevent my recognising who he was'.

The Marlborough exhibition brought out the critics in force, with Nigel Gosling in the *Observer* describing Nolan as 'an English eccentric outside the

New Guinea, *1966*

mainstream of art'. His review stated, 'He appears to have been around London so long it is surprising to see it is only fifteen years since he descended on us with his obsessive visions of the Australian outcast Ned Kelly'. Gosling stated that since then Nolan had become something of a phantom figure: 'His original myths having been mined to the point of exhaustion, he tackled new ones but never with the same thread of inspiration running through even the smallest drawing'. A small section of *Snake* was shown in the Marlborough exhibition — some 200 individual images — and Gosling thought that the panels were 'vividly alive, and the whole conception adds up to a decoration which would look fine in any big space'. Edward Lucie-Smith, writing for the *Sunday Times*, was more pointed, admiring the enormous energy required to produce such a large-scale work, but remarking that 'the end product looks dismayingly like the foyer decoration of a smart new hotel'.

This burst of attention received by Nolan in Britain was echoed at the other end of his art axis when, on the same day, the two morning newspapers in Sydney carried separate stories of his activities. The *Sydney Morning Herald* ran a report of critical reaction to the Marlborough show under the heading 'Faint British praise damns Nolan works', while the *Daily Telegraph* gave news of *Dog and Duck Hotel,* one of the Queensland outback series, being sold for an Australian record of $60,000, easily exceeding the previous highest price for a local work of $45,000 for Russell Drysdale's *The Cricketers.* Nolan's painting was sold by the Sydney collector Mervyn Horton through the Southern Cross Galleries and Sweeney Reed in Melbourne to the wealthy British collector Alistair McAlpine, who previously had attempted to acquire the original Kelly series from the Reeds, causing concern in art circles that an essential part of Australian culture might be lost overseas. It was reported at the end of November, a few days before the other sale, that McAlpine had offered $500,000 for the Kelly series without creating a ripple of response from the Reeds. It was said he went as high as $800,000 but John Reed stated categorically that the series was not for sale. These fiscal skirmishes, however, generated discussion about the future of the paintings because the Reeds were getting old — John was now 72 and Sunday 67 — and it was disclosed that they probably would sell or bequeath them to the Australian National Gallery in Canberra, which had a growing collection but no gallery space, as a new building was still on the drawing boards. One thing was made perfectly clear, the National Gallery of Victoria would not be considered as a home for Ned Kelly and his painted exploits because of a long history of argument between its successive directors and John Reed. This was confirmed by the Reed's adopted son, Sweeney, who was an art dealer: 'The Victorian Gallery will definitely not get the paintings', he declared.

Over on the other side of the continent, Nolan had intended to present a group of sixty-four panels of wildflower pictures to the Western Australian Art Gallery in Perth, but his act of benefaction became a long-running scandal when the wife of the museum's director, who was both a flower painter and an art critic for a local newspaper, was unduly critical when they were exhibited in the city's leading commercial gallery run by Rose Skinner, who had been Nolan's representative for many years. She had an unerring eye for good paintings and was so incensed by the review that she vowed not to make a bequest of her own extensive private collection to the State art gallery, as previously intended, presenting it instead to the university. Nolan then offered the panels, totalling 384 pictures, to the Perth Concert Hall on the basis that he would receive some recompense for the cost of the frames, which in their heavy brass construction had been extremely expensive and, as he joked, helped set up the manufacturer in a nice five-bedroom house in England. When news of the proposal to pay Nolan $50,000 for the frames was made public it resulted in letters to the newspapers suggesting this was a confidence trick by an opportunist from the eastern States. The works went on display for three months in the Concert Hall,

216

but they were indifferently mounted and rather badly lit, so reactions were unfavourable. Nolan's mind was made up about the gift, valued at $640,000, after he was invited to see the mayor to discuss the possible benefaction. He said to him, 'Well, you're an honest man, Mr Nolan', and then added after a pause, 'At least you've expressed yourself like one'. Nolan felt his motives and honesty were being questioned and this violated the basic tenets of his upbringing. In the end the Perth City Council turned down the artist's offer and although he had second thoughts and subsequently offered a free permanent loan, that was rejected because of concern about possible legal complications.

The Kelly series, central to Nolan's career, would not be part of the largest exhibition of his work to be shown during the early summer of 1973 in Dublin, although *Paradise Garden* would. The impetus for the show came from the Australian ambassador Keith Brennan. His surname suggested an Irish heritage, and he had received his education at St Patrick's College in East Melbourne before becoming an associate to Mr Justice Evatt at the High Court of Australia. Nolan regarded him as a profound believer in Australia who, like himself, also had a strong commitment to Ireland.

Funding for the exhibition came from the Australian Department of Foreign Affairs and almost the entire year's budget of the Irish Arts Council. A considerable sum was needed because the show was to be housed in the Royal Dublin Society's vast premises at Ballsbridge, famous as the venue for the Royal Dublin Horse Show. Nolan had visited a couple of exhibitions there and was impressed by the elegance of the Georgian building, which was capable of being transformed into a splendid gallery, with plenty of natural light streaming down from windows high above. It was planned to hang gauze around the walls and construct partitions to give a more intimate atmosphere to the open spaces. An anonymous donor contributed £10,000 towards the considerable costs. Nolan heard he was a successful Australian mining man who owned racehorses in Ireland, but the funds came through Ambassador Brennan on the understanding that their source would remain undisclosed to everyone, including the artist.

Because of the generous space, the three huge constructions, comprising 4,260 separate images, could be exhibited for the first time together under the collective title of *Oceania*: *Paradise Garden*, *Snake* and the previously unseen *Shark*. Special scaffolding was designed to hang the many hundreds of individual brass frames that made up these works and a squad of university students armed with forklift trucks was marshalled to assemble them. The Irish prime minister, Mr Liam Cosgrave, agreed to open the retrospective and Kenneth Clark would make an introductory speech.

In the meantime, five unknown Nolan paintings that had been gathering dust in a Sydney storeroom for fifteen years had been taken out and entered in a Christie's auction in Melbourne to take advantage of the high prices the artist's

217

work was reported to be bringing, following the astronomical offer for the Kelly series and the sale of *Dog and Duck Hotel*. The story read like a major archaeological discovery because these unknown Nolans, each approximately 28 by 36 inches and painted on Masonite, had been exchanged by Nolan in 1956 for a Qantas round-the-world air ticket, then worth about $1,200. Nobody could remember details of the arrangement but it was thought that the paintings were meant to be reproduced as illustrations for a calendar. As the works were expected to bring a total of about $24,000, some thought the airline had put economic considerations where its artistic nationalism used to be. The five signed paintings — *Tower Bridge, London; Temple of Dawn, Bangkok; Jain Temple, Calcutta; Colosseum, Rome* and *Golden Horn, Istanbul* went on sale and reflected the fickleness of the market by reaching only $12,800 in total. The auctioneer commented it was lucky they had been sold at all because 'Sidney Nolan is a very overrated painter'.

Back in Dublin, the Australian Foreign Affairs Department and the Irish Arts Council had reached a very Irish solution to guard their investment in the Nolan retrospective by charging 20 pence admission to ensure that there would be a good public response. An official explanation was 'We had to charge something, otherwise people would think it was not worth going to see'. The huge throng who turned up for the opening on 18 June 1973 was dazzled by the sight of the three great panels surrounded by the brilliant imagery of nearly thirty years of sustained work. St Patrick may have banished snakes from this land, but here before their eyes was a 150-foot serpent stretched magically across an escarpment of paintings. Ambassador Brennan read out a message from the Australian prime minister, Gough Whitlam, then Kenneth Clark delivered his speech. Much of it was based on material used in the Thames and Hudson monograph published twelve years before and it seemed to go down well with the audience, although a few Australians present, including Peter Bellew who had flown over from Paris, thought Clark was being excessive in talking about two revolutionary heroes, Ned Kelly and Che Guevara, in the same breath. Conor Cruise O'Brien was also seen to raise an eyebrow at this reference.

Clark continued, 'The fact is that Sidney Nolan is a genius and a genius cannot do what he wants, still less what his admirers want him to do. He is under orders ...' Nolan squirmed with embarrassment as Clark proceeded to pour out compliments. '... Genius comes from somewhere else. Of course, then there is a confluence of visible experience and personal experience. All Sidney Nolan's work is to some extent autobiography. But what dictates that confluence, what makes the confluence happen, comes from somewhere else.' The speech was getting rather long and the building, which was not equipped for displaying art at night, became darker as the sun set, while Clark continued in the clipped delivery that had become almost a caricature of himself since *Civil-*

From left, Nolan, Lady Clark and Ambassador Brennan at the Dublin retrospective, 1973

isation: '... and since I have used the word "disturbing" I will add that Sidney Nolan's painting is and always has been essentially disturbing. He is not simply a rebel, that is something we can all share and rather enjoy sharing. He sees very deep into the recesses of the mind and he finds there is a feeling of menace.' Clark's lengthy monologue came to an abrupt end when a loud Irish voice suggested he shut up. There was absolute silence in the hall as Clark responded to the interjector then abandoned his prepared text and concluded, 'Leaving art aside, you are standing in the midst of a phenomenon about which I will say no more because, quite obviously, you could all say it better than I'.

Nolan was dazed by Clark's words and thrilled by the sight of his three large panelled constructions, realising on seeing them together for the first, and perhaps the only, time that he had paid his debt to the Mexican muralists. The Dublin retrospective proved to be a great summertime attraction for local art lovers and students, together with many visitors from the United States, Britain and Australia during its three week run.

When it was announced that Patrick White would receive the 1973 Nobel Prize for Literature it was after a long vetting by the Swedish Academy, not because of any doubts about the Australian author's stature as a writer, but because of his apparent indifference to the honour. White recoiled at what he regarded as the excessive attentions of press, radio and television, most of which wanted only superficial headline stories. He resented this intrusion into his life after many years as a reclusive professional writer and realised that after the prize, life would never be quite the same again. When the distinguished Argentine writer, Jorge Luis Borges, who might have been considered a leading contender, was asked what he thought about an Australian winning the prize, his succinct reply was, 'There are no Australian writers!' Patrick White, in fact, had long regarded the award as a rather debased literary honour, although he accepted that there was national prestige associated with it. He decided to accept the prize and turn the $80,000 cash award into a foundation to assist fellow Australian writers, although he could not face the prospect of a long journey to wintry Sweden to accept it. He had the idea of asking the Nolans to represent him, thinking that his painter friend might enjoy donning white tie and tails to be part of the glittering ceremony under the Stockholm chandeliers, and Nolan readily agreed, although he became extremely nervous as his moment approached, finding it far more daunting than the opening of a major new exhibition or even his first retrospective. He had to resort to some unaccustomed alcohol to steady his nerves as he stood and waited to accept the award from King Carl Gustav XVI. The citation described Patrick White as 'a bold psychological explorer' and paid tribute to his contribution to 'an important body of Australian literature', including the writings of Henry Lawson and Henry Handel Richardson. Cynthia sat in the audience sharing her husband's tensions of the moment, delighted that her good friend and fellow writer was receiving the highest honour for literature. She knew that much of what was being said about Patrick's use of language to define a national character applied equally well to Sidney's interpretations of Australia in his paintings. 'For all his originality', the citation continued, 'there is no denying that the work of Patrick White displays certain typical features of Australian life in general, sharing with it the background, natural history and ways of life of the country'.

Cynthia had just received a review of Nolan's latest exhibition at the David Jones Gallery in Sydney where four huge tapestries woven in Portugal from the original Kelly series and twelve oil paintings from the 1972 Miners series were on show. Kenneth Clark previously had described the miners' heads as amongst the most moving of Nolan's works, 'the ultimate expression — so far — of the stoic defiance of a cruel and miserable existence that men and animals share'. The review by John Henshaw in the Sydney *Sun* was complimentary about the tapestries, noting that the increase in scale amplified their emotional impact to a monumental degree. He was not so favourably inclined towards the miners, while admitting that Nolan had grasped the aggressive physical presence of the men who, to quote Robert Melville's catalogue introduction, 'live in a squalor of work, drink and copulation'. As Cynthia watched Sidney stiffly receive the award from the Swedish king, hoping he would not drop it in his nervousness, she wondered, as only an Australian expatriate could, what future there could be in the face of continuing attitudes such as Henshaw's, for herself, her husband

Nolan accepts the 1973 Nobel Prize for Literature on behalf of Patrick White from King Carl Gustav XVI

or even Patrick White after his moment of supreme recognition.

Nolan's main painting activity during the previous couple of years, well away from the glare of publicity in his Putney studio, had been preparing a large show for the 1974 Adelaide Festival where the major official exhibition was to be 'Ern Malley and Paradise Garden', two apparently different themes, although closely linked in Nolan's mind because much of their emotional content referred to his days at Heide. The Ern Malley paintings covered several rooms of the State Art Gallery, starting with a 1944—47 group of portraits of his circle of friends and colleagues from the *Angry Penguins* period, including Max Harris, Albert Tucker, John and Sunday Reed, and two self-portraits characterised by enormous searching blue eyes. The exhibition contained a variety of other works; two from 1944 and others from 1964—66, which Nolan felt related to some of the lines in the Ern Malley verses. The third and fourth rooms contained Nolan's latest paintings and drawings embracing a maze of images unlike anything he had done before; an intimate cartoon-like statement full of references to sexual passion and tenderness, hate and disillusion. All were suggested by the Ern Malley poems and many of the drawings had a verse or line inscribed on them. Max Harris pointed out that this imagery held a code which had to be cracked if the exhibition were to make sense to the viewer. In the midst of graffiti depicting Kelly and Mrs Fraser, Anzacs, snakes and elephants, was another chapter of the artist's biography. Genitals were in abundance with Ern Malley sporting in one image testicles for epaulettes and a penis in place of an amputated arm.

221

From the Ern Malley series, Dürer: Innsbruck, 1495 *(left), and* Portrait of Ern Malley *(right)*

Nolan regarded this exhibition as one of his best; it was large and he had taken an inordinate amount of trouble to make a reasoned analysis of the Ern Malley story. However, the Australian poet Peter Porter, who was also a guest at the festival, was openly critical of Nolan's use of such myths as the basis of a painting series. Porter suggested that the use of material such as Malley, Burke and Wills and Kelly was the wrong way for a painter to approach twentieth century painting. It was, as Nolan interpreted the criticism, 'Trying to ride in on the back of Ned Kelly's horse'. He had become tired of defending himself by repeating that he *was* part of the *Angry Penguins* group, he *did* travel over much of the route of the ill-fated explorers, and his grandfather *had* pursued the Kelly gang. Furthermore, he found the Australian outlaw a very interesting character. But it appeared from many people's opinions that nothing could atone for his apparent indiscretion in committing the Kelly story to paint. Nolan had long admitted that the act of painting was complex and difficult to follow in rational terms. He pointed to Picasso, who had evolved other forms from the original concept of Cubism, often reversing the initial approach, apparently destroying the purity of the style he and his colleagues had initiated. They chopped into their own creations, but Nolan accepted this was their privilege. He grew to feel the same about Kelly after hearing so often the clichéd comment, 'Nolan has never painted anything since Ned Kelly and never will'. He said with feeling, 'They didn't allow me the possibility that I did them as a continuing expression of myself and my circumstances. All lives and all works of art have hidden sub-plots and mysterious other reasons for their being, although that's probably a failed film-maker's view of life — looking for the plot.'

Although Nolan usually refused to express publicly his political thoughts and sympathies, he made an exception in 1972 when Gough Whitlam swept the Labor party into power for the first time in twenty-three years and his broad vision eagerly embraced the arts as an integral component of life. Like many Australians, Nolan regarded the new regime as the beginning of a golden age. 'For the first time in my life', he said, 'the potential of Australian artists seems to fit the great Australian dream'. Whitlam came as a breath of fresh air, dispersing the cobwebs of the conservative coalition's long reign. Nolan had always resented Robert Menzies' rigid attitudes in the late 1930s and early 1940s when he was attempting to form an academy of art. Nolan's father had once made him promise never to shake Menzies' hand because he could not approve of a style of government that appeared unsympathetic to the working classes. 'Never shake the bastard's hand whatever you do', was the request and his son agreed. Years later Nolan was invited to a parliamentary gathering in London at which Menzies was present. He caught sight of the painter in the crowd, recognising him from press photographs, and, thrusting out his hand, approached him with the greeting, 'So you're the one who's the famous Mr Nolan!' There was no alternative but to shake hands and Nolan knew he had failed his father at that moment. He could have kept quiet about it, but there were photographers and journalists from the Australian press present and their meeting might be reported in Melbourne. The next time he returned home, Nolan bought his father a pair of field glasses on the stopover in Singapore as a gift to soften the blow of his impending admission. 'Pop, I've got a confession to make', he said when they met. 'I was cornered at Westminster the other day and, well ... I couldn't avoid shaking Bob Menzies' hand'. There was a pause while his father unwrapped the present and then, without looking up, replied offhandedly, 'Well, son, he hasn't done so badly by us senior citizens, so I wouldn't worry too much about that'. Nolan suddenly felt ashamed of his father and himself.

Gough Whitlam opened Nolan's Adelaide Festival exhibition with his usual style and wit, and the artist, feeling a little euphoric, promptly donated all the paintings to the Art Gallery of South Australia. Nolan had already offered Whitlam a selection of early works owned by himself and Cynthia if a suitable place could be found to exhibit them. They had just been to visit an old homestead, Lanyon, on the Murrumbidgee River some fifteen miles south of Canberra, which had been acquired by the federal government in 1971 with the intention of preserving the 1858 building and its surrounding property as a fine example of nineteenth-century rural architecture and farm layout. It was tucked away in the rolling blue hills at the gateway to the Australian Alps and Nolan thought the homestead would make an ideal gallery for the paintings. The property's attractions had not escaped the attentions of Lionel Murphy, the federal attorney-general, who envisaged Lanyon becoming an official residence. Gough Whitlam would need to claim a significant alternative use for the property to avoid this happening and he was able to assure Nolan at the Adelaide opening, 'Don't worry about Lanyon, Sid, it will be all right'.

A couple of months later it was announced that Sidney Nolan and his wife would give the Australian government paintings from their personal collection conservatively valued at more than a million dollars. In making the statement, the Minister for the Capital Territory, Gordon Bryant, confirmed that the historic Lanyon homestead would house a permanent exhibition including some of the artist's 'middle bushranger period'. This generous gift brought extensive publicity in the newspapers, with the *Australian* making the best assessment of its impact. In an editorial on 19 May 1974 headed 'Gift of genius', the writer observed that many expatriates were now returning home to participate in a boom in arts and literature that would have seemed impossible a few years before. 'Even if we cannot welcome Sid Nolan home, his paintings are now to be an integral part of the nation's capital. What's more, they will be seen in a building which a few years ago, under a different environmental climate, might well have been bulldozed.'

The same newspaper accepted a full-page advertisement from a Sydney commercial gallery capitalising on the Nolan publicity at a time when the value of traditional investments was depressed. Under the bold heading 'The New Currency' the advertisement stated, 'National share markets slumped to their worst day last week, but we sold our complete collection of NOLAN'S [sic] — ($18,000) in one afternoon. Exchange your portfolio, and reinvest in The New Currency the Australian Art Boom, internationally recognised, and currently soaring.' No wonder fellow painters sometimes regarded Nolan with suspicion.

On his return to England Nolan set about selecting the paintings for Lanyon, choosing sixteen early Kellys, two of his best St Kilda pictures, the idiosyncratic *Woman and Tent* from 1946, *Death of Captain Fraser* from the Mrs Fraser series, a Burke and Wills subject, a Central Australian landscape and a couple of 1953 carcass works. There were twenty-four paintings in this first batch which Prime Minister Whitlam agreed to take home with him on his aircraft after an official visit to several European countries. He welcomed Nolan's gift, saying it would 'add immeasurably to the artistic heritage of the nation, whose reputation he has done so much to enhance and whose landscape and distinctive tradition of folklore and mythology he has unforgettably preserved in his art'. The artist, now almost 58, had given away more pictures than any other benefactor in the country's history and during the heady atmosphere of the early Whitlam years, his motives went unquestioned, at least publicly, with the paintings accepted in a spirit of altruistic nationalism. Nolan knew there was a kind of immortality to be won from his action, providing the works remained on display, there were no leaks in the gallery roof and the quality of the paintings was high enough to retain the public's interest. A large body of his output was already scattered around the world in private and public collections and, having made enough money to feed and house himself, he felt it was best to present the work to the widest audience, as in a forthcoming retrospective for Stockholm. Immortality did not come cheaply, however, and Nolan complained to Cynthia, 'You know, I don't get a penny out of all this; in fact, it costs me for time and materials, framing and freight'. As a professional painter he received no financial benefits from benefaction in the way of tax credit.

Another problem soon became apparent: the donations appeared to be out of all proportion to his real financial standing because the figures put on his work in the press were often highly inflated and were, in reality, just paper values. It was perhaps inevitable that after the overwhelming public praise for his generosity, carping criticism should start to be heard, reflecting an attitude deeply entrenched in the Australian psyche. The visual arts in Australia traditionally had been stunted by a dearth of generous benefaction because of a community impression that giving things away with no strings attached must be something of a confidence trick. A typical reaction to the celebrated art collections in so many American cities, based on a long tradition of gifts, was that they had been engineered to salve the consciences of robber barons who openly cheated both their workers and the State.

The awareness of these attitudes, together with growing tensions in his private life, contributed to an air of restlessness and disillusionment when Nolan arrived in Australia in March 1975 for the first exhibition at Lanyon. He told a news conference in Canberra that his days of hustling to sell a painting were over and that he could not give a hoot whether he sold another one or not. 'I think it was Picasso who said you can only eat three meals a day. I'm happy to live a simple life, to be happily married and to stay at home listening to records.' He added, 'Art appreciation is like happiness, it either comes along or it doesn't'. As so often happened, Nolan's words would prove to be prophetic.

CHAPTER TWELVE

Decline and Flaws

§

The approach of Nolan's sixtieth birthday had few of the big events associated with his fortieth and fiftieth anniversaries. There were to be selling exhibitions in Australia, an honorary doctorate from Sydney University, and a co-production television film was planned under the predictable title *Nolan at Sixty*. Now in her early sixties, Cynthia was finding life at Putney increasingly claustrophobic and even her beloved garden began to lose its appeal. She suggested they look for an apartment in central London and, although Nolan was quite happy to remain by the river, he agreed to consider a move, knowing he could reorganise his working life around a large picture store and studio he had established in Fulham. He suspected, however, that his wife was in the process, consciously or unconsciously, of dissolving their relationship, and moving from Putney was the first step. They heard of an attractive proposition at Whitehall Court, a splendid late Victorian building of town apartments, situated between Scotland Yard and the Ministry of Defence on the Embankment at Westminster. The available apartment, which overlooked the river, was within walking distance of the West End theatres and galleries as well as the South Bank arts complex, and the Nolans planned to move in as soon as renovations were complete. Nolan had looked at the terms of the contract being prepared for the long lease and as they seemed to place him in an ambiguous situation for future possession if anything happened to Cynthia, he suggested some changes to his solicitors.

Nolan's next London exhibition was to be a group of twenty-five paintings in a common format called Notes for Oedipus, which had been done at a time when his mind was in turmoil as a result of increasing domestic tensions. This was reflected in the paintings themselves, although it might not be obvious to others because, as Kenneth Clark had noted years earlier, much of his work displayed a sense of menace and disturbance. With the series, Nolan had deliberately set out to nullify opinions for and against his reputation. When Robert Lowell first saw the paintings his comment was, 'Twenty-five posters for the stages of the Passion', which made the painter think of the use of 'posters' in this respect; it was a typical Lowell remark. During the opening at Marlborough Fine Art, the painter Lucien Freud, who had obviously interpreted the imagery as an attack on his celebrated relative, passed Nolan a note which read, 'Lay off my grandfather'. Nolan had no such intentions, although he had read extensively about psycho-analysis, particularly in relation to Cynthia's mental state. She had dedicated her early life to being a psychiatric nurse and even after she ceased to practise professionally, remained close to the subject and its principles, which continued to rule her life. Nolan thought he could link some of her behavioural patterns with those of their close friends, Benjamin Britten, Robert Lowell and Kenneth Clark because, like them, Cynthia had suffered an unhappy childhood. Hers was dominated by a martinet of a father, who rarely spoke with kindness in a family that became rich nomadic pastoralists, moving from one Tasmanian sheep station to another. Some of this story was told in her book, *Daddy Sowed a Wind*, published by Shakespeare Head in 1947. Nolan had studied it carefully, page by page, seeking clues to her character, and joked that her father had indeed sowed a wind and as a result reaped a whirlwind. With a brilliant razor-sharp mind, her striking beauty and vivaciousness combined with the love of flowers and a joy of life, Nolan thought it a tragedy that such a gifted creature should be so affected by childhood experiences, although he found it hard to accept the view that difficult upbringings should lead inevitably to disastrous lives. Cynthia's problem, as he saw it, was being in love with the world but not with mankind.

Although their relationship was increasingly tense, they were inextricably bound by admiration for each other's work. She had always been his strength during energetic bouts of painting when he had to be shielded from external pressures, and Nolan was constantly supportive of her writing. But now she became preoccupied with her mother's origins, about which she had known almost nothing in a home atmosphere of paternal domination where women were relegated to the sidelines. Cynthia had been working hard at following up various leads and discovered the maternal origins of her family in the Orkney Islands off the coast of Scotland.

In his catalogue introduction for Notes for Oedipus, Robert Melville described Nolan's iconography, based on the Egyptian story of Oedipus' meeting with the Sphinx and solving the riddle of his personal dilemmas, as a black comedy, calling Oedipus a comedian 'whose antics are as scarifying as the jokes of Lennie Bruce. Oedipus has already solved the riddle of the Sphinx and is now impudently acting out his answer in front of her and slyly inferring that she is his mother and wife.' Nolan, ever the myth-maker — or in this case perhaps the myth-breaker — introduced a sinister new figure into the story, a giant cockerel dominating each picture, differing in colour and form from frame to frame and facing the monster Sphinx with woman's breasts and lion's head in a sexual confrontation. This striking creation came from Nolan's reading of Freud's *The Interpretation of Dreams*, in which the author refers to 'bird-beaked figures', combined with the more mundane sight of the poultry run at a friend's farm.

The exhibition with its repetitive imagery and chameleon-like colour changes confused everyone, including Kenneth Clark, who seemed to be genuinely concerned that Nolan had revealed his mental state in the paintings, which were now displayed for all to see on the walls of Marlborough Fine Art. 'What do they mean, Sidney?' he pleaded at the opening and Nolan replied a little too sharply, 'I'll get you Robert Melville's catalogue introduction'. When he first told Clark he was planning to paint the Oedipus myth, the response had been immediate and welcoming, but when he discovered that Nolan was using the Egyptian not the Sophoclean version, he was most upset.

The show resulted in only one sale, to Nolan's dealer Frank Lloyd. However, a few months later he telephoned, coughed nervously, and asked if Nolan would mind if he returned the painting. The sequence was sent for exhibition at Realities Gallery in Melbourne, where it not only remained unsold but also suffered a *Bulletin* magazine review headed, 'Too many cocks'.

Nolan continued to see Benjamin Britten as his health rapidly declined during 1976 and in November he was allowed to spend five minutes with him, although the composer knew the end was near. He was stoical about it, however, and Nolan tried to overcome the impression this was to be their last meeting. The nurse left them together and then there seemed to be nothing to say. As he was sitting there Nolan remembered for no apparent reason that in Britten's opera *The Turn of the Screw*, the orphan boy Miles sings a nonsense song in which each line begins with the Latin word *malo* as part of a lesson in grammar. Nolan knew it could mean 'bad' or 'sick' and looked at his watch, commenting, 'Well, I suppose I have to be going. This is all a bit *malo*, isn't it?' He realised this sounded foolish, although what he had intended to express was the thought that it was a bad deal having to die. However, Britten thought Nolan was saying he, Nolan, was *malo*, and with an effort he smiled, raised an index finger to his lips and whispered, 'I won't tell anybody'. It was a moving finale to their friendship.

One grey chilly day late in November the Nolans travelled up to town together; he to talk over some gallery business and she to spend some time in the public records at Somerset House, followed by a visit to a couple of libraries in the continuing research into her family. It was a routine they had followed on many occasions since living at Putney, ending with the usual arrangement to meet at Fortnum & Mason's for tea before going home. Nolan entered Fortnum's right on 4 o'clock, the appointed meeting time, ordered tea and cakes for two and sat reading a book he had just purchased. Time passed and Cynthia failed to arrive. It was approaching 5 o'clock when the tea rooms would soon be closing, as Nolan decided to pay his bill and return to Putney, assuming that Cynthia had been delayed by her research. He opened the door of their house to be greeted by the two French bulldogs and a telegram lying on the doormat, which he ignored for the moment, assuming it to be one of the many he received from dealers in Britain and Australia. Nolan fed the dogs, switched on the radio for some music and then idly opened the telegram, to find it was from Cynthia. It read: OFF TO THE ORKNEYS IN SMALL STAGES. LOVE CYNTHIA. He thought it rather unusual to be contacted in this way, but assumed she had found a good lead about her mother and had decided in her enthusiasm to follow it immediately. Nolan was sure she would call him as soon as she could.

By the following morning there had been no contact and he set about locating Cynthia, ringing every hotel and guest house in the Orkneys. Each call drew a blank and, remembering that a journey to the Orkneys would involve considerably more than a day's travel, Nolan decided to wait at home until Cynthia called, not worrying unduly until there was an urgent rapping at the door, which gave him a chilling bolt of apprehension. He turned the latch to be confronted by two police officers, who asked if he was the husband of Cynthia Nolan. They revealed that Cynthia had been found dead in a hotel room in central London. Nolan was numbed at the news, totally confused as if he had been suddenly forced to inhabit some of his own nightmare imagery, not believing what he was hearing. One of the detectives offered to make some tea and Nolan was able to steel himself to hear their explanation of what had happened.

They informed him that the previous day Cynthia had booked into the Regent Palace, just off Piccadilly Circus, a few minutes walk from Hatchards and Fortnum & Mason. It was a large, impersonal hotel, favoured by British tour parties and package tourists from abroad. As the hotel was on the edge of the red-light district of Soho, the management had an inflexible rule that women could not stay on their own for fear of the premises being used by the many prostitutes operating in the area. The register showed that a couple had checked in the previous day, although the man's identity remained a mystery. After sending off the telegram to Putney, and writing a note with the family doctor's name on it, Cynthia must have taken an overdose of barbiturates. She had been discovered late that morning when a maid arrived to service the room.

The police officers asked him to report to Vine Street police station as soon as possible to sign the routine documents that would lead to a coroner's verdict of suicide. Nolan collected the two dogs to take them to the vet so they would be left in good hands. He gathered a few personal possessions, including several bottles of barbiturates Cynthia had left prominently positioned in the bathroom, and crammed them into a small overnight bag. He turned his back on Putney never to return, spending the night at his doctor's residence in Regent's Park. Nolan had no idea what the future would hold and, after retiring to bed, took the cap off a bottle of drugs and swallowed a handful of them to add to the sedative his doctor had already given him to assist sleep. He needed to ease the shock of Cynthia's dreadful action and eliminate the searing pain of her sudden absence. His action failed and, although he was in no state to reason why his own attempt at suicide did not succeed after such a determined effort, he later assumed it was because his constitution proved stronger than his willpower. A period of maudlin self-pity followed, then an agonising questioning of what had gone wrong with their lives. He began to drink after years of abstinence and was convinced that he would never want to paint another picture. Nolan refused to return to Putney because it was haunted by too many ghosts and his friend Alistair McAlpine suggested he move into his family suite at the Dorchester Hotel where he would be well looked after, giving him time to recover from the emotional shock and plan his future. Friends rallied round and messages of sympathy poured in when Cynthia's death was announced in a small obituary in the *Times*, stating she had died in her sleep on 23 November.

Patrick White was particularly supportive in his letters, mourning the passing of a fellow writer as well as the end of a precious friendship. He wrote an obituary for Cynthia which was published in the national newspaper the *Australian*, recalling the many occasions when what he described as her kingfisher spirit enriched the lives of Manoly and himself. White reminisced about the last summer they had spent together; an almost too perfect time of simple meals, happy conversations and visits to the opera, including a memorable *Don Giovanni* when the set gave way under the singers before the Don could make his descent into hell. Above all, there were the drives to some of southern England's finest gardens, including Sissinghurst in Kent where Vita Sackville-West had created her masterpiece, and visits to the great houses and grounds of Knowle and Petworth. There had been a sense of finality about those carefree times, the faint shadow of a suggestion that Cynthia's increasing physical frailty combined with an erratic nervous energy was controlling her tormented destiny. White and Manoly had visited the Nolans at Putney, enjoying the glorious garden she had nurtured over a period of nearly twenty years, sloping down to the Thames with its myriad moods changing on the turn of every tide. White understood how she had been happier here in this muted world far away from the harsh glare of Australia where, even in the more temperate latitudes of Tasmania, the bright sky and the sun could cause harsh contrasts to shatter the harmony of landscapes. He wrote, 'I shall remember her in the shimmer of her Putney garden beside the river, amongst the magnolias, the hummock of pinks and tussocks of cornflowers, the Persian roses with their spiny canes, the perfumed cabbage-roses forgotten except by those who remember what is out of season and who are obsessed by roses'. White recalled this setting and the powerful yet disturbed presence of Cynthia herself, talking and laughing in the dappled sunlight filtering down through the boughs of a stately elm. There was a sense of almost Georgian order disturbed only by an undercurrent of melancholy that seemed to rise like an invisible mist from the river whose dark, flat surface broke into occasional ripples reflecting the hazy sunshine. But it was another novelist who made perhaps the most eloquent comment about the Nolans' tragedy. Lord Snow wrote, 'She was, you could say, his muse'.

There was a further shock to Nolan when his wife's will revealed that he was not a beneficiary. This happened because of a company structure that had been set up many years before when their main assets were placed in Cynthia's name to ensure the most favourable tax situation for their erratic incomes and expenditure. After a while it had become obvious that the arrangement was unworkable and, following a change in British company law, Nolan assumed the original scheme had been negated when he made no effort to re-register the business name. However, the will made it clear that except for the apartment, little was actually owned by Nolan and Jinx was the sole beneficiary. It was an appalling situation and he engaged a Queen's Counsel to unravel the legal complexities and discover if he had any claim on his own home, where many paintings and possessions were located. Nolan was advised that under the terms of the will and the company articles he had no rights. There was a meeting with the lawyers representing Cynthia's interests and they came to a general agreement that as the will was unconventional and, in its present form, would attract considerable death duties, an obvious solution was to split the estate, allowing Nolan possession of half the property with a consequent large reduction in death duties. The two trustees, one of whom had drawn up the original document and was a close friend of Cynthia, agreed this would be the best course of action, but for a reason that was not explained it was never carried out. The full death duties were paid rather than sharing the assets. This left Nolan with few of his personal possessions, although he had paintings in store in London and Australia and owned a few other valuable works of art collected over the years which would be sold off to cover expenses until he could again earn an income.

He was shattered by these events and in no state, mentally or financially, to fight a legal battle over domestic rights and possessions. When Nolan had left Putney on that November day he had turned his back on perhaps a hundred completed pictures in the studio, together with a considerable collection of correspondence and many hundreds of photographs. He was not informed where they went, leaving a huge gap in his life and work for he had kept no inventory of pictures or other personal records. Very slowly, in spite of these chronic worries, Nolan managed to pull himself together in the face of rapidly mounting bills at the Dorchester, one of London's most expensive hotels, where he had been led to believe he was staying 'on the house'.

The strangely elliptical nature of his life displayed itself again when Mary Perceval came back into his life, inviting him to stay at her home, named The Ruthland, on the Welsh border. Here he could enjoy sitting in front of roaring log fires as winter snowstorms swept over the hills and gradually regain a passion to paint. He had first known the beautiful young Mary Boyd with her long blonde hair and quick wit as a girl of fourteen when she visited Sunday Reed at Heide and, of course, he and her brother, Arthur, were lifelong friends. Nolan thought it a wonderful twist of fate that she should turn up on the scene because, apart from Arthur, she was the only person from that period thirty years ago he had any contact with. She had come to live in England in the early 1970s with her son and daughters after her marriage with John Perceval had broken down, living at first in London and then buying a remote sheep farm in southern Herefordshire, high on a hill overlooking the valleys and the Black Mountains of Wales. Mary had discovered a simple grey stone farmhouse with extensive outbuildings and, after some hard work improving the accommodation and the grounds, had created a comfortable home in one of the most beautiful corners of England.

It was a changed Nolan who arrived in Australia with Mary during April 1977 to celebrate his sixtieth birthday with exhibitions in Sydney and Melbourne and to begin filming sequences for the ABC-BBC co-production television documentary for which Kenneth Clark agreed to record the narration.

The newspapers marked Nolan's return with interviews, feature articles and pictures; every journalist found him disarmingly considerate, although close friends could tell that the shock of Cynthia's suicide had taken its toll, ageing him and giving him a look of frailty and an air of vulnerability. Melbourne was now a lonelier place with both his parents gone — Dora had died in May 1975, aged 79.

His sixtieth birthday was a time for both receiving and giving gifts, including the decision to donate his personal collection of Gallipoli paintings to the Australian War Memorial in Canberra. The offer came through a chance letter written by the director requesting information about where the Memorial might acquire a selection of those works to add to its comprehensive collection of war art by many Australian artists. Nolan replied within a week that he would be delighted to donate his whole collection of paintings, sketches and drawings as a dedication to his brother, Raymond. The critic and buyer for the Australian National Gallery, James Gleeson, was quoted as saying Nolan's gift would be worth at least two million dollars on the open market at current prices.

At the same time as the Gallipoli announcement, the Australian National

Mary Perceval and Nolan, Sydney, 1977

Gallery became the recipient of the remaining twenty-five paintings of the original Ned Kelly series to add to the one already acquired: *Death of Sergeant Kennedy at Stringybark Creek*. Sunday Reed presented the collection to the gallery and her husband was inundated with press interest at this announcement, but would not be part of any publicity, even refusing to allow any of the paintings, which were still at Heide, to be photographed. 'She wants to leave the gift simple, and doesn't want to elaborate on it', John Reed explained. 'If you must say something about us, just say I'm a gardener'. Newspaper stories the previous year, claiming the Kellys were locked away in a bank vault, had stirred the usually reticent Reeds to action. He had made a public statement outlining their exhibition history, starting with Melbourne in 1948 and then being shown twice again in that city, twice in Sydney, throughout New Zealand, once in Rome, once in London and twice in Paris. He said the Kelly series had played 'an intimate and active part of our day-to-day living'. Reed had criticised Nolan, however, for one of the *Paradise Garden* poems titled 'Fidelio' which was accompanied by an illustration showing the

233

outline of Ned Kelly behind bars with a small bird perched beside him. The
poem read:

> In the bank vault
> the paintings
> like prisoners
> face each other,
> the man
> with the iron head
> and the robin
> on the fence,
> buried without
> being dead.

The Reeds had invited Mary to see them when she was in Melbourne but
Nolan was unable to bring himself to come face to face with them again after a
separation of thirty years. On the appointed day he drove Mary out then sat in
the car a discreet distance from the new Heide, next to the original weatherboard cottage where Sweeney Reed now lived. He remembered the day he had
left Heide, the Reeds, the Kellys, and many tangible reminders of their close
association, including all the correspondence between himself and Sunday. Her
letters to him were personal and passionate, but most of what he had written to
her was in a detached mood and style, conveying his reactions to the new
environment in the Western District of Victoria and how he could realise it in
paint. An exception was two letters Nolan had written from Fraser Island, full of
doubts about leaving Heide and blaming Sunday for his sorry situation. By the
time he had settled down to a calmer domestic life in Sydney, those emotional
letters began to concern him and he became increasingly ashamed of having
expressed himself so openly and revealed his vulnerability. Nolan knew it was
unlikely that Sunday would part with them, but thought he should at least have
her letters to him, which he knew were safely stored at Heide. A couple of
weeks after his request for their return, a large package had arrived at
Wahroonga which contained their entire correspondence. It was a mysterious
action which was either a mistake or a pointed comment. Nolan took the two
letters he was worried about and burned them under a camphor laurel tree at the
bottom of the garden. As the ashes were blown away by a brisk breeze he felt
relieved to have expunged the record of an unhappy period in his life. He had
repacked the parcel and posted it back to Heide so that Sunday again held their
entire correspondence, except for two letters.

Now, sitting in the car waiting for Mary, he idly wondered if Sunday still
kept all those mementoes of the past. During their meeting Sunday had asked if
Mary could persuade Nolan to telephone her that evening. He was reluctant to
break the silence after such a long time, but Mary finally persuaded him to make

234

the call. Sunday answered the phone and Nolan identified himself. There was a moment of hesitation and then she asked, 'Why did you leave me, Nolan?' There could be no adequate reply thirty years later and the conversation was short-lived. Nolan parried by saying he would turn up one day as normal, 'You'll see me coming through the lavender bushes and the sun will be shining'. Sunday replied, 'I don't understand'. 'Well, when I come back, I'll explain to you why you don't understand'. She hung up. Nolan had been holding the phone so that Mary could hear and he now put it down with a gesture of finality. That night the open fire in the Reeds' sitting room burned brighter for a while as Sunday destroyed all her letters to Nolan, watching tearfully as the record of some of the most precious moments in her life disappeared in smoke.

His selling exhibition in Sydney at the Rudy Komon Gallery during this visit showed the poetic side of Nolan's nature in a series of paintings that celebrated his status as a godfather. His old friend Douglas Cairns, who was now a successful orchardist on the Mornington Peninsula near Melbourne, had some eight years before taken his young grandson down to one of the dams on the property and, holding the child in one arm while flourishing a reproduction of Piero della Francesca's *Baptism* in the other, proclaimed to the surrounding gum trees as he baptised him in the muddy water that Nolan was the godfather. It was only recently that Nolan had learned of the event, as he was starting to paint again in Mary Perceval's farmhouse after recovering from the shock of

From the Baptism series, 1977

235

Cynthia's death. The pictures of flowers and bush in vibrant colours on a joyful theme were summed-up admirably in the Vice-Chancellor's oration at the degree ceremony in the Great Hall of Sydney University. Nolan sat in his academic robes about to receive his fourth doctorate, following those from universities in York, London and Canberra. After the ceremony Nolan talked about the pretensions surrounding painters and art, which he said tended to alienate many people. 'The average person, so to speak, shouldn't have to be put through an intellectual process in order to understand paintings. The appeal should be immediate, like people one to the other.' He emphasised the importance of emotional response, saying that as far as he was concerned, it was the same for everybody.

Sidney Nolan and Mary Perceval were married in February 1978 at the Euston Road Registry Office in London. Arthur and Yvonne Boyd were the witnesses and, as Nolan had played the same role with Yvonne at Mary's first marriage more than thirty-four years before, he joked that this latest arrangement must look like 'an in-house job'. With the stability and security that marriage provided for him, Nolan was able to settle down to his familiar routine of working and travelling.

In June 1981, at the age of 64, he was elevated from Commander of the Order of the British Empire, which he had held for eighteen years, to Knight Bachelor in the Queen's Birthday honours. Sydney art dealers estimated that the price of his paintings rose by 10 per cent overnight. At this time he was working on the final designs for the Royal Opera of Elijah Moshinsky's production of *Samson et Dalila* at Covent Garden. Sir Sidney prepared designs for everything from backdrops and gauzes to the costumes for principal singers. One striking image among many for Saint-Saëns' rather neglected work was the blinded face of Samson with his eyes blocked out by two giant red crosses, while Israel in bondage was represented by a blackened hand rising from the desert. There was even a suggestion of *Moonboy* in one of the gauzes for Act II. The production was widely praised by the critics and Nolan joined the cast on stage at the end of the premiere performance when six curtain calls were taken. It was nearly twenty years since he had last stood here on the first night of *The Rite of Spring* and he looked forward to his next engagement at Covent Garden in 1984 when an opera based on Ned Kelly's exploits, to be composed by Edward Cowie, was due for presentation. After that, there was talk of designing a *Ring* cycle, but the vagaries of the opera world made all these projects less than certain.

On Cynthia's death in late 1976 Nolan had telephoned Patrick White to tell him of the circumstances and the writer was distraught at the news of her life ending in such a way. He felt it was an utter waste of a person who had become increasingly dear and close to him. He suspected that such a drastic step had been the culmination of the tension he had observed building up between the

Nolan receiving honorary degree at the University of Sydney, 1977

Nolans to the point where White felt it was inevitable there would be a violent conclusion, although he had not anticipated such a grim result. In his heart he blamed Nolan for the situation, feeling he had driven Cynthia to the point of desperation, although he kept these thoughts to himself and wrote a friendly letter of condolence. Nolan and Mary had dinner with Patrick White on their 1977 visit to Australia, some five months after Cynthia's death, and felt the relationship between the two men had remained intact. Simmering beneath the surface, however, was White's distaste of the artist as a public figure. He saw Nolan as constantly in the limelight, often accompanied by a film crew. He was always being quoted in the press, courted by society; the name on everybody's lips. To White, Nolan's return visits to Australia had the brashness of a travelling circus; but more than that was the revulsion of seeing another woman on his arm in place of Cynthia, so soon after her death. This became too much for the writer to stomach and his relationship with Nolan entered a period of uneasy calm with contact gradually ceasing. It was a lull before the storm.

In 1981 Charles Osborne, the Australian-born writer and editor, telephoned Nolan to tell him he had received an advance copy of Patrick White's autobiography titled *Flaws in the Glass* from the publishers Jonathan Cape and had just read the final section, *Episodes and Epitaphs*, a sequence of penetrating vignettes of various people who had made a strong impression on White. The author's encounters with the Queen, Sir John and Lady Kerr, and Dame Joan Sutherland were almost all unfavourably reported. There were also a few

237

paragraphs headed *The Nolans*, in which White gave a brief sketch of the painter and Cynthia from the time they all met in Florida. Osborne read out excerpts over the telephone. They were amusingly observant until it came to criticism of Nolan's behaviour after Cynthia's death, with White accusing him of rushing to another woman before the memory of his wife had even slightly receded. Nolan could not believe what he was hearing; it sounded worse than any of the arguments and emotional tussles that had occurred at Heide. None of White's letters, or their last meeting, had prepared Nolan for the shock of the comments in *Flaws in the Glass*. He had certainly been a bad correspondent over the years of their friendship, which was another of White's accusations, but he had always acknowledged that flaw in his own personality, leaving the letter-writing to Cynthia because he was the painter in the family and she the writer. Nolan was mystified that White had apparently harboured this intense dislike of him for a number of years, while giving the appearance that little had changed.

Nolan obtained an advance copy of the book and was only slightly relieved to confirm he was just one of a number of well-known identities criticised by White. He was amazed that such material could have been published and wondered how he could forestall its imminent release because, once public, it would cause considerable pain to himself and to Cynthia's family when it was revealed she had committed suicide. Nolan thought Oedipus must have returned to haunt him when he read White's statement that Nolan had probably never needed a wife but an eternal mother as his companion. He had never tried to hide the fact that he closely identified with his mother, although their relationship had gone through many strains, particularly during his late teens. But before that, and afterwards, he had enjoyed her company immensely. He remembered discussing this on a number of occasions with Patrick White and realised that the novelist had stored the information for future use. He thought the accusation was a strange comment to come from a man whose depiction of his own mother in *The Eye of the Storm* was so ruthless that he had her die on a mahogany commode.

Nolan thought there might be a case to answer in court and he sought informal advice from two of his friends, who were both eminent QCs: John Mortimer, equally well known as a writer, and Lord Goodman, one of the leading figures in the arts. They both advised him to take no action over White's words because libel or defamation cases were always protracted and expensive and, even if successful, usually subjected the victims to more pain than the original material. Nolan knew one of the editors at Cape who had worked on the book and asked him how such personal comments had been passed for publication. The blunt answer was that a great deal had been deleted and, if he thought himself hard done by, he should see some of the material that had been left out.

Nolan had hoped that White might realise the pain he had caused and, being a grazier's son, would back down and make an apology. That was an article of Nolan's working-class faith. But it did not happen and against his better judgement he found himself planning his own comment in the only way he could: in a painting. Mary was anxious to avoid any more trouble and suggested he avoid public show, but as he explained to her, 'In the ordinary course of events I would never think about doing this, but White revealed a personal and family matter for all the world to read and I feel committed to making my own statement about him'.

Nolan was invited as guest of honour to the annual Perth Festival in January 1982 where he was represented by three exhibitions: a new series based on D.H. Lawrence's *Kangaroo*, thirty-one drawings inspired by the early convict novel by Marcus Clarke, *For the Term of His Natural Life*, and a selection of the Ern Malley paintings from 1974. *Kangaroo* proved to be one of his best series for a number of years, a lyrical treatment of themes from Lawrence's Australian novel, combined with incidents from the author's brief stay in Perth in the 1920s before he and Frieda travelled to Sydney and then made their home in the coastal township of Thirroul where much of the book was written. Lawrence had been intrigued by the ghostly quality of the Australian bush and this, together with myriad wildflowers, were woven into Nolan's work. One picture, titled *Nightmare*, although based on an incident in the book where the hero, Somers, tells of his mistreatment in the army, had a further significance. The picture was painted in two separate sections, intended to be hung together. The figure on the left, staring out of the frame with sunken eyes and a helpless look of defeat, was made ridiculous by a small airforce cap perched precariously on top of his head. To the right, the hindquarters of a pig-like creature intruded into the portrait. The complementary picture revealed the remainder of the gross, indeterminate animal, bearing the head of a dark-haired man of Mediterranean origin, wearing glasses and an expression of subjugation to the sour-faced individual next to him. On the body was inscribed the image of a crucifix and the whole impression of the diptych was one of disgust turning to hate. The image of the ageing man with the drooping eyes and look of defeat was unmistakably a likeness of Patrick White, while the face on the shape beside him was that of Manoly Lascaris. The work was reminiscent of one of the more lurid panels by the fourteenth-century Flemish master Hieronymus Bosch and had the immediate effect of generating a scandal, not only in Perth but right around Australia and in London, where the vendetta was reported in the pages of the *Sunday Times* together with a photograph of *Nightmare*. All Patrick White would say was, 'There are rules and rules — horses for courses'. Nolan explained how he had painted the work at The Ruthland, 'Usually I put on some Mozart when I'm in the studio, but on this occasion I thought I'd better do it in cold blood'. He said that the painting was not for sale, 'Because it's not for burning'.

The public was prepared to be entertained and the press was eager for any further developments that might cause the smouldering passions to burst into a new conflagration. Nolan, regarding the incident from England, saw it in terms of a passing storm, 'You just batten down the hatches and ride it out'. He had experienced some awkward moments in his life and many of them were in Australia where there seemed to be a particularly destructive intensity in relationships he had not observed or experienced elsewhere in the world. 'There is nothing I can do about it', he admitted to Mary, whose ties with home were not nearly as strong as his, 'I enjoy Australia a great deal and I love being there, but it is a community that brawls more than it should'. A couple of months after the Perth exhibition, he showed at the Rex Irwin Gallery in Sydney a group of drawings which poured further scorn on the writer. He employed an episode from Dante's *Divine Comedy* about the committing of enemies to the pit of hell in the Seventh Circle, or Sodomite Division, with the writer depicted in sparse, telling strokes as a sinner against both Nature and Art.

Nolan revealed that he held the film rights to *Voss* and intended to make a feature movie on his own terms in association with Stuart Cooper. The novel's translation to the screen had been the subject of speculation for many years and there were countless reports of famous directors being engaged for what was regarded as a great Australian subject. The English playwright David Mercer had provided a fine screenplay and now that the rights were under Nolan's control, he felt he could steer the production 'towards an Australian feeling', while admitting that his experience with feature films was non-existent, except as a member of the audience. He also stated that the novelist would certainly not be involved, 'unless he wants to play Voss!' Over the next few years White declined to make any public comment about the film, suggesting only that a German actor be engaged to play the leading character, based on the explorer Ludwig Leichhardt, who disappeared on his second attempt to cross the Australian continent from east to west in 1848. The seven expedition members were never seen again and nothing was known of their fate. Nolan assumed that White had no control over the choice of director if the film were made outside Australia, suggesting it could be shot in Libya and adding darkly, 'There are more deserts than Australian ones'. White's literary agents countered by pointing out that the author retained the right of veto on a director anywhere in the world. Most of this skirmishing would subside when the big-budget movie *Burke and Wills*, the story of yet another ill-starred exploration of the Australian wastes, failed to live up to its commercial expectations when released in 1985. The potential producer had to admit, 'It has probably set back *Voss* by ten years'.

Nolan presents Serge Lifar with a recent drawing on the subject of Icare, *Sydney, 1981*
(News Ltd)

When Sunday Reed had presented the Kelly series to the Australian National Gallery she had requested that they be exhibited with an inscription stating they had been given 'with love'. This was followed by a letter from John Reed in June 1977 proposing a more appropriate way of stating the origins of the gift, to be known as 'The 1946–47 Group of Ned Kelly Paintings by Sidney Nolan'. He suggested an inscription reading,

> In 1977 these paintings (with the exception of *Death of Sergeant Kennedy at Stringybark Creek*) were given with love to the Australian National Gallery by Sunday Reed. Nolan painted them and gave them to her when he was living with her and her husband, John Reed, at 'Heide', Heidelberg, Victoria.

The suggestion was put to the trustees and they thought it a fitting statement which was incorporated in a plaque to accompany the paintings when the gallery was officially opened by the Queen in October 1982. Soon after, Nolan began hearing gossip that the wording made people snigger and wonder what had been going on while the Kellys were being painted. On one Canberra visit, much to Mary's embarrassment, he asked the attendants to look the other way while he tried to prise the inscription from its backing, but the plaque remained firmly attached.

It was an opera plot that engaged Nolan's next efforts, designing the sets for the Australian Opera's 1983 production of *Il Trovatore* with Dame Joan Sutherland in the role of Leonora. The Nolans had been staying with the Boyds in the country and when out walking he had tripped and broken a small bone in his foot, necessitating a strapped ankle and the assistance of a walking stick to attend the opera's rehearsals. Then suddenly it seemed as if the curse of Azucena, the gipsy in Verdi's masterpiece, was deflected in Nolan's direction instead of the wicked Count di Luna. Nolan was negotiating a ramp between the auditorium and the stage during the final dress rehearsal when he tripped and fell about three metres into the orchestra pit, breaking three ribs. He was admitted to Sydney Hospital for a week, missing the premiere of the opera, although he was able to attend one of the later triumphant performances in the Sydney Opera House in a wheelchair.

On their first trip home together in 1977 Nolan and Mary had stayed with Arthur Boyd. His life, too, was divided between Australia and long periods of painting and exhibiting in Europe. At that time the Boyds were building a house and studio overlooking the Shoalhaven river upstream from Nowra in southern New South Wales. In country inaccessible without a four-wheel drive vehicle, they were creating an earthly paradise on a hill conveniently high enough to avoid the flooding that sometimes isolated the property. Arthur Boyd had plans to turn the extensive tracts of native bush surrounding a former dairy farm into a nature reserve and, in the longer term, to establish a museum to display his own work, together with that of the entire Boyd dynasty of painters, potters, sculptors and writers. Later, Arthur and Yvonne Boyd moved a few kilometres along the rough track into Bundanon, a fine colonial sandstone mansion dating from 1866, its broad wooden verandahs facing south over river flats to the tree-lined Shoalhaven flowing beneath a rocky escarpment. A spacious studio was added at the end of a formal garden to be used during return visits from the Boyds' English home in Suffolk. A few years later Nolan became interested in acquiring 400 acres adjoining his brother-in-law's land, comprising some impressive wooded country high on a plateau with its cliffs overlooking the river valley. Then in 1985, the two artists would buy another property together, known as Earie Park, which made their individual holdings contiguous. They intended to preserve the whole area, covering a peninsula formed by a broad sweep of the river and giving a water frontage of fourteen kilometres. Nolan was taking steps to secure a significant foothold in the country — if not the State — of his birth.

242

CHAPTER THIRTEEN

Rewards and Honours

§

In November 1983 it was announced from Buckingham Palace that the Queen had conferred on Nolan the rare distinction of the Order of Merit, limited in number to twenty-four eminent statesmen, writers, scientists, artists and musicians. He became only the sixth Australian to receive the award in its 81-year history and the first in the arts. The four new appointments to the Order, the Queen's personal gift, filled vacancies left by the deaths of artist Ben Nicholson, composer Sir William Walton, engineer Lord Hinton and, significantly, Lord Clark. An editorial in the *Australian* newspaper headed 'Distinction for a genius', pointed out that Nolan's sharp wit often had made him unpopular with his fellow artists, but the public had taken him to its heart. 'The suburbs, motels and office blocks of this country are filled with Nolan prints. Ned Kelly rides through the drawing rooms of houses from Manchester to Melbourne.' The writer ended with the hope, 'It is perhaps time we begin celebrating our geniuses instead of cutting them down'. Nolan commented to Mary, 'I've no idea how I came to be mixed up with British honours and I can only assume Kenneth Clark had something to do with it before he died. There are people who might have been more suitable for an OM — like Victor Pasmore — and I don't doubt that he would think so, too.'

With immense perseverance and inherent good taste, Mary had created a wonderfully sympathetic environment at The Ruthland, far away from the nearest habitation, on a hill overlooking the Black Mountains of central Wales. It became rather crowded at times with visits from her grown-up son and daughters, who often brought their young children to stay, but Nolan was happy there, having converted an old stone barn into an efficient studio by installing lights and central heating. He also supervised extensions to the 300-year-old farmhouse including the addition of a new kitchen with a sitting room above. He had plans to build a large gallery on land below the house to accommodate *Snake*, which he imagined would look interesting in this unusual setting. When estimates were made for the construction, however, it became obvious that the costs would be prohibitive, even though the structure was also intended as a working studio.

Just before leaving England in 1983 for a sojourn in Australia, the Nolans learned about the sale of The Rodd, a seventeenth-century manor house about an hour's drive from The Ruthland. They had visited the house on a number of occasions together because Mary was a friend of the widowed Lady Rennell who lived there. She invited them to a Christmas party and there had also been a poetry reading in the great tithe barn and a guitar recital in the library. When Lady Rennell died the house was put on the market and the Nolans took a brochure with them on their journey with the idea of perhaps acquiring this larger property in the part of England Mary had grown to love. Their decision was made during a stopover in Singapore and negotiations to purchase began in Sydney.

Nolan had seen potential in The Rodd's fine complex of barns and outbuildings, together with its extensive walled gardens, greenhouses and twenty acres of lush grazing land. He envisioned the tithe barn being converted into a theatre for music recitals, and the other farm buildings around a courtyard as ideal for storing paintings and installing a lithographic press. Mary, as a keen gardener, could accept the considerable challenge of establishing a new vegetable garden and developing the lawns, flower beds and shrubberies.

On their return to England the Nolans set about putting their rambling new acquisition in order. Although in good condition, this fine example of a late Elizabethan manor house — completed in 1629 according to an inscription over the porch — was denuded of Lord and Lady Rennell's furniture because by the terms of sale it was to be auctioned separately. The new owners had to attend the sale in Chester, many miles away, where they managed to buy back some of the original contents, although the purchasing power of the American dollar saw them outbid for several fine pieces of early English oak furniture, which found new homes in the United States.

Inside, the house looked very much as it must have done for the past 350 years, its white plastered walls inset with massive oak beams darkened over the centuries by smoke from huge open fireplaces large enough to roast a side of beef on the spit. There were stout oaken floors, mullioned windows with latticed panes, and arched doorways. The principal rooms were wainscotted and contained handsomely carved wooden fireplaces, including one outstanding example representing Adam and Eve with the serpent coiling around a central column of flowers and foliage. The house was constructed of thick stone walls, roofed with stone slates that had acquired a patina of orange-coloured moss, and surmounted by several clusters of tall brick chimneys. There had been additions over the years, such as the library converted from a wain house in 1956. The Nolans soon introduced some changes by removing an internal wall to open out

The Rodd and the library, showing Nolan's Dog and Duck Hotel

the kitchen. This allowed more natural light to enter, because none of the original windows faced south as it was believed in the early seventeenth century that sunshine attracted the plague. Now from new windows they could look towards the sun, south and west down a broad valley to a distant vista of hills which, at certain seasons, took on the shapes and tones of many parts of the world where Nolan had painted: Kenya, China, New Guinea, Greece and, of course, Australia.

Nolan's association with another Australian novelist had proved to be a more satisfying and lasting relationship than that with Patrick White. Several years before, Xavier Herbert had written asking if he would visit him next time he came to Australia and Nolan promised he would. Herbert was the author of the best-selling *Capricornia*, first published in 1938, and his most recent work was a huge novel of 850,000 words, *Poor Fellow My Country*, which Nolan had read and annotated, marking aspects of the text and references that interested him. It was a practice he followed for many years, particularly with the novels of Patrick White. He was glad to spend a day in March 1981 with Herbert because he had the reputation of being a colourful character and Nolan had wanted to meet him for many years. Herbert lived at Redlynch near the north Queensland city of Cairns, a considerable distance from Sydney but, unlike the trip Nolan had made to this area in 1947, he was now able to arrange a return journey on the same day.

245

It was after 1 o'clock when Nolan arrived and he had only a couple of hours before the return flight to Sydney. He had not eaten on the journey and was feeling very hungry as Herbert drove him to his house. Over lunch — a toasted sandwich that Nolan did not eat for fear of indigestion — Herbert launched into a rapid account of the book he was writing following the death of his wife, Sadie, and its effect on him. At first it was intended to be called *My Grief for Sadie* (later changed to *Me and My Shadow*) and every reminiscence would be punctuated with the line, 'and that's part of the story of my grief for Sadie'. Xavier Herbert had been a hospital pharmacist as a young man in Western Australia where he was born, acquiring considerable medical knowledge, and part of the worry about his wife's death in her late seventies concerned an argument with doctors over the exact nature of her illness. This resulted in the withholding of a death certificate and he claimed to Nolan she was cremated without one. Nolan listened to this long and rather morbid story, wondering if they would ever get around to talking about the main reason for his visit, a new production of *Poor Fellow My Country*, which he had been asked to illustrate. But perhaps it did not matter because Nolan imagined the market was not yet ready for another edition of this *magnum opus*, fully a third longer than *War and Peace*.

The writer continued to pour out his experiences and Nolan was interested to hear them, becoming for once a better listener than talker. He regarded Herbert with fascination; uniquely Australian with a colourful past as an aviator, deep-sea diver, sailor, stock rider and miner. He refused to own a passport because he said it demonstrated subservience to the British Crown. He vowed never to have one again until Australia became a republic and, in the meantime, asked if Nolan could possibly arrange for him to get an Irish passport instead. During the course of these ramblings Herbert explained he once had an arrangement with a local schoolteacher, who was one of his closest friends, to assist him to take a death pill when Herbert thought he was ready to die. He claimed he had prepared the poison himself, using his dispensing knowledge, and the agreement was for the schoolteacher to drive him far out into the bush, where he would take the pill and then wander off until its fatal effects worked, never to be found at his last resting place. The problem was he had now fallen out with his friend and needed a replacement to carry out the scheme. He asked if Nolan would agree. 'Certainly Xavier', he replied, as if it were a routine request. 'Give me twenty-four hours' notice and I'll come from anywhere in the world and drive you wherever you want to go.' He added, 'But I'll have a revolver with me'. 'Oh, don't worry about that, son', the old man replied, 'I'll have the pill and it's guaranteed to work'. Nolan smiled, knowing he would have the last word during this short visit. 'The revolver, Xavier, is to prevent the pill being forced down my throat!' The writer enjoyed this knockabout Australian humour and Nolan

246

decided he would like to return to hear more from this fascinating old character. Nolan left with a copy of the 1979 paperback edition of *Capricornia*, containing a note on its flyleaf from the author. It read, 'Inscribed with joy for Sidney Nolan, that man, of few men, after my own heart'. A scribbled addendum stated, 'Our association, although not in the flesh, ante-dates this by many years'.

Later in the year the Nolans visited Herbert on their way to the Barrier Reef, and Nolan continued to keep in touch with him, although the proposal for illustrating *Poor Fellow My Country* came to nothing. He rang Herbert one day from England to say he was coming to Australia soon and suggested they meet. In the meantime, he had received his knighthood and when he identified himself on the telephone, Herbert's greeting was, 'And how are you, *Sir* Sid?' and then hung up. Nolan was taken aback by this response, even if Herbert was an outspoken republican who objected to imperial honours. Nolan then set about dialling Herbert's number every hour during the rest of the day, which was through the night in Australia. He would let the phone ring three or four times and then put down the receiver, cutting off the call before it could be answered. He finally allowed the telephone to ring long enough to be answered and at 6 o'clock in the evening, when it was 7 a.m. in Cairns, a woman's voice came on the line. Nolan asked for Herbert and she explained wearily that he was unwell and could not come to the phone. 'Nonsense', Nolan responded, 'he's a bushman and always up at the crack of dawn'. 'Well, I'm afraid he's sick in bed after a terribly disturbed night when the telephone kept ringing, and he's had to cancel a trip to Darwin'. The matter rested there, with Nolan feeling ashamed that he had expended so much energy in attempting to reap a small revenge on another republican writer.

Their paths did not cross again for a couple of years. Nolan had been asked to look after Herbert's papers in the event of anything happening to him and had agreed to see that the manuscript of *Me and My Shadow* would be published. In 1983 Nolan was passing through Alice Springs and was being seen off at the airport by a journalist who had just interviewed him. She mentioned in conversation that Xavier Herbert was at a camp on his own at Docker River. Nolan would have liked to see him again, but there was no time on this visit. The journalist knew that Herbert was to give a lecture soon at the Alice Springs library and promised to pass on Nolan's greetings. He and Mary were back in the area during 1984, accompanying a large team of actors and technicians shooting a film about the Burke and Wills expedition, which would be the subject for a new series of Nolan's paintings. He heard that Xavier Herbert, now 83, was extremely ill in the Alice Springs Hospital and refusing to see visitors. Nolan and Mary got to see the old man through the intervention of a friend and found him in a sad condition, suffering from rheumatoid arthritis with ulcers all over his legs. They caused him constant pain and would not heal. Herbert was glad to see Nolan, welcoming him enthusiastically and making up their differences in a warm embrace. He seemed to enjoy reminiscing again, talking about a whole range of subjects including the clarity of the Alice Springs light and the new book he intended to write, *Billygoat Civilisation*, the title derived from the main promontory in the town, Billygoat Hill, because Herbert had the strange vision of a great new nation originating here and spreading out across the world.

Herbert passed Nolan the completed manuscript of *Me and My Shadow* with considerable pride mixed with an air of relief. It was obvious that finishing the manuscript had been a great strain, driving him to the point of exhaustion, but his deeply lined and tanned face seemed to relax a little now that his labour of love was over and he could think about making a start on *Billygoat Civilisation*. When the Nolans left, Herbert got up from his bed and insisted on walking the length of the hospital with them and then painfully across to the car park. He held open the car door for Mary, then raised his arms like a biblical prophet, his shock of white hair lit from behind by the pink glow of the sunset. As they drove off Nolan remarked to Mary, 'That's the last time we'll see Xavier'. He died ten days later. The film unit had moved on to Cooper's Creek and although Nolan wanted to attend the funeral, it was almost impossible to get to the Alice from their remote location. The writer's last wish was to be attended by nobody at his demise, just as would have happened with the planned suicide pill. His request was granted, except that four Aborigines attended the final rites to place symbolic pieces of paper-bark on the grave in homage to the old man, a ferociously proud Australian.

Although he always played the part of a loner in art, Nolan maintained an interest in observing people come together to work on a common project, such as the men in the Antarctic, the miners in Western Australia or the movie team filming *Burke and Wills* in the Australian desert. He observed the camaraderie involved and likened it to the atmosphere he'd experienced in the army, and during the production of a ballet or an opera.

'I don't know what other painters are like', he admits, 'because I can't pretend to understand the secrets of most of them. But I find looking back over my own career that although I've made a lot of mistakes and produced hundreds of paintings that didn't come off, there are a few I don't mind sitting in front of and simply enjoying.' When he has completed a painting Nolan usually places it on the floor facing the wall and ignores it while he gets on with the next. Hanging on the wall of his apartment at Whitehall Court is one of his Central Australia landscapes from 1949. At first glance it seems a rather dark painting, but after one sits and looks at it for a while, as he sometimes does, it will catch the light reflected from the Thames below and begin to reveal details. Nolan finds that in concentrating on a small section of the picture's technique he can

248

take his mind back nearly forty years to when he painted it in the garden studio at Wahroonga. He can re-live moments of its composition he was never conscious of at the time because of the pressure to complete the picture for an exhibition. He says, 'I hear that most painters don't stand back and admire their work at the time, but much later I get the contemplative, idle pleasure of doing just that, and I suspect the Proustian sense of seeing one's life spread before one has something to do with it'. Nolan regards this experience as similar to that of watching a spectacle unfolding, serious and committed on the one hand, but basically showbusiness on the other.

These elements seemed to have blended perfectly with his gift of *Paradise Garden* to the Victorian Arts Centre, whose concert hall was the next stage in the complex after the National Gallery of Victoria. The interior designer, John Truscott, was delighted to receive such an impressive decoration but wondered how to place the individual brass frames into the available space. A total of 186 of them, each containing six paintings, fitted perfectly into the foyer, except for a couple of airconditioning outlets and, with Nolan's approval, this little snag was overcome by a slight re-arrangement. The remaining sections were to be hung in the building that would house the theatres, to be completed a couple of years later. Truscott, an Oscar-winning designer for the Hollywood film *Camelot*, with a long and successful career in the theatre, was amazed at the way Nolan's work blended with the decorative schemes of brass and timber and carpet already established. When the concert hall was opened in 1982, the splendour of its foyers attracted huge crowds who came just to see the decor and, after being in store for much of its life, *Paradise Garden* suddenly became one of Nolan's best-known works.

When the foyer of the State Theatre, the new home for opera and ballet in Melbourne, was about to open, Nolan and Mary were staying with the Boyds at Bundanon, where Arthur Boyd had painted his commissioned works for the foyer. A little more than a month before the new paintings by Roger Kemp, John Olsen, Jeffrey Smart, David Rankin and Noel Tunks were to be unveiled to the public, Nolan was approached by John Truscott to see if he would contribute five large panels to complete the interior decor of the State Theatre. There had been some gossip in art circles about another painter, Charles Blackman, having received a commission but his work had been rejected and Nolan, known as a quick worker, was being called in to fill the gaps and save the day. There was always a surfeit of this type of art talk and he took no notice of it. Certainly the fee offered — $25,000 for five large canvases — was extremely modest with much of it being used to purchase paints. He had to regard the money as a token gesture, although the proposal for a group of landscapes based on regions where some of the overflow panels from *Paradise Garden* originated, seemed a brilliant idea.

Nolan went to Melbourne to discuss the project with Truscott and was met by one of the city's leading art dealers, who claimed he had organised the commission and would take a reduced fee of 10 per cent for his participation. Nolan assumed this was a standard arrangement for all the art works in the State Theatre and regarded the charge as reasonable. At very short notice, Truscott had stretchers and canvas made to the correct size and they were despatched on the tortuous journey to Bundanon, where Nolan would borrow Arthur Boyd's studio. His enthusiasm for the project led him into what he calls 'a lucky streak' and he was able to work at a rapid pace with few interruptions. After a sustained effort he was quite pleased with the results that dominated the lofty, wood-panelled studio; five large-scale canvases of glowing Australian landscapes, at once bright and muted, combining bold forms with intriguing small details that characterised a new, loosely relaxed style that had been seen in his recent works from China. Nolan imagined his pictures fitting the bill admirably: landscapes in a consciously operatic style to go into the foyer of a large and luxuriously appointed theatre where opera and ballet were to be performed.

That had been his concept from the start and provided the motivation to work so fluently and rapidly, linking his latest techniques and style with the *Paradise Garden* images of some fifteen years ago. There were vivid landscapes of Ayers Rock, Mount Olga, Mount Conner, the jagged Bungle Bungle in the Kimberleys of Western Australia, and a valley of ancient palms outside Alice Springs. Nolan had used big brushes and both his hands to complete the paintings in time. The paint would take two weeks to dry, but the works were needed in Melbourne and Truscott had arranged for them to be packed and transported in their wet state for the unveiling to the press at the end of October 1984, just prior to the official opening of the theatre.

The occasion promised to display one of the largest collections of contemporary Australian art outside the State galleries. One of the main attractions was to have been the presence of Sir Sidney Nolan and his new work, but in the event neither turned up. The general manager of the Centre, George Fairfax, explained in a short informal speech to the invited guests that Nolan had been delayed in Sydney. He reminded them that Sir Sidney previously had made the generous gift of *Paradise Garden* to the Centre and that he would also be donating other works which were not completed yet. It was a strange comment to make when the five finished landscapes were somewhere in the building, locked away out of sight. All John Truscott would say about the empty spaces on the wall where they were intended to hang was that Nolan's works had proved to be 'so powerful they diminished the effects of *Paradise Garden*'. The designer said he had spoken by telephone to the artist who had agreed that his desert paintings would have done a disservice to the earlier work. 'Sir Sidney

250

will paint another series compatible with *Paradise Garden'*, Truscott informed the press.

Nolan dismissed the affair from his mind until May 1985 when he was in New York to receive honorary membership of the American Academy and Institute of Arts and Letters, with the Chinese novelist Ba Jin, Italian composer Luciano Berio, and British art historian E.H. Gombrich. He was asked if Australia had a similar institution and had to admit there was nothing of the sort, even in Melbourne where the director of the National Gallery of Victoria was able to claim, 'We live in a philistine nation but a civilised city'. Nolan felt increasingly irritated about what had happened the previous year and during an interview let it slip that he thought he was the victim of a set-up because there was something odd about the affair of the rejected landscapes. He had asked several influential people in the Melbourne art world how his paintings looked when hung in the State Theatre and everybody was evasive. Truscott had told him they were displayed for a couple of days and a number of experts were consulted about their effect. Nolan made it his business to telephone or personally talk to those who might have been expected to be present, but nobody would confirm having inspected them. Nolan was also infuriated by the fact that, without reference to him as the artist and constructor, non-reflecting glass was placed in the *Paradise Garden* frames, flattening out the forms and bleaching the colours and making them look like rather ordinary prints instead of original paintings. He thought that the original perspex, although giving a wavy line of reflection, was far from disagreeable, and that was how the work had always been displayed. In addition, the colour of the mounts backing each image was changed. This had been carefully controlled by Nolan in a shade of blue designed to enhance the overall look of the construction, but now the mounts were an unpalatable shade of green, making the *Paradise Garden* wall in the concert hall foyer completely unacceptable in his opinion. He thought this action taken in the name of complementary decor was not so far removed from the director deciding to alter certain sections of the great Tiepolo in the adjacent National Gallery of Victoria, or perhaps touching-up the Rembrandt painting to make it lighter and appeal to a wider audience. Nolan was at a loss to understand how such a thing could happen, assuming Truscott must have an inherent sense of muted colour that precluded his enjoyment of anything too bright, although he could not remember *Camelot* looking that way. He described the experience as 'another Melbourne situation in which nobody comes clean'. There was no formal statement from the board of the Victorian Arts Centre that his commissioned landscapes had been unacceptable, no official indication that he would paint an alternative group of pictures, just a deafening silence and blank spaces on the walls of the State Theatre's foyer.

Nolan did not receive a fee for the completed work and presumably the dealer lost out on his anticipated 10 per cent commission. 'I thought that even an informal letter of explanation would have been nice', Nolan said, 'but nothing eventuated'. The Nolans became angrier about the incidents and the likelihood of any further gifts for Melbourne seemed remote. 'In fact', he says, 'I've now scrubbed the whole thing, but what I would really like to do, but can't legally, is to get the rest of *Paradise Garden* back and have it on display as part of my trust at The Rodd'. He describes these events in Melbourne as 'a kind of dying fall', a sensation experienced so many times in the past he is certain it will be repeated. As he puts it, 'I will not have to make peace with them because nothing will have been formalised. No war, no further skirmishes, just a void except for "How are you, Sid?" next time I'm in town.' He sees an analogy with Australian Rules football, regarding his situation in Melbourne rather like a tactic in this game where a player is 'minded' and every now and again, when the play is at the opposite end of the ground, 'you get a sharp jab in the kidneys which nobody sees because it's not where the action is, but nevertheless it plays its part in the final outcome'.

The landscapes painted for the Victorian Arts Centre were retrieved and exhibited at the gallery housed in Heide II during April and May 1985 where they created considerable interest, although they were not for sale. In the end, however, one of the large canvases, titled *Bungle Bungle* after a spectacularly serrated sandstone massif in the far north of Western Australia, and an appropriate name, Nolan thought, to describe the whole affair, went to a buyer in Perth. It was sold, as Nolan says, 'In a meaningful way, to show whoever cared to notice, that the pictures were in demand and I could make money out of them'. This combined commercial and symbolic act of defiance meant that one of the five works found a good home and its selling price far exceeded the promised fee for the five paintings. Of the other four, *Ayers Rock* will go on display at The Rodd, while the others remain stored in Sydney. Despite discussions with Truscott, Nolan never seriously considered doing a series on operatic themes for the State Theatre and no formal commitment was made. He discovered during 1986 that another artist had been approached by Truscott and that the overflow panels of *Paradise Garden* would be accompanied by the works of Colin Lanceley, an abstract painter not noted for his muted tones.

Nolan ascribes the problems he has faced in Melbourne to the inherent attitudes of Australians towards benefaction, although he knows that whatever he thinks about the subject is irrelevant and that anything the press writes is likely to sensationalise his motives. He has no idea where such suspicions and animosities spring from, but accepts that by being in the public eye he has to live with them.

With his working-class background and State school education in Australia, followed by working in a factory and connections with the trade union movement and political groups, Nolan has always believed that popular art has its roots in the ordinary people, while high art is simply a refinement, and both are a means of communication. When art is displayed in a gallery it immediately becomes a communication between the painter and the viewer. If that is not the artist's intention, then the work might as well be kept at home for personal viewing only. He recalls the Balzac story *The Unknown Masterpiece* where a great artist works on a picture for so long and in such secrecy that he makes an utter mess of it. He is discovered one day dead in front of his intended masterpiece, which looks like an indecipherable muddle, except for one beautifully-painted foot.

Nolan never considered what he was engaged in — the so-called high art — to be anything more than a stage in the evolution of a tribal statement whose equivalent in music is Haydn, Mozart and Beethoven borrowing from dance forms. Nolan is well aware that Beethoven's late quartets do not seem to bear much relation to dance origins, but is sure there is a connection. Rather than high art inspiring the masses by filtering down to them, Nolan regards the process the other way. He feels a commitment to explain his approach as much as possible, although he knows that few artists break the rules of their game by revealing secrets of painting they consider should not be told. In the 1960s, his dealer at Marlborough Fine Art warned him against too much exposure on television after the success of the Leda and the Swan exhibition. The painter's predictable reaction was to tell him to mind his own business and state firmly that he intended to utilise the medium increasingly, talking about art and explaining his views on the subject. The audience must be interested in hearing him, otherwise he would not continue to be invited. Nolan saw no harm in this and, although he is the first to admit he is not the world's greatest performer, often using elliptical language and difficult concepts, he felt the need to explain his work to anyone who cared to listen. As he says, 'You learnt as a child that nine nines are eighty-one by rote and it became a fact of life. I happen to think that Cubism is also a fact of life, although Picasso and Braque chose not to enlighten the public about it and the movement remained an impenetrable mystery, but that was their prerogative, which led one to assume there must be a bit of hanky-panky involved.'

Nolan has countless ideas for series of paintings that have been maturing for many years. He would like to continue with themes based on the Greek myths for the good reason that he finds them fascinating, particularly Troy. A series based on the myth of a man allowing his daughter to die in order to get a fleet on course is nearer to realisation than many of Nolan's other ideas. In preparation he has already done a series of drawings based on this theme. 'I was going to methodically plough through all these myths', he explains, 'and will still try it, but I'll have to hurry up'. At seventy he senses the time left to finish projects is beginning to run short and he still has many unrealised dreams.

In Paris there is a graphic series on Hellenic themes that has never been printed, with the plates in storage. 'If I'm going to get through Mycenae and have another go at Gallipoli, I'll need to sprint a bit'. He remembers his interest in these subjects being awakened when he read *Mourning Becomes Electra* and *Long Day's Journey Into Night*. He then read many of the myths in a superficial way at the public library in Melbourne and it was the time on Hydra that crystallised his thoughts: 'It's only when you live in Greece', he explains, 'that all of this starts to haunt you'. Nolan's problem in 1956 was that he was not mature enough to deal with the subject matter in a methodical fashion. He now says he will make a list of what remains to be done and the items will be ticked off on completion. 'If I'm defeated in one line of development, I'll just switch to another; the Long March and the Silk Route are subjects which are equally challenging.' Nolan suspects these intentions sound more like the words of a schoolmaster than a painter, but they are what he thinks about most nights before he goes to sleep and they keep him cheerful.

Another subject that he would like to paint again is the Antarctic. He plans a tragic allegory, incorporating his previous thoughts on the subject with a new dimension: the crash of the Air New Zealand DC10 on a tourist flight to Antarctica when a computer routing error caused it to fly into Mount Erebus and all on board were killed. Nolan sees this event, and air crashes in general, as part of the twentieth century's mythology. Then there are new African paintings that he sees incorporating elements suggested by Romain Gary's novel *The Roots of Heaven*, the story of an elephant hunter, Jewish by birth, who survives the horrors of Auschwitz by thinking about the freedom of the elephants he once hunted.

Nolan returned to the subject of Burke and Wills in 1984, the result of an invitation to travel on location while the film was being shot. He was interested to observe the interaction of the film crew at work, while they recreated the tragic story of the ill-fated explorers. He found the juxtaposition of modern film technology with the bizarre features of the saga of Burke and Wills an extraordinary spectacle and seized the opportunity of painting another allegorical statement which linked the two. He describes his approach to all these recycled subjects as 'taking a long swing around some of my basic themes and trying to show that in the first instance I wasn't just a tourist taking snapshots'. Nolan also feels that this demonstrates that he hasn't left his native roots behind in Australia even though he lives somewhere else.

The quality of Australian light continues to intrigue him,

It isolates objects, disperses them, giving them emphasis, but not equal emphasis. It probably isolates them more than any other light that I've ever seen and that's a problem which confronts Australian painters, because painting is essentially about the cohesion of forms and objects on a given surface and when light produces completely disparate objects in space you have problems not encountered by painters in the European tradition and light. The light will not let you amalgamate the forms, whereas in Europe you have the unity emanating from floating skies.

Because of this, Nolan thinks that Australian art is, by nature, unpredictable and, therefore, exciting, and he finds it impossible to speculate on the direction it may take in the future.

His continuing interest in China as a painting subject goes back to his youth when he first heard about the revolutionary ferments at work in what was then a remote part of the globe. He has now visited the country on seven occasions, often as the guest of the government with permission to travel to many places closed to foreigners. His interest has become centred on two main themes. One of them is the Silk Route, which he has travelled in Afghanistan and through the Gobi Desert, where great wall paintings reminded him of his preoccupation with the work of the Mexican muralists. These Buddhist frescos in the middle of a desert were also reminiscent of Aboriginal cave paintings in the centre of Australia and set his mind racing to make a juxtaposition of the two. Another element which fascinates him is the European exploration of the great trade and religious route that had existed for more than 2,000 years. Nolan found himself identifying with these subjects, as he had with Burke and Wills in Central Australia, and Shackleton in the Antarctic.

In recent years Nolan has become interested in collecting small Egyptian antiquities and this keeps alive a determination to return to the story of Oedipus. He was walking through the Piccadilly Arcade in London at the end of 1985 and noticed a small bronze in a dealer's window attributed to Barye, a nineteenth-century French sculptor. It was only about eight inches high and depicted an African elephant, which made him think immediately of *The Roots of Heaven*. The little bronze was, in fact, by Barye's son and had the figure of a woman riding on its back, representing Cleopatra. Nolan had never heard of anyone riding one of these elephants before and, equally interesting, was the fact that the beast was standing with a foot placed firmly on a fragment of the Sphinx, half buried in the sand. In this one figure, which he bought, were reminders of two of his themes, the Egyptian Oedipus myth and *The Roots of Heaven*. He wondered if he might connect the two, perhaps incorporating a third element — his continuing interest in Sigmund Freud whom Nolan now regards as something of a mythical figure.

Nolan's visits to China have resulted in a considerable number of landscapes, and many misgivings. It was as if the territory was meant to remain foreign and, therefore, untouched by an Australian painter. Nolan felt he was being asked to give up his artistic passport for activities contrary to the cause of the nation's culture. As he put it, 'Most people regard my paintings from China as part of my eternal search for another place to plonk my Australian nose in'. What evolved, however, was the idea of using the poetry of Mao Tse Tung as the inspiration for a visual odyssey, incorporating the words of this soldier taking part in one of the greatest events in human history. Nolan is fascinated by military men who are able to express themselves in literary forms; Caesar had done it, Wavell was a good writer, and Nolan considered the Chinese leader equally outstanding as a poet, politician and soldier. Nolan's version of the man's thoughts would never be as the Chinese themselves regarded them and that was justification enough to persist with an allegorical series.

Nolan is aware that many of these subjects tend to the sombre and are often heavy with tragedy: the elephants in Africa, the senseless loss of life in an Antarctic air crash, and the rigours of the Long March. He feels that each contains elements of hope for the survival of the human spirit, although he concedes that 'As you get older, I suppose the choice of subjects does get more sombre, even though I feel lighthearted in approaching them'.

When the Nolans returned to England from New York in May 1985, their immediate preoccupation had little to do with art or a forthcoming trip to Australia. It was about the future of The Rodd and its environs. The surrounding land, which formed part of the original estate operating as an independent farm, suddenly came up for sale and was offered in a number of lots rather than as one unit of 500 acres. This raised the spectre of building developments starting to spread across the fields in front of the house or on the wooded hillside at the back. They faced a similar situation on the other side of the world at Bundanon: how to halt ribbon development. The main problem was that this land in England, made valuable by generous EEC subsidies to farmers, had become prohibitively expensive and the Nolans had nowhere near enough money to purchase it. There was the added consideration that rather late in life Nolan might have to take on the unwelcome responsibility of becoming a farmer.

One solution was to raise a mortgage and form a trust to purchase the parcels of farmland immediately around the house, ensuring that the manor and its collection of farm buildings remain intact in a completely rural setting. At the same time the activities of the Sidney Nolan Trust were devised to stage public exhibitions in the tithe barn with associated lectures and concerts. There is a five-year plan of development based on the buildings now signed over to the Trust and the fifty paintings that must be owned by it. No profit is allowed to be made, but under the complex government regulations that control such organisations, the artist can donate more of his pictures and other art works without incurring extra personal tax. Nolan is amused that such organisations are not usually established until a painter or sculptor is dead, and because of this

256

Nolan's studio at The Rodd

he intends to make the Trust's activities as lively and stimulating as possible.

Nolan admits to growing increasingly fond of England, enjoying the pace of life in the country and appreciating its subtle seasonal changes. He had to make an effort to come to terms with the tight and aloof communities of his corner of the country, otherwise he would have remained an outsider. London, of course, requires no effort in assimilation, although he finds the easiest relationship with people is in Ireland. Apart from the two or three months of winter when he finds the climate disagreeable, Nolan likes being at The Rodd, although it brings the question of exile into sharp focus. He describes his life from the 1950s to 1970s as a yo-yo existence when he was a regular traveller through what seemed like an unbroken succession of airport terminals. Although the pace has slackened, his curiosity has remained constant since he first left his home shores more than thirty years ago. He thinks Australia has now reached the point that the United States had achieved at the beginning of this century, becoming a melting pot of cultures from which the nation will continue to draw strength and grow. He remembers a comment made by Peter Bellew when he went to live and work in Paris during the late 1940s. He brought out his diary in a Left Bank bookshop one day and the owner, noticing a kangaroo embossed on its cover, remarked, 'Oh, you come from Australia. How wonderful! It must be a marvellous place to live, this great land and with such a future.' Bellew could only think to himself, in the face of this unexpected enthusiasm, that it was indeed a country with both a future and a past, but unfortunately an ill-defined present. Nolan agrees with those sentiments.

Until recently, he has shown little concern for any personal records, leaving it to others to document his achievements, as best they can, but admitting he should have been more responsible about preserving his books and letters, and especially his paintings. What remains of his extensive correspondence with the Reeds during the 1940s is part of the Reed estate, although it is a one-sided view of a relationship because Sunday's letters to him were destroyed. For many of his peripatetic years he was convinced he should travel light, taking his cue from Rimbaud who was said to have walked across Europe with an English dictionary, learning the words on each page and then tearing it out and throwing it away. This approach to personal possessions has left Nolan a scrappy archive with not even a reasonable documentation of his friendship with Robert Lowell, Kenneth Clark and Benjamin Britten, to mention only a few who corresponded regularly over the years. He now feels the need for some of this material 'purely because I have somehow lived to be as old as I am, and there were various experiences and relationships in my life that I haven't been able to express in paint. And now I'd rather like to gather them.' With this in mind, a large room has been set aside at The Rodd for his memorabilia, which he and Mary are gradually assembling.

Records of his painting life are firmly anchored in Australia at Lanyon and in permanent displays in public galleries and arts centres. Although Nolan does not regard himself as part of Anglo-Saxondom, he is very grateful to England after spending more than half his life there. He is aware of the perils of becoming institutionalised with a trust named after him and the establishment of a Nolan collection in Dublin, although this attention only adds to the acceptance of his work in the country where he was born, the place where he has spent most of his professional life, and in the land of his Celtic roots which, probably as much as any other influence, helped to mould his personality. Through everything runs a thread of music which becomes increasingly important for him. He counts many musicians among his friends including Alfred Brendel, Julian Bream, Yehudi Menuhin and Ravi Shankar, and music will become an increasingly important facet of the Trust's activities. Nolan cannot define the precise connection between his art and a passion for music, but sums it up jokingly as the expression of an 'Ocker Australian wanting to be worldly — the civilising of Sid!'

But it is the city of his birth that often commands his thoughts as he gets older.

Most of our lives, indelibly influenced by the Melbourne experience, didn't turn

Sir Sidney and Lady Nolan, Sydney, 1985

out too well. Some of the principal players, including the Reeds, Joy Hester and Sweeney Reed, are already dead. Nobody got off easily and most of the battles were fought for a forlorn cause. You cannot know what makes or unmakes you, although when I return, get up on the 44th floor of the Regent Hotel and look out over the city, I become quite elated, but that can quickly change to the thought, the bloody joint looks just like a cemetery. I alternate in this ambivalent situation, feeling at home, liking the look of Port Phillip Bay and enjoying certain breezes I must have experienced as a boy. Then the uselessness of so many years sweeps over me, with memories of the determined young people who were going to be painters and poets, all talented and all intending to change the world. They either drank too much or missed out for other reasons, their aspirations severely attenuated. There's an unresolved part of me that cannot relate to Melbourne, and most likely never will. I have to say I don't think Australians are very fair fighters, but must add that I don't consider myself one either. That means we're well-matched.

On the subject of public recognition and official honours, Nolan is equally outspoken. His citation as honorary fellow of the American Academy and Institute of Arts and Letters in May 1985 reads:

Predominant among Sidney Nolan's themes are the ancient mystery of the Australian continent and its precipitate modernity — a paradox that he has brought into the mind's eye of his countrymen over the past forty years. He is a poetic and highly accomplished painter, whose power rests on an ability to suggest simultaneously the might and the fragility of life.

He is humbled by such attention paid to him in the United States, Britain, and certain parts of Australia, but says, 'I still find Melbourne contains more booby traps than Sydney. I've had an honorary doctorate from the University of Sydney for a number of years and another from Canberra before that, but nothing of the sort has ever been offered by Melbourne, and I've a fair hunch it may never be.'

He says that when he gave his Wimmera paintings to the National Gallery of Victoria in 1983, 'Everyone accepted them nicely, there was a good dinner and I was made a life member of the gallery, being hailed as the missing link in Australian landscape between Arthur Streeton and Fred Williams'. An artistic gap was neatly bridged and Nolan regarded the recognition of his gift as 'the small-town boy finally accepted'. He has had second thoughts since then and in retrospect says, 'I think I was probably foolish to let go of those valuable paintings in the light of what happened afterwards. But that's Melbourne!'

Australia's most honoured painter approached his seventieth birthday having to admit, 'I've never been offered an Australian award, high or low. Not even a hint of one.' He assumes it is because he has lived abroad for half of his life and that those who look after such matters say, 'Oh well, he's been doing his stuff over in England for such a long time, and the Queen's looked after him pretty well. He can't have it both ways.'

However, Nolan is delighted with the prospect of ending this act of his personal opera in a major key. The city of his birth, which played such an irritatingly ambivalent role in his life, has honoured him at 70 with the most comprehensive survey of his work in a retrospective exhibition at the National Gallery of Victoria, to be seen at other centres in Australia before travelling abroad. It would be easy for the artist to regard this as a fitting finale to his long career, but truths remain to be learned about life and art and music. Quite obviously this painter's quest for communication will continue until the compact disc player in his studio is silenced and he no longer has the energy to wield a spray can or brush.

Such is life for Sidney Nolan.

Select Bibliography

Sidney Nolan

Badham, Herbert. *A Study of Australian Art*. Currawong, Sydney, 1949.

Barber, Noel. *Conversations with Painters*. Collins, London, 1964.

Bonython, Kym (ed.) *Modern Australian Painting and Sculpture 1950–1960*. Rigby, Adelaide, 1960.

—— *Modern Australian Painting, 1960–1970*. Rigby, Adelaide, 1970.

Clark, Kenneth, MacInnes, Colin and Robertson, Bryan. *Sidney Nolan*. Thames and Hudson, London, 1961.

Dutton, Geoffrey. *The Innovators: the Sydney alternatives in the rise of modern art, literature and ideas*. Macmillan, Melbourne, 1986.

Fry, Gavin. *Nolan's Gallipoli*. Rigby, Adelaide, 1983.

Haese, Richard. *Rebels and Precursors: The Revolutionary Years of Australian Art*. Allen Lane, Melbourne, 1981.

Horton, Mervyn. (ed.) *Painters of the 70s*. Ure Smith, Sydney, 1975.

Hughes, Robert. *The Art of Australia*. Penguin Books, Harmondsworth, 1970.

Luck, Ross K.A. *A Guide to Modern Australian Painting*. Sun Books, Melbourne, 1969.

Lynn, Elwyn. *Sidney Nolan: Myth and Imagery*. Macmillan, London, 1967.

—— (intro.) *The Darkening Ecliptic*. R. Alistair McAlpine, London, 1974.

—— *Sidney Nolan: Australia*. Bay Books, Sydney, 1979.

—— and Bruce Semler. *Sidney Nolan's Ned Kelly*. Australian National Gallery, Canberra, 1985.

MacInnes, Colin. *England, Half English*. MacGibbon & Kee, London, 1961.

Melville, Robert. *Ned Kelly*. Thames and Hudson, London, 1964.

—— (intro.) *Paradise Garden*. R. Alistair McAlpine, London, 1971.

Osborne, Charles. *Masterpieces of Nolan*. Thames and Hudson, London, 1975.

Pringle, John Douglas. *Australian Painting Today*. Thames and Hudson, London, 1963.

Reed, John. *Australian Landscape Painting*. Longmans, Melbourne, 1965.

—— *New Painting 1952–62*. Longmans, Melbourne, 1963.

Robertson, Bryan and Snowdon, Lord. *Private View: The Lively World of British Art*. Nelson, London, 1965.

Smith, Bernard. *Australian Painting 1788–1960*. Oxford University Press, Melbourne, 1962.

Thomas, Laurie. *200 Years of Australian Painting*. Bay Books, Sydney, 1971.

Turnbull, Clive. *Art Here: Buvelot to Nolan*. Hawthorn Press, Melbourne, 1947.

Cynthia Nolan

Lucky Alphonse (novel). Reed and Harris, Melbourne, 1944.
Daddy Sowed a Wind (novel). Shakespeare Head, Sydney, 1947.
Outback. Methuen, London, 1962.
One Traveller's Africa. Methuen, London, 1965.
Open Negative. Macmillan, London, 1967.
A Sight of China. Macmillan, London, 1969.
A Bride for St Thomas (novel). Constable, London, 1970.
Paradise, and Yet. Macmillan, London, 1971.

Filmography

Ned Kelly, Australian Paintings by Sidney Nolan. Dir. Tim Burstall. Eltham Films, Melbourne, 6 mins. 1960.

Sidney Nolan (Monitor). Dir. Peter Newington. BBC London, 40 mins. 1960.

Sidney Nolan. Dir. Dahl and Geoffrey Collings. Qantas, Sydney, 21 mins. 1962.

Toehold in History. Dir. Dahl and Geoffrey Collings. Qantas, Sydney, 21 mins. 1965.

This Dreaming, Spinning Thing. Dir. Storry Walton. Australian Broadcasting Commission, Sydney, 60 mins. 1967.

Kelly Country. Dir. Stuart Cooper. Sidney Nolan, London, 60 mins. 1972.

Beyond is Anything. Dir. Paula Nagel. Australian Broadcasting Commission, Adelaide, 50 mins. 1974.

Nolan at Sixty. Dir. Brian Adams. Australian Broadcasting Commission, BBC Television, RM Productions, Munich, 50 mins. 1977.

Sidney Nolan: An Australian Dream. Dir. Don Bennetts. Don Bennetts and Australian Broadcasting Commission, Sydney, 75 mins. 1982.

It is of Eden I was Dreaming. Dir. David Muir. Film Australia, Sydney, 23 mins. 1983.

Such is Life. Dir. Brian Adams. NVC Arts International, London, 60 mins. 1987.

Theatre Design

Icare. Ballet by Serge Lifar. Theatre Royal, Sydney, 1940.

Orphée. Jean Cocteau. Directed by Sam Hughes for Sydney University Dramatic Society, 1948.

Ned Kelly. Douglas Stewart. Directed by John Sumner. Elizabethan Theatre, Sydney, 1956.

The Guide. Harvey Breit. Directed by Frank Hauser. Oxford Playhouse, 1961.

The Rite of Spring. Ballet by Kenneth MacMillan. Royal Opera House, Covent Garden, 1962.

The Display. Ballet by Robert Helpmann. Her Majesty's Theatre, Adelaide, 1964.

Samson et Dalila. Opera by Saint-Saëns. Directed by Elijah Moshinsky. Royal Opera House, Covent Garden 1981.

Il Trovatore. Opera by Verdi. Directed by Elijah Moshinsky. Sydney Opera House, 1983.

Die Entführung aus dem Serail. Opera by Mozart. Directed by Elijah Moshinsky. Royal Opera House, Covent Garden, 1987.

Index

268